EMPOWERING YOUR HEALTH

EMPOWERING YOUR HEALTH

DO YOU WANT TO GET WELL?

DR. ASA ANDREW

THOMAS NELSON
Since 1798

NASHVILLE   DALLAS   MEXICO CITY   RIO DE JANEIRO   BEIJING

Published in Nashville, Tennessee, by Thomas Nelson. Thomas Nelson is a registered trademark of Thomas Nelson, Inc.

Thomas Nelson, Inc., titles may be purchased in bulk for educational, business, fundraising, or sales promotional use. For information, please e-mail SpecialMarkets@ThomasNelson.com.

KING JAMES VERSION, AUTHORIZED STANDARD VERSION, and DOUAY-RHEIMS BIBLE are in the public domain and do not require permission, but should be noted on the copyright page. No publisher's name required.

Holy Bible, New Living Translation. © 1996. Used by permission of Tyndale House Publishers, Inc., Wheaton, Illinois 60189. All rights reserved.

Library of Congress Cataloging-in-Publication Data

Andrew, Asa.
    Empowering your health : do you want to get well? / by Asa Andrew.
        p. cm.
    Includes bibliographical references and index.
    ISBN 978-1-4016-0372-4
    1. Health. 2. Naturopathy. I. Title.
    RA776.A5485 2007
    613—dc22

2007034672

Printed in the United States of America

08 09 10 11 12 QF 7 6 5 4 3 2

DEDICATION

I read this dedication to my dad the last week of his life. He couldn't talk anymore because he had an oxygen mask over his face. But as I read this to him he looked at me, smiled, and slightly squeezed my hand. I knew what he was trying to say. He was one of the greatest men I ever knew.

This is what I wrote.

This book is dedicated to my father. He and my mother adopted me as an orphan, and gave me a home. He taught me many valuable lessons in life—usually not in his words, but always in his actions. Principles like love, forgiveness, perseverance, faithfulness, and belief in myself. I gleaned these qualities from him, and they have made me the man I am today. My father's unfailing love has helped me achieve all my goals in life, including this book.

So thanks, Dad, thanks for choosing to love me when I had no one. For giving me a name when I didn't have one. For giving me a home when I didn't have one. For providing for me when you didn't have to. For giving me a life when I seemingly didn't have much of one. For giving me the greatest title a little boy and man could ever ask for. Thank you for calling me your son. I am so grateful God handpicked you to be my father. You empowered my life in so many ways, so that I could empower the lives of others. I will always love you.

CONTENTS

PART I: WHAT IS NATURAL MEDICINE?

PART II: MENTAL HEALTH

PART III: CHEMICAL HEALTH

CONTENTS

ACKNOWLEDGEMENTS

As with any major project, it takes a great team to make all of the elements come together in a book. I want to extend my deepest gratitude to:

Ken Abraham—Thanks to your team, including Jennifer Lill. Ken, your insight, expertise, and guidance made this project possible. Thank you for challenging me and getting to the core of my heart and this message. I admire your character, passion, persistence, and integrity. You are the absolute best at what you do.

The Entire Thomas Nelson Team—I am more humbled than words can say for your passionate belief in me and this project. Thank you to Mike Hyatt, Larry Stone, and especially to Pamela Clements for your faith, friendship, encouragement, enthusiasm, and support. And to Geoff Stone for your patience through this process. Thank you all for giving me a publishing home.

Empowering Your Health Radio Show—Thanks to Cumulus Media and Nashville's Supertalk 99.7 WWTN programming and the sales teams, especially John Columbus, Leslie Pardue, and John Mountz. Without your friendship, support, belief, and positioning, this message would not be reaching the masses.

Empowering Your Health Radio Staff—Thanks to my producer Kortland Fuqua, and the team including Stu Gray, Craig Jolly, Matt Collins, and the gang. Your persistence and creative efforts have made this show grow quickly and impact peoples lives.

Dave Ramsey and The Lampo Group—Thank you Dave Ramsey for helping start my radio show, Suzanne Sims, and Joe Leavitt for your

Godly wisdom, guidance, and being exceptional examples of what a great organization is made of—great people with great integrity.

The Staff of The Center for Natural Medicine—You are giving so much hope to the world. I am blessed and privileged to work alongside you.

Rebekah Hubbell—Thank you for managing "my world" and helping impact the lives of many. If we have angels on this earth, you must be one of them.

Christopher Schmidt—Your unprecedented counsel, wisdom, and perseverance have been a huge attribute to this project and in my life. Thanks for being such a great friend.

Dr. Jeff Hall—Thanks for your friendship, faith, and support. You are one of the best in Natural Medicine.

Drs. James Andrews, John Anderson, Patch Adams, John Hainesworth, Lou Obersteadt, TAB, and Tim Adair—You are the physician "dream team" who have been amazing peers and mentors in this process.

Coaches Bobby Bowden and Dave Van Halanger—For allowing me to work alongside you in the Florida State University Seminole football program and pointing me toward the greatest decision in my life— a relationship with God.

Keith Harrell, Larry Winget, John Jacobs, and Mike Hagen—Thanks for teaching me about what being a communicator is all about and never giving up on me.

Dr. David Cooper—Your friendship, faith, Godly wisdom, and unique insights have made me much of who I am today.

To my immediate family, especially my mother—You know me the best. You love me the most and have supported me in all my endeavors. I love you all very much.

To you, the reader—For picking this book up and taking the most difficult step toward your health—the first one. I wrote this for you because I believe in you.

FOREWORD

JUST LIKE OUR WEALTH,
HEALTH IS REALLY JUST GOOD OLD COMMON SENSE

Winning with money is 80 percent behavior; it's only 20 percent head knowledge. For years I've been teaching common sense concepts people can follow to change their behavior and get control of their money. The problem is that common sense isn't very common anymore.

It's the same thing with healthcare—you have to take responsibility for your behavior. Just as I teach about money, Dr. Asa Andrew reminds us we can't rely on anyone to take care of our health for us. We have to take responsibility by choosing to make healthy lifestyle choices each and every day.

A while back, I saw myself on TV and wondered who that fat guy was. I had been working so hard I had abandoned the care of my physical condition. I knew that I had to do something to change the habits that made me look like that. I made the choice to eat better and exercise more. It wasn't rocket science—it was common sense. You lose weight if you eat less and exercise more.

Now I feel better, have more energy, and am more excited about life than ever. And as a result of my commitment and hard work, I ran my first (and probably last) full marathon earlier this year.

Asa is a doctor but he's also a teacher. In my opinion, he is teaching a Common Sense approach to health that is critical to us living the healthy life we all deserve.

—Dave Ramsey
New York Times best-selling author and
nationally syndicated radio talk show host

MY STORY
The Power to Change

"Every human has four endowments—self-awareness, conscience, independent will, and creative imagination. These give us the ultimate human freedom . . . The power to choose, to respond, and to change."

—STEPHEN COVEY,
best-selling author and motivator

It was 1994, and I had just entered school to become a physician. I was an avid bodybuilder, standing at about six feet one inch and weighing 215 pounds with a twenty-seven-inch waist and 6 percent body fat. I worked out six days a week and I was in the best shape of my life. I maintained a healthy diet, or so I thought, including absolutely no fat because fat will make you fat, right? That was the health and fitness mentality in the 1980s and early 1990s. Grains and carbohydrates were the craze and, at all cost, we stayed away from fat. Sure I was lean, but when you're working out as much as I was and had the fast metabolism and the hormones of a twenty-three-year-old, any diet and exercise program would have worked.

The body can generally take some abuse in our younger years, apparently without too much consequence; there is, however, always a breaking point. Too many carbohydrates, good or bad in quality, can lead you toward one of the most challenging diseases diagnosed in America today—Type 2 diabetes. Although I was unaware of it, that was the direction I was heading.

Initially, I pursued the fitness craze to enhance my health, but of course there was some vanity involved as well. Lean and mean was my goal. I was involved in athletics in college and being in top shape was critical.

1

When I began working on my doctorate, school became much more serious. I had to buckle down, and I did. Eight hours per day of classes, up to twenty-six hours of credits per quarter, and up to eight exams in one week kept me stressed and frazzled. Not surprisingly, my body eventually said, "No more!"

As I walked to class one day, the hallway started spinning out of control. Everything went black, and I woke up to one of my classmates slapping me and pouring water on my face, as I lay stretched out on the floor.

I feared that something was seriously wrong. All sorts of frightening thoughts raced through my mind. *Did I have a stroke? Oh, no! I must have cancer! Or maybe something is wrong with my heart.* I quickly assumed the worst, and even began expecting it! (I've since discovered that this is a negative mindset that many people develop—one ache, one pain, an odd or funny feeling— and they leap to a potentially disastrous conclusion.)

I made an appointment with a primary care physician. I was expecting him to run all sorts of tests and put me through the ropes, but much to my surprise and chagrin, he simply examined me and asked me some basic questions about my symptoms and what had happened to me in the hallway. Once he had assessed it all, he merely chuckled.

"What?" I blurted. "What's so funny?"

The doctor looked at me and smiled. "Okay, son. Welcome to the world of studying medicine and wanting to become a physician. If it were easy, everyone would be doing it. Your schooling is extremely intense and you must pace yourself. Now, go home and rest for three days. Do as little as possible, and try to keep your mind off your school work. You'll be just fine."

I recognized the wisdom in the doctor's words. I knew I had been teetering precariously on the verge of a more serious breakdown, so I regarded this incident as a warning. Looking back, I now see that moment as a turning point in my thinking that health was more than merely causes and symptoms. Our health, I realized, is highly integrated mentally, chemically, and structurally. A whole person was involved, not simply various bones, muscles, organs, or other parts of the body.

In the spring of 1995, my life, medical studies, and pursuit of good health took another turn. I was asked to be a part of a group called The Power Team, a worldwide organization and ministry. The Power Team was a group of large, muscular men who performed feats of strength, such as crushing through walls of concrete and breaking seven-foot walls of ice, to young

2

people at high school assemblies across the country. After the feats the group shared with young people about believing in themselves, holding on to their dreams, and avoiding the pitfalls of drugs and alcohol. The Team was also extremely popular on the corporate motivational speakers' circuit, sharing platforms with the likes of Zig Ziglar, Tony Robbins, and other successful motivators.

No wonder I was excited when I received a phone call from a friend named Big Tommy, who lived in Los Angeles. "The Team wants to do an interview with you," Tommy said. One of the main guys on The Power Team was leaving to pursue new opportunities, and they needed another member. The team members and I hit it off great, and it seemed that we might enjoy working together. Little did they know that I was wearing five extra T-shirts under my starched dress shirt to make me look bigger than I was!

I was in my second year of my doctorate program, which for many students is frequently the most grueling, and I was faced with a decision. Should I leave school and accept the position with The Power Team? Sometimes what looks like the easiest route is not always the road you should take. The road filled with adversity will often bring you the greatest joy.

I knew that if I left school to join The Power Team, I could always come back and finish my doctoral program. Beyond that, something deep inside of me was saying this is the road I had to take. God was calling me into this area to further His plans for my life. So I accepted The Power Team offer with a resounding *yes,* but there was one major challenge to overcome. At 210 pounds, I was the smallest guy to ever be on the team. I had to get bigger.

What could I do to build up my body? Again, I had a decision to make. Should I take anabolic steroids? I could quickly gain the fifty pounds or more that I needed, but I'd be destroying my body and lying to all those to whom I was going to be speaking. Basically, I would gain the girth but lose my integrity. No, instead, I had to get my body's metabolism to slow down so I could pack on the pounds.

Through my knowledge of how the body works and my experience in bodybuilding, I knew I had to purposely overeat and ingest massive amounts of calories to gain the weight. The challenge was that plain tuna and brown rice just wasn't going to do it. I needed foods that were full of calories. So I went against my conventional wisdom of eating only healthy foods and began eating *everything.* If there was a buffet, I was there. When we were on the road, our hosts would always take us to a buffet to eat because of the large amounts of food that we consumed. I mean, think about trying to feed six hungry guys, each one weighing over 300 pounds! I ate three and four helpings until my stomach ached, constantly feeding myself to pack on the pounds. I was willing to do whatever it took to gain the necessary massive amounts of weight.

The guys on the team joked and called me "Baked Potato" because I snatched a baked potato wherever we were eating. I never wanted to miss an opportunity to get those extra calories in my body.

Nowadays, I always say that food is the greatest drug that we have. It can literally change our bodies for the good or the bad. I know this from my own experience. Back in my Power Team days, I would eat at McDonalds twice a day, and enjoy large pizzas before bed every night. It was insane. I'd do anything to catch up with the guys and not be the smallest guy on the team.

After about two years, I weighed in right at 300 pounds. I was incredibly strong, bench-pressing well over 400 pounds and leg pressing over 2000 pounds. However I began to notice some disturbing physical changes. I became extremely sleepy after meals, to the point of having to lie down, yet I would feel famished an hour later. I perspired profusely at night, often waking up on soaked sheets. And worse yet, instead of a body bulging with muscle, I noticed some "love handles" forming around my waist.

The fatigue factor was frustrating, too. I could not even run down the aisle to get to the stage sometimes. I would be breathing so hard I thought I was going to pass out. Something was very wrong. Eventually I started fainting and nearly slipping into mini-comas.

I went to see a doctor. While sitting in the waiting room, my mind rationalized, *I'm studying to be a doctor! How can I be so unhealthy? I'm still a young man.* The doctor ran some basic tests and came back with some alarming news. My blood sugar was close to the 200 range; a specific test called the hemoglobin A1C looked dangerously high—according to the test results, I was clinically diabetic. The doc wanted to start me on light doses of insulin.

How could that be? I'm so young! I silently cried out.

How did it happen? I ate myself into diabetes. I had established habits of eating the wrong kinds of foods, and too many of them. My body could not handle the rising and falling of the blood sugar and my pancreas said, "I just can't do this anymore." And it began to shut down. I was facing a life-altering diagnosis and had to make a decision. Indeed, this was one of the pivotal points in my life. Was my health and life worth making the changes necessary to save it? I had to make up my mind, "Do I want to get well?"

I decided, *Yes, I want to get well!*

I knew that with the intensity that it took to gain the weight, I would have to do at least the same to take it off. But my eating had to change radically. *Radical changes equal radical results,* I reminded myself. I began eating lean sources of proteins, low-glycemic carbohydrates in the form of fruits and vegetables, and good fat. I realized how important fat was to our bodies and all the hormonal systems that it controls. I also reduced the amount of food I ate by half and gave my digestive system a rest. It took me six months to drop from over 300 pounds down to 235. I didn't do gastric bypass, stomach stapling, the lap band, or any other unusual or mysterious weight loss programs. I simply made a decision to get well, to lose the weight, so I would be able to accomplish all that God had for me to do. I realized that being healthy was important if I hoped to be around for my family. I became more concerned about others than my biceps.

I took responsibility for my own health, because no one else could do it for me. The doctors couldn't, my family couldn't, and my friends couldn't. I was the one who had put myself into a diabetic state, not my genetics, and not my circumstances. I ate and "lifestyled" my way in, and by making radical changes, I ate and lifestyled my way out.

At my next yearly physical, my doctor was astounded. He hadn't heard from me since he had pronounced his bleak diagnosis. "Asa, I haven't seen you in quite a while," he said, rubbing his chin as he looked over my medical charts. "You were supposed to follow up with me a month after we saw your test results. Did you ever go on the insulin?" he asked.

"No," I replied. I knew that the body had the ability to fully regenerate itself. That means that each day old cells are constantly dying and new cells are forming—so essentially we can eventually get a new body and all of its parts. I continued, "I made radical changes in my diet and lifestyle, and now my blood sugar is under control, my pancreas is working normally again, and I am no longer a diabetic."

He was shocked. Was it a miracle? Not really. I simply made a decision that I wanted to get well.

The great news is that what worked for me can also help you, whether you suffer heart disease, cancer, high blood pressure, high cholesterol, skin diseases, allergies, arthritis, or something else. Our bodies are constantly regenerating; they grow and change by the daily food and lifestyle choices that we make. Do genetics play a role? Sure, a little. Your choices, however, will outweigh genetics. You *can* take responsibility for your health. That is the foundation of this book; it is the essence of Natural Medicine. It is a new medicine, a new approach, based on the simple, foundational ways the body works combined with good old common sense. And don't forget that you have the greatest gift with which to work—hope that today is a brand new day, and tomorrow can be even better.

The choices you make today will affect the health you will have tomorrow. Remember, your body is constantly regenerating from the foods you eat, the exercise you choose to do, the good air that you breathe, and the purity of the water that you drink. Your health is your greatest wealth.

You *can* be well, healthy, and whole! The question is: Do you want it? You have the power to choose, and my hope is that as you read the pages of this book, you will be empowered to choose good health.

Friend, I believe in you. You can get your health back; you can be well. If I can do it, you can, too.

Why is your health so valuable? Because you are valuable. Ask yourself, *What am I good at?* Look at your gifts and talents to discover where you excel, and then do that with all your heart. Get up off your "blessed assurance" and do something. Stop doing what you don't want to do and start doing what you are meant to do. When you begin to live your life *on purpose*, other people around you will notice. They will see you glow because you are living the life for which you were designed.

Empowering your health, empowering your life. That's what this book is all about. You are the only you there is, and you can do something great while here on earth. Natural Medicine is designed to take you from where you are to where you want to be. You can get your health and your life back.

PART I:

WHAT IS NATURAL MEDICINE?

1

IN SEARCH OF A NEW MEDICINE
The Quest for Extraordinary Health

"The Doctor of the future will give no medicine, but will interest his or her patients in the care of the human frame, in a proper diet, and in the cause and prevention of disease."

—THOMAS A. EDISON

ere we go again—here comes the latest doctor and his incredible discoveries in health, wellness, and medicine. Read his new answers, and then go buy his revolutionary line of vitamins, pills, potions, and miracle meals. All we need is another health book, right? A new diet. A new pill. A new "nine keys" or the only "ten steps" you need to a healthier you.

Today we are overwhelmed with studies, researchers, and test groups who tell us that butter is bad and broccoli is good. Then we open the newspaper to discover that a new study concludes they may both cause cancer. *What are we supposed to believe?*

We are told to exercise every day—better yet, exercise three times a week. *Eat high fat . . . no, eat low fat . . . never mind, eat no fat. You need high protein, or is that low protein? Forget protein—be a vegetarian! The real answer is to avoid sugar, but only certain kinds of sugar . . . no, now all sugar is bad.*

Am I the only one who is tired of new studies apparently conducted with no other purpose than to prove the old studies wrong?

And yet you are still searching. You remain optimistic, still out there looking for the answers, in spite of all the conflicting advice fed to us on a daily basis. You may have bought this book because you or someone you know is suffering from a health challenge, a disease, or some terminal condition. Or maybe you know someone who simply needs to lose some weight and wants to attain better health. You are thinking, *Maybe, just maybe, this is the answer, the one I have been waiting for.* If this book is not the answer you've been looking for, then you are thinking that somewhere out there is the secret to finding the kind of health you either used to have, or the kind you desire.

Am I right?

We are looking for a type of medicine that triggers instant change, the kind of change no doctor or pharmacy has ever been able to give us.

What we are looking for is a new medicine.

We want to believe there is a prescription out there that will finally put us on the path to living out of the *ordinary* . . . and into *extraordinary* health. We are looking for the kind of medicine that will take us from where we are to where we want to be. We are looking for the best medicine that anyone could ever find. Get your pen and paper ready because here it is—it's the greatest doctor that has been inside of us our entire lives.

The prescription is HOPE.

I'm sorry if this isn't the complicated answer you've been waiting for, but why does it need to be complicated?

So you need to lose weight.

You need your cancer to go into remission.

You need your cholesterol level to lower.

You need your blood sugar to be under one hundred.

You need a new kidney.

You need a tumor removed.

You need your heart to work right.

You need your fibromyalgia and arthritis pain eliminated.

The question is not what you need to do. The real question is: What are you willing to do? This is the pivotal question for finding the health you desire and need.

Dr. Jerome Groopman, M.D., practiced hematology and oncology for thirty years. Throughout the years, his patients taught him one of the most valuable lessons in life and in medicine, and that is the power of hope. He writes in his book *The Anatomy of Hope*:[1]

> Hope is one of our central emotions, but we are often at a loss when asked to define it. Many of us confuse hope with optimism, a pre-

vailing attitude that things will turn out for the best. But hope differs from optimism. Hope does not arise from being told to think positively, or from hearing an overly rosy forecast. Hope, unlike optimism, is rooted in unalloyed reality. Although there is no uniform definition of hope, I found one that seemed to capture what my patients had taught me. Hope is the elevating feeling we experience when we see—in the mind's eye—a path to a better future. Hope acknowledges the significant obstacles and deep pitfalls along that path. True hope has no room for delusion.

COMBINING THE OLD WITH THE NEW

The new medicine is not based on counting on others to take care of your health or make decisions for you, but for you to take responsibility for your own health and have the hope that it can be achieved. It's a new way of thinking. There is an example in the Bible about wineskins. It says that you can't put new wine into old wineskins or they will burst (Matthew 9:17). Likewise, we can't have new ideas of medicine in the old way of thinking. We need a whole new way of thinking about medicine and our health.

So if this is the new medicine, what is the old medicine? It's not that our traditional setup of medicine today is wrong in its efforts. We need all fields of medicine to achieve the best health care for people. However, a pill or a potion is not going to give us extraordinary health. Traditional medicine doesn't place much importance on lifestyle choices, diet, clean air, reducing toxins, and exercise. Instead it focuses on treating a specific symptom once an illness has arrived. And with antibiotics, steroids, allergy medicine, cold medicine, hormone medicine, and the like, we have done a great job managing people's health—allowing them to survive with minimal discomfort. Old medicine helps people cope with their diagnoses and health challenges, but does not offer much hope of eliminating those problems. Nor does it lead to an extraordinary life.

All the specialists—from the "-ologists" to the surgeons—are vitally important to our health and our health care system. We need all types of health care professionals and their specific knowledge and expertise to make a great team. However, a new mind-set of medicine is emerging that involves keeping people as far away from sickness and disease as possible so they can thrive. If and when their health is challenged, we give them hope as well as a positive prognosis.

Today, people with Type 2 diabetes (the preventable type) are usually given insulin and told to watch their blood sugar levels instead of being told that they need to make radical changes in diet and lifestyle habits, which is often what produced the diabetes in the first place. (Perhaps because doctors got tired of patients ignoring their advice to lose weight, change eating habits, and increase exercise.) Patients with high cholesterol are put on a statin drug to lower cholesterol, which reduces liver function—and it does work. However, nothing is done to help restore the liver (where cholesterol is made in the body), which would allow cholesterol levels to normalize.

The old style of medicine is doing a great job of maintaining, but we need more. We were created to thrive. We were designed to live an extraordinary life where raising kids does not rob us of our precious energy and playing with our grandkids doesn't hurt our hips. We were made for more.

You can move on with your life, take responsibility for your own health, and find the hope to see it through—and this book will help you.

SIMPLE HEALTH

I have a different way of looking at health. People say that I'm simple. They say that my approach is too easy. Well, I am simple, and health really is that easy. The human body is extremely complex; however, good health is nothing more than common sense.

I have been a physician and health coach for years, treating people just like you with major health challenges including migraine headaches, allergies, high cholesterol, arthritis, fibromyalgia, high blood pressure, diabetes, hormone imbalance, overweight, and lack of energy. I help them have the life they were designed to live. I help people find the best health insurance policy available in America today—making healthy choices—and consciously choose health.

I can help you take responsibility for your health.

In the midst of a schedule that includes a nationally syndicated radio show, speaking appearances, TV and media appearances, ongoing research, writing articles and books, and spending quality family and personal time, I still spend that special one-on-one time with patients at my clinic, the Center for Natural Medicine, in Nashville, Tennessee. Why? Because I believe in my patients. I never want to be unavailable to help those who want to get well. *When you leave the people, you leave yourself.*

Am I some "big shot" doctor? No way. I'm just a regular person like you who has a passion to use the talents and gifts that God has given me to make the world a little better.

WE NEED YOU

I call myself a health coach for several reasons. First, the word "doctor" actually means "teacher"—it comes from the Latin *doc re*, to teach—rather than the connotation that most people have of a doctor: someone who heals you or rules over you with a white coat. So if I carry the title of doctor, that means I must teach you something, or I am not really doing my job. I call myself a health coach because I am your number one fan, your own personal cheerleader, and I won't let you slip up for a second—it's my job to coach you to win.

When you say negative things such as "I'll never get well," use the term "my diabetes" like it's your pet, put toxins or the wrong kinds of foods in your body, or don't exercise and rest properly, I am here to hold you accountable, because this whole life thing is not just about *you*. It's about the team that needs you. "Us" includes your spouse, your children, your grandchildren, your friends, your coworkers, me, and most importantly—God. We all need you to be healthy because you make this world a better place. Yes, I said we *need* you. So as your coach, I'm not going to let you slip.

It's also my goal to equip and empower you so you can take responsibility for your own health. As a doctor, I want to *teach* you the way to extraordinary health, and how to thrive instead of just survive.

Years ago when I began my practice, an old family physician shared with me a valuable piece of information that I still use today. He said, "Asa, when you are taking on the responsibility to treat someone with their health challenge, make sure to let them know that you will be able to get them about 50 percent better—make sure they're okay with that. As human beings, that's about all we can do with our own abilities and training. God is the other 50 percent in their healing process. He is the 'Great Physician' and will have to do the rest."

His words stayed with me throughout the years. So now when a new patient comes into my office I say, "I can help you get about 50 percent better through treatment. Are you okay with that?" Most people reply with a resounding "Yes!" After all, most would be ecstatic to achieve a 5 percent improvement in their health. Then I always add, "Great, then we'll let God take care of the rest—because I'm not God." Remember, doctors are just men and women like you. We have the same human limitations as everyone else, and we are only as good as the books we've read, the seminars we've attended, and the other doctors who have taught us. But like my old mentor and friend said—God is the "Great Physician."

SURVIVING ISN'T THRIVING

After going through school, working the rounds in hospitals, practicing in the field, and seeing how the traditional health care system works, I became frustrated. I knew that health had to be more than just surviving. It's about thriving. But how can we find a way to achieve optimal health?

In close to two decades of research and treating patients, I found that we spend more time trying to repair our health than preserve our health. During this time, I realized a powerful yet simple principle. Our health is our greatest wealth. And when this dawned on me, I finally understood what people were constantly searching for. It wasn't to look like the hottest Hollywood star—it was to live a high quality life, full of energy and vitality for as long as we are here.

Based on a foundational principle of hope, I have developed a new medicine designed to restore people who are challenged with their current health. I want to lead those living in ordinary health on a lifelong journey to the extraordinary health they rightfully deserve. This new system is called Natural Medicine. Working in conjunction with traditional medicine, it is designed to empower and restore those suffering with most health conditions and challenges. Instead of treating the symptoms, my goal is to get to the root of health challenges.

Health is integrative; it is interconnected. Therefore I look at each individual from a holistic approach. The holistic approach emphasizes the importance of the "whole" and restoring balance to the body rather than simply focusing on a symptom or what part of the body has problems. There are three basic elements to every person: mental, chemical, and structural. All three areas have to be addressed before we can experience the vibrant health for which we're searching.

FORGET WHAT YOU THINK YOU KNOW

Forget all the doctor talk, the labels, and the titles as you read this book. Please allow me to take off my white coat and stethoscope, walk beside you in your health journey, and just be Asa. I'm your health coach, and most importantly, I'm your friend. Keep in mind, there is a purpose for your life. Regardless of how you have been living, there is a more excellent way. Regardless of the challenges you are facing, there is a way out. Remember, your past does not define you. The choices that you make today *will* define you.

I'm here to coach you toward your health goals. But be aware that no one else can do it for you. The doctor can't do it for you, your spouse can't do it for you, your kids can't do it for you, and your friends can't make the right choices for you, either. Only *you* can take responsibility for your health. The choices you make today can and will determine the health you will have tomorrow.

Wherever you are in the health process—beginning the journey, along the way in the quest for extraordinary health, struggling to get your health back, absolutely thriving, or challenged in a hospital bed—keep reading and don't lose one of the greatest prescriptions God ever gave you—the prescription of Hope.

This book is your starting point. Keep reading with an open heart and open mind, and you will clearly see how you can reach the next level in your health transformation.

Your health is your greatest wealth. You can get it back. That's why we're here, and that's why you are reading this book.

And now for the most important question you have ever been asked . . .

2

DO YOU WANT TO GET WELL?
Taking Responsibility for Your Health

*"If we could give every individual the right amount of nour-
ishment and exercise, not too little and not too much, we
would have found the safest way to health."*

—HIPPOCRATES

Do you *really* want to get well? If so, then why are you still struggling with high blood pressure, diabetes, obesity, insomnia, or high cholesterol? Forgive my bluntness, but you are still struggling because you still *want* to be struggling. Before you throw down this book in disgust, allow me to explain. You are comfortable right where you are, and you have been for quite some time. Like many people, you believe the hype. You believe that your problem is genetic—your parents or grandparents had it, it's inevitable, so you just have to live with it. But the truth is, for the most part, people don't stay sick because they can't get well; people stay sick because they don't want to get well.

I went to visit a friend's grandmother who was in the hospital with a severe case of bronchitis. She was ninety-five years old but had been as energetic as the Energizer Bunny. However, instead of seeing the vibrant woman I knew, I saw a downcast, saddened soul. She began to complain about how badly life had been treating her and the horrors of aging. She yelled at the nurses and spewed a barrage of negative comments at anyone who crossed her path. Something had shifted in her mind, and she was giving up and giving in. She had been in the hospital for a week and seemed to want to stay there. When I pulled her doctor aside, he confided, "She still has some bronchitis in her chest, but her attitude is really what's keeping her here."

I went back in to let her know I was thinking about her and would be praying for her quick recovery. She replied, "Everybody needs to watch out! I'm going down like the Titanic!"

It's sad to see that defeatist mentality take over. She had so many people who loved her and needed her around, and yet she grew increasingly negative and selfish. She didn't want to get well, and she reached a point where she just didn't believe anymore. Unfortunately, when we develop that kind of outlook, we are not the only ones who suffer. All of those around us fall victim to this attitude of defeat and despair.

STOP MAKING EXCUSES

"But Dr. Asa, you don't understand. I try to eat well. I try to exercise. I try to get more sleep. I try, I try . . ."

In *Stars Wars, Episode V: The Empire Strikes Back*, young Luke Skywalker did not believe what Yoda, the Jedi Master, was teaching him about the power of the mind. When asked to raise his sunken star fighter from the swamps by the power of his mind alone, Luke responded he would "try."

"No," scolded Yoda. "Do, or do not. There is no try." Unfortunately, Luke failed to "unlearn" his preconceptions and he did not believe; that's why he failed.

Yoda is a fictional character, but the message is clear. The word "try" should not be in your vocabulary. In fact, I'm convinced it needs to be eliminated from our vocabulary entirely. I am so adamantly against a "try mentality" that whenever anyone says, "I'll try," I always stop and ask for clarification. "What do you mean you'll *try*?" Just see the word *try* for what it is—an excuse—and decide to rise above it.

NOBODY'S GONNA MAKE YOU

Let me put your mind at ease for a minute—I haven't come to take away your fried chicken. I haven't come to take away your pork, your shellfish, lobster, or fried catfish (especially if you grew up in the South like me). I can't make you do anything you don't want to do—no one can. I won't tell you to get rid of those foods, but after you become more educated you may no longer desire them. So I'll let you decide.

The Bible records an account of a healing pool called Bethesda in John chapter 5. Crowds of the sick, the blind, the lame, and the paralyzed would lie at this pool to be healed by its waters. One sick man had been lying beside the pool for thirty-eight years. Jesus came to Bethesda and saw him, fully knowing how long the man beside the pool had been sick. Jesus asked him one question, one rather intriguing and somewhat surprising question: "Do you want to be made well?" (John 5:6)

"I can't," the sick man told Jesus, "for I have no one to help me get into the pool when the water is stirred up. While I am trying to get in, someone else always gets in ahead of me."

Jesus looked at the man and said, "Get up; pick up your mat and walk." In an instant, the man was healed! He rolled up his mat, and began to walk. (Author's rendition.)

Regardless of your religion or creed, the story of the sick man at Bethesda makes a convincing point. Like many of us, the man had his excuses for why he wasn't healed. It's always someone else's fault, right? It's genetics, or it's the hormones in our food supply. But the question, "Do you want to get well?" doesn't leave room for excuses. It requires a simple yes or no—and you get to choose.

The body constantly regenerates itself. That's right—every few years depending on each individual's specific makeup, we have completely different bodies. We may essentially look the same on the outside, but internally speaking, we don't have the same bodies we had a few years ago. We have new hearts, new lungs, new livers, and new skin because the old cells are gone and new cells have been made. Once you learn that concept, you will begin to realize that what you put into your life every day—food choices, what you drink, and exercise habits—affects what you are going to have tomorrow. I can motivate you, encourage you, and share my knowledge with you, but only *you* can make the decision to thrive.

I can imagine a time in the not too distant future, when every headline in the media, every *Time*, *USA Today*, *CNN*, and *Fox News* cover story will tout "Americans, the healthiest people in the world!" Americans will have fewer cancer cases, less heart disease, less diabetes, and live more abundant lives. We can't achieve that in beaten, broken-down, sick bodies, so we must treat our health like the gift that it is. Right now, this nation is one of the unhealthiest countries in the world; to achieve better results we must shift the way we think, act, and live.

TAKING RESPONSIBILITY

Cyndi had been to every top allergist in the country. She was suffering from a variety of symptoms associated with allergies—chronic sinus problems, hay fever, itchy eyes, and even digestive issues. Dealing with her allergies was a continuous, year-round ordeal for Cyndi. Specialists looked at her symptoms, but no one thought to look at what might be the *root* of her symptoms. She was about to undergo surgery in an attempt to alleviate her *symptoms* and came to see me as a last resort. I asked her if she wanted to get well, just as I ask all my patients. She started crying and was unable to speak.

Her husband, who was sitting next to her, looked at me and said, "I want her to get well, but no one seems to have the answer."

I asked them if they would try the Natural Medicine protocol for eight weeks and then make their decision about surgery. They agreed.

After only four weeks, I began to notice Cyndi's eyes sparkling—her countenance was glowing. She told me with excitement, "I haven't sneezed in two weeks!" She brought a small gift into the office to thank me, and I asked her what she was thanking me for. She replied, "For giving me my life back." I protested that I didn't do anything, and she said, "I realize you are just a man and a doctor, but you gave me the guidance, wisdom, and hope that helped me take responsibility for my own life and health. I don't care as much for just me, but I need to be healthy for my family because they need me."

Was it a miracle? Perhaps some would say it was. But ultimately, Cyndi took responsibility for her own health. She didn't expect God to do it; she didn't expect doctors and allergists to do it; she didn't expect a diet and exercise guru to do it. She took responsibility and did what was necessary to bring health back to her body.

THE AMAZING REGENERATING HUMAN BODY

You may be saying to yourself, "Listen, I'm seventy-five years old. I've been eating junk my whole life. I've already got cancer, had a heart attack, and I'm probably going out soon, so I'm going out eating and living how I want."

I understand that mentality—I see it every day. But if that type of thinking is really your mind-set, then hear this: The body regenerates itself about 1 percent every day. That means that the heart, pancreas, and lungs that you had a few years ago are not the same ones you have now. It also means that the foods you ate over the last few years determine the body you have today.

We age because our food, environment, and personal choices are not perfect. Even if you were to eat the highest forms of organic foods, problems still exist within the soil. We are not looking for some "fountain of youth." Instead, Natural Medicine focuses on doing the *best* we can with what we have and not settling for a mediocre life. Knowing that our body regenerates itself, and with a new mind-set of faith and hope, we may have cancer, but changes in our lifestyles can literally cause the cancer to go away.

How does that happen? Some doctors may call it a miracle—and maybe it is! However, it is also as simple as taking responsibility for your health, with the realization that you do have the power inside you to get well.

YOU "LIFESTYLED" YOUR WAY INTO THIS

Our lifestyles are responsible for the physical conditions we are living with today. Eight out of ten of the major diseases Americans suffer are diet related. A person doesn't just *get* diabetes or just *get* heart disease. Are there genetic factors associated with some diseases? Absolutely. But for the most part, they are diet and lifestyle related. That's right; you have *eaten* and lifestyled your way into illness (with some help from being sedentary).

Here's some great news. You may be seventy years old, and although you have eaten a certain way your whole life, you can change today, and start creating a different body now. If you can lifestyle your way into something, *you can lifestyle your way out!*

I'm bringing you this message of hope because I believe in transforming the health of this nation one life at a time. Take care of your body just as you would take care of your new home, boat, or car. In doing so, you are setting yourself up for success, and great things can happen.

CHOOSE TO BE EXTRAORDINARY

There is an ordinary way to live, and then there is a more excellent way. There *is* a more excellent life that will come to you based on the smart lifestyle choices you make. It's completely up to you. You've eaten or lifestyled your way into illness, so you can eat or lifestyle your way out.

When Jesus asked the man at Bethesda, "Do you want to get well?" the first answer out of the man's mouth was, "I can't, I can't."

You too could easily say to yourself, "I've had diabetes for thirty years. I've already had two heart attacks and another one is coming. I can't get well." You might think, "I've already had a stroke, and part of my mouth doesn't move. I can't get well." Or you could say, "I'm in a wheelchair because of osteoarthritis. I can't get well." But I am asking you the question: "Do you *want* to get well?" I am not looking for excuses, and neither is God—just a desire to live an extraordinary life.

Besides the obvious benefits of living a life free of pain and disease caused by poor diet choices, there are three main reasons to make a change today:

1. YOU WILL LIVE LONGER!

When I ask people how many of them want a long life, generally a few respond—but when I ask those same people how many of them want prosperity, many respond. People want prosperity, but they are not so sure about long life. You may be going through trials and tough times, but let me tell you—it's not over. Even if you are sick and feel you don't have anything else to live for, it's not over. By realizing that health is a gift, you can adopt this philosophy: *"I value my health. I value the gift of this body that's been given to me. I desire a long and healthy life."*

2. YOU WILL LIVE BETTER!

Too often, we believe the lies that our taste buds tell us: "Eat this fried chicken; the baked chicken doesn't taste as good. Eat the shellfish; it tastes much better than baked fish. Eat this piece of pork; it's delicious. Eat the pasta; it's so much tastier than fruits and vegetables." Your health is your wealth, and these lies will take your health from you. Making healthy choices gives you a better quality of life.

3. YOU WILL LIVE A FULLER LIFE!

Your life is not about you. You have a family and friends, and they *need* you. They can't handle losing you at age forty-five from a heart attack because of a lifetime of unhealthy choices, or because you have lived selfishly. Leave a health legacy for your family. Your kids are going to learn how to eat from two sources: first, from watching you. Children don't do what we tell them—they do what we do. Second, they are going to learn from the media. If they see commercials touting professional athletes or popular actors eating a Big Mac or other unhealthy foods, they will do the same thing. We must teach our children the truth about healthy choices. The choices *you* make today affect everyone else around you.

Recently a close family member suffered from lung cancer. In a short period of time, he went from being wonderfully healthy and vibrant to becoming extremely ill. He had major surgery and was preparing for chemotherapy. I visited him as much as my schedule would allow. I flew to speaking engagements and came right back to stay at the hospital.

One night as I was leaving, he called to me. With tubes protruding from his body, he rasped, "There are no guarantees in life." Sadly, he had the same mind-set that many others have today. When you become hurt or angry because life has "dealt" you certain blows, it is easy to think that there are no guarantees in life. There may be no ironclad guarantees on this earth, but you do have a choice. You can struggle through life, feeling the insecurity of each step you take, or you can choose to live an abundant life, no matter what circumstances come your way. As Abraham Lincoln once said, "Happiness is a journey, not a destination. Most people are about as happy as they make up their minds to be."

You can eat as healthily as you can; you can exercise every day; but if your soul and mind are not healthy, you will never be fully well. No matter where you are in life, don't come to the point that you are lying in a hospital bed with tubes in your body before you finally understand that you have the power to choose sickness or health.

"I can't," the sick man responded, lying next to the healing waters at Bethesda. Like him, we seem to live in an "I can't" world, and most of us act as "I can't" people. But you *can* if you want it. You may still be thinking, "Oh, I can't, Asa, it's too hard, I've tried every diet and it's too hard." Or, "I was on a diet for a while and then I got off; it's just too hard."

Too hard? Let's talk about what's too hard for a moment. Visit your local hospital's cancer floor and watch patients as they struggle to stay alive—in pain and full of tubes—all the time wondering how this happened to them. They are enduring the pain with no promise of tomorrow. Then go to your local children's hospital and witness a young child dealing with a terminal illness, and ask him if exercise, an organic diet, and a few healthy lifestyle choices would be too difficult if it meant he could one day go home again and play outside. You don't know what hard is until you must face the reality of death. Giving up doughnuts, fried chicken, shellfish, or pork is not really that hard. Exercising a little each day is not hard. Having your life cut short is hard. Leaving loved ones behind is hard—and it's selfish. Your life is worth more than that. Your family needs you. This world needs you. There is only one you, and you are the best you that we have. Take responsibility now.

Ask yourself this one simple question the next time you think making the right choice for your health is too hard:

"If it meant living free from struggle, depression, pain, or disease, is there anything I *wouldn't* do?" I hope your answer to that question is "no," and if it is, you are already on your way to empowering your health and living an extraordinary life.

THERE IS A PLAN FOR YOUR LIFE

Every one of us has a plan and purpose for our lives. You are custom designed; not one of us has the same thumbprint, the same retina, or the same body shape. Whether you are seven years old or ninety-seven, it doesn't matter what your life has been like before now; it only matters what it becomes when the pages of this book are closed. What your life becomes will be based on the decisions that you make starting today.

As a whole, Americans think money is everything—but our real *wealth* is our health. A person can work all his life to build up an estate with many possessions, but if that person loses his health, he'll spend all his money and time in an attempt to get his health back.

We all get sick and make poor choices at certain points in life, but if we really want to commit to taking care of our bodies, we have to start making the right choices. That's why we must not focus on what happened yesterday; today is a new day.

FIND YOUR PASSION

People often ask me, "Why do you do what you do?" That's easy—I do what I was created and designed for. When I respond this way, they usually ask, "How do you know that?" Again, the answer is simple. I believe in living a life of purpose. I am a communicator, and I have an intrinsic talent for it. I am also educated and have a passion for seeing people get well. I combined my talents with my education, and here I am. I believe in being more than a space-filler in this world. I also believe that every person was created and designed with a specific purpose in mind. Everyone has unique gifts, talents, and abilities. The greatest thing you can do in life is to take those gifts, talents, and abilities and use them to do something great.

Determining your purpose in life is one of the greatest keys to achieving optimal health. It's amazing how many people work year after year to take care of their families, but they still don't know why they are really here. Steve was one of those people. He sat in my office with a look of despair on his face. He had some basic health challenges such as chronic fatigue, high blood pressure, and high cholesterol, but those weren't my main concern. It was his downcast demeanor and lack of enthusiasm for life that had me puzzled. On the surface, Steve seemed to have it all—he had a lovely wife and two beautiful daughters, had a great job, and played golf three days a week. What more could a guy want?

At the beginning of his treatment, Steve's body was hardly responding at all. This baffled me—his health challenges were nothing out of the ordinary. About a third of the way into the program, I began to really get to know him. I discovered his goals, what he had achieved, and who he wanted to become. He finally confessed he was miserable in his job, he and his wife were not getting along, and he was emotionally disconnected from his daughters. I knew then why the treatments were ineffective. Human beings are only truly effective when they are living the life for which they were designed.

"What are your strengths?" I asked him.

He replied, "I'm good at sales."

"Okay, and what do you enjoy?"

"I really enjoy golf. It's my passion," he said.

I told him to go and find the work he loves in the golf industry and watch what would happen. Many of us gain our self-worth by what we do—our purpose in life. Because Steve was miserable at work, had no purpose, and felt passionless every day, his wife, daughters, and health suffered. All the treatment in the world was not going to correct his health until he got his mind right. Living your purpose is essential to the extraordinary health for which you are seeking.

I know about purpose—I had to discover my purpose on my own. I was placed in an orphanage as a baby, and shortly thereafter, two wonderful people adopted me. They gave me a home, loved me, and raised me to be the man that I am today. When I was adopted, I realized that I'd been set apart— I was special and not like other children. I couldn't see a reflection of myself in my adoptive parents, and I couldn't see my characteristics in them. I always felt loved, but there was a separation in knowing that I didn't come from them. Because of that, I sometimes felt as though I had to stand alone in life, and by standing alone, I began to *stand out*. It was then that I began to realize my full potential.

I could try to play NBA basketball; but as I am only a little over six feet tall, that probably wouldn't be the best choice. I could try to be a country music singer, but the fact that I can't sing would likely keep me in poverty, sitting on the side of the road playing a banjo for tips.

I knew that my biological parents gave me up for their own reasons, but I also knew that God created me and gave me special characteristics, gifts, talents, and abilities to use for something great. I didn't know what those were growing up, but as I defined what my talents were—what I was good at, what made sense, what I could use to help other people—my purpose on earth became clear, and it was then that I found my true vision.

EXPANDING YOUR VISION

When I speak of vision, I am not referring to the physical ability to read letters on a chart—we'll call that eyesight. Eyesight allows us to physically see where we are going, but our *vision* is what shows us our true direction in life. If our physical eyesight is impaired in some way, we need corrective measures to restore our sight. This help usually comes in the form of glasses, contact lenses, or laser eye surgery. I could give you some tips today for helping your eyesight, such as taking vitamin E or eating organic foods with high concentrations of vitamin A and beta-carotene. But there is a greater issue at hand; your physical eyesight is important, but your *vision* is critical to your life.

Proverbs 29:18 (KJV) tells us, "Where there is no vision, the people perish." The question today is *How is your vision?* How do you see yourself? How do you see your life? Where will you be in five years? If you can see it in your mind, it will come to pass, but you will never achieve what you cannot see. You need a vision that is bigger than your circumstances, your problems, or your past. To enlarge your vision, what you see must be bigger than you. In other words, your vision must be larger than what you think could really happen. *Think big.* This can be accomplished even if you are a pessimist. When your vision is bigger than yourself, you will know that it took God's hand to help you do it. God likes to be needed, and he loves faith. He likes to see us stretch ourselves and grow.

People find many reasons for their lack of vision:

"I grew up in lower income housing." Oprah Winfrey grew up in an inner-city ghetto, and look what she has accomplished.

"I'm partially deaf." Beethoven began to lose his hearing in his twenties, yet continued to produce masterpieces throughout his life.

"I just went bankrupt." Developer Donald Trump filed for bankruptcy in the nineties, but came back, rebuilt his financial empire, and became a billionaire again.

"I've been in prison." Nelson Mandela spent twenty-seven years in prison, but maintained his integrity and continued to influence his country.

"I am unable to have children." Mother Teresa, herself childless, became a mother to millions.

What do all of these people have in common? Celebrity status? Riches? No, they enlarged their vision and saw something in life beyond their circumstances. They didn't see where they were; they saw where they could go. Your health relies on having vision for your life—it is the critical component.

My goal in life was to become a physician. However, my grades in high school were low due to my attention deficit and lack of effort, and my guidance counselor told me I would be lucky to get into a technical college. But I didn't listen to her negativity, and I didn't let it hold me down. Even at seventeen my vision was bigger than my circumstances, bigger than negative words, and contained a big God. With hard work in college, I achieved a high GPA, and earned two bachelor's degrees, a master's degree, and two doctorates.

You are either striving toward something or you are dying. You have to make that choice every day. Remember, no one can do it for you. It is *your vision.* Become clear-sighted and watch what God will do in your health and in your life.

It is my desire that Natural Medicine will empower you to take responsibility for your health, give you hope, and instill in you the truth that no one else can do it for you. Once you have learned the basics, you can overcome your health challenges and then continue to apply the principles throughout your life. I want you to live an empowered life, not a doctor-dependent life. You have the greatest doctor inside you. You can take responsibility for your health, and gain hope and reassurance that with your body constantly regenerating every day, your best days are truly still ahead.

3

NATURAL MEDICINE
The Health Triangle

Everything in life seeks balance. The Health Triangle is the diagram I use to illustrate the integrated nature of Natural Medicine, which focuses on all three aspects of the body when bringing it into the natural state of balance and total health. This method thoroughly investigates patients' problems and determines if they arise from mental, chemical, or structural sources. The Natural Medicine approach does not just treat the symptoms, nor does it attempt to cure any disease. The cause of a health problem is identified and corrected accordingly using advanced testing techniques that have substantial documented research.

This approach is not symptom-oriented, but instead employs a "cause and effect" system of diagnosis. In other words, pain or discomfort is a symptom (the effect) of a mental component, nutritional deficiency, or structural malfunction (the cause). Focusing on all three sides of the Health Triangle is a time-proven system used to restore patients back to optimal health. All aspects of the body are evaluated—like putting together pieces of a puzzle. One side may affect one or both of the other sides depending on the health challenge; however, all sides must be addressed to achieve extraordinary health.

THE MENTAL SIDE

Stress is an inevitable part of life, but that does not negate the fact that stress affects your entire body and overall health. The *mental* aspect of the Health Triangle focuses on the body's ability to cope with daily life, changes in attitude, and the way stress is managed. The relationship between mental health and its physical consequences is called the "mind-body connection." You must strive for a hopeful and positive mental attitude, and the body's neurotransmitters (hormones in the brain that transmit information) must be evaluated to avoid mental challenges such as depression and other psychological disorders.

Studies have shown that 80 percent of all illnesses start in the mind. Edward Bach, a pioneer in the field of alternative medicine, believed that "health is our natural state, and disease indicates that our personality is stuck or in conflict." Bach suggested that we must "treat the person and not the disease; the emotional state that presages the pathological changes of illness."[1]

You will learn about my system of *Natural Medicine* as you read this book. There are protocols for each area of the Health Triangle. In the area of mental health, there are several primary areas that must be addressed:

Attitude. Our reactions to life stressors determine the level of health that we have. Most people react to health challenges with fear, and as a result, they will try any drug or any treatment, no matter the long-term consequences, to avoid disease. But fearing a disease will only make it worse. The right attitude involves replacing fear with hope. It is more beneficial to understand the root or cause of this disease so you can combat health challenges with the knowledge of how to beat them for good rather than use the Band-Aid approach and mask the symptoms. Band-Aids will eventually come off, and you will be left with the same problem until you address the root cause. Attitude is discussed further in chapter 4.

Lifestyle choices. One of the best things about the philosophy of Natural Medicine is that you get to decide how healthy you will be (discussed further in chapter 5). Genetics does play a role in your health, but because your father had heart disease or your mother had breast cancer, it does not mean that you inevitably will. Through deciding to make specific food and lifestyle changes, you have the power to choose the kind of health you will have.

The mind-body connection. The role of both the conscious and the subconscious mind is discussed in chapter 6 and must be addressed for total health, as well as identifying the underlying imbalances in neurotransmitters (brain chemicals) and ways to regain balance. The mind is powerful, and it goes far beyond simply having a positive attitude. Your state of mind can help heal you or make you sicker. We will discuss some positive steps you can take to give your brain the right fuel it needs for health.

THE CHEMICAL SIDE

The *chemical* side of the triangle deals with your overall blood chemistry, hormone function, and how well the body processes the foods that you eat. Natural Medicine uses a seventy-plus-component laboratory blood test, which I designed, that provides key information regarding any nutritional deficiencies; genetic tendencies toward heart disease, cancer, and diabetes; and the overall status of your body's chemical health. The chemical side can be most simply defined as vitamin and mineral deficiencies that result in the accumulation of toxins that can lead to health problems and eventually disease. Chemical imbalances can result in common ailments such as headaches and allergies and more serious health conditions such as cancer, obesity, heart disease, and diabetes.

The traditional medical approach for deficiencies in our chemical makeup is to use an array of prescription and over-the-counter drugs. This is a symptoms or "branch" approach, which we will learn more about in chapter 7, "The Tree of Life." Medication can be useful and at times necessary. However, medication many times masks symptoms, and can also block normal physiological functions in the body, as well as create other problems and severe side effects. The goal of Natural Medicine is to determine the basic cause (root) to address the effect (symptom) of a health condition. Chemical health has several fundamental areas to address, and the protocols for this section include:

Food choices. Your body forms new cells based solely on what you feed it, which you'll learn more about in chapter 8. That means you really are what you eat. The strength of the chemical side of the triangle depends greatly on your food choices. We will discuss the best food choices and what foods to avoid.

The most common diseases. The diseases that are most prevalent in America today are cancer, heart disease, diabetes, and obesity. However, you can beat the odds, and we will discuss the protocols to help you do so in chapter 20.

Diagnostic blood work. Blood work is the "gold standard" in Natural Medicine. You'll learn more about blood work and your body chemistry in chapter 14. Through comprehensive blood tests and thorough examinations of the results, you can finally discover the underlying cause of your health challenges. There is real power in the blood, and this section will educate you on just how much you can learn about your health from your own blood.

Inflammation. Inflammation is more than just a term used in a sports injury. Inflammation is your body's way of telling you something is wrong. In chapter 13, you will learn about the Anti-Inflammatory Diet and how to effectively eliminate inflammation in the body.

Supplementation. Chemical imbalances and disease ultimately stem from deficiencies of essential vitamins and minerals in the body. No matter your state of health, every person needs to supplement his or her diet with what we call the foundational four supplements. In chapter 9 you will learn about those four supplements, other important supplements, and the best kind of supplements to take.

When mentioning supplementation, I often refer to vitamins in their "active" or "activated" form. This means they are in their simplest, most broken-down forms, ready to be used by the body. Most vitamins have to be broken down by the body in multiple steps before they can be used. During that process, much of the potencies of these vitamins are lost. Therefore, we need the simplest version we can get to avoid unnecessary conversion steps that reduce effectiveness.

For example, flaxseed oil must go through a two-step process before it can be used. The liver must convert it to alpha linoleic acid before the body can use it as an omega-3 fatty acid, which is why we take it in the first place. Because of the conversion process, we only absorb 15 to 20 percent of all flaxseed oil intake.[2] Cod liver oil, however, requires no conversion in the body before it can be used as an omega-3 fat. Another example is vitamin B6. You can take it as pyridoxine, but it must be broken down before the body can absorb it. That is why I frequently mention pyridoxal-5-phosphate, or P-5-P, which is the active, or simplest, form of B6 and is ready for assimilation by the body.

Toxins. Toxins are everywhere. We find chlorine in our water, mercury in our fillings, and pesticides in our foods just to name a few. They enter the body, cause damage to every system, and rob us of our good health. However, there are ways to eliminate them from the body as well as ways to limit our exposure to them in everyday life, and we will address specific ways to avoid these deadly substances.

Hormone regulation. Hormones are more than estrogen or testosterone. Hormones keep our bodies in balance; they are the powerhouses of the bodies. We will talk about the different hormone systems, how their malfunctions can harm you, and how you can control them in chapter 11.

The pH scale. Striking the right balance of alkaline and acid in the body is what the pH scale is all about. It is more important than you may realize. When pH is in balance, you will experience unlimited energy and optimal health. In chapter 12 we will discuss which foods to eat, which foods to avoid, and which supplements to take to balance your body's pH.

THE STRUCTURAL SIDE

The *structural* side of the triangle deals with our muscular, skeletal, and nervous systems. The muscular system is responsible for movement in the body; the skeletal system is the framework supporting the body; and the nervous system provides the electrical power that controls every function in the body, including eye movement, heartbeat, skin sensation, breathing, and brain function. This is the third piece of the puzzle in determining the status of your overall health.

Stress and injury wreak havoc on the body and ignite a vicious cycle: An injury occurs or constant stress is placed on the body for extended periods of time; the nerves then become irritated and muscles tighten up; and those tightened muscles pull on the spine and misalign the spinal column that houses all our nerves. In short, nerve interference brought on by injury or ongoing stress equals malfunction and eventual disease. Traditional medicine's approach for these injuries is to prescribe medications such as anti-inflammatory drugs and muscle relaxers, use physical therapy, and implement surgery. But this doesn't remove the nerve interference. As with most modern-day treatment, it simply masks it for a while.

When the nerve interference is removed rather than masked, and communication from the brain to the muscles, organs, and tissues can now function at full capacity. Uninterrupted communication from the brain to the body's systems leads to 100 percent function, which in turn leads to 100 percent health. There are several fundamental structural health areas to address, and the protocols for this section include the following.

Nervous system. Every muscle, organ, and tissue in the body has nerves that control it. Chapter 16 covers how the nerves carry communication from the brain to the body and back to the brain through the spine. Nerve interference occurs when the vertebrae misaligns due to injury and causes pressure to the nerve root. The signals going from the brain to the muscles, organs, and tissues are now disrupted and the resulting systems cannot function properly—and a malfunctioning system leads to disease.

Muscular system. Muscles are more than big biceps. They carry energy throughout the body through pathways called energy meridians. In chapter 17 you will find out more about these pathways and how to harness the maximum power of your muscles, and the answer is not hitting the gym.

Skeletal system. Our bones are our core foundations. They house every other system and keep us standing tall. But just like every other part of the body, they weaken over time: Osteoporosis, the degeneration of bone, can cause a weakened skeletal system. But there are specific ways to keep your bones healthy and strong, no matter what your age, and you'll learn these ways in chapter 18.

Lymphatic system. Inside our bodies at this very moment, a silent war is being waged. Toxins, bacteria, and pollutants relentlessly enter the body through the food we eat, the air we breathe, the water we drink, and other ways. The lymphatic system is your body's army. It is the first line of defense against harmful substances that try to steal your health and is discussed further in chapter 19. Our lifestyle choices have weakened our lymphatic system, but there are specific ways to make them strong again and keep our bodies' strong fortresses against disease.

INTEGRATED HEALTH

Our health is integrated, which means that each side of the Health Triangle affects the other two. Being stressed can cause you to get sick or have a headache. Being nutritionally deficient in a vital mineral or vitamin can cause you to get depressed. A hurt knee can affect the function of your gall bladder. Our bodies are integrated, and everything that happens to one side of us—whether mentally, chemically, or structurally—affects our health in a variety of ways. Maintaining balance between all three is the key. When we do that, we will find the great health we are looking for.

Natural Medicine can be the foundation of how we attain and maintain extraordinary health. It's when we stray too far from our foundation that we need traditional medicine to help. If blood pressure gets out of control, cancer develops, or you suffer a heart attack, traditional medicine can be an immediate lifesaver. Natural Medicine and the Health Triangle are the day-to-day foundational systems used to keep the body where it needs to be in order to avoid these conditions. In medicine, we all have our specialties, and all doctors can work together as a team to help you live the life that you desire.

The two leading causes of death in America today are heart disease and cancer; two out of three Americans will develop one or the other.[3] In 2006 1.2 million people suffered a heart attack or died of cancer. The Health Triangle identifies health problems to help prevent these diseases and others. The underlying principle behind the Health Triangle is that all systems in the body affect the other systems, and to get healthy and stay healthy, you must determine what part of the body is not functioning properly and thereby affecting your overall health. Once the root cause is corrected, the body can once again find balance.

I walked in my office recently to find a new patient in tears. She had been to eleven doctors from all the top fields and medical specialties. She went to one doctor, who would just send her to another. She went to an internist, who sent her to a gastroenterologist, then to a neurologist, and to a psychologist. She said, "Dr. Asa, I've been doctor hopping all over this town. They say I have Crohn's disease, and that it's incurable, but I just want to feel better. No one sent me here. I heard you on the radio, and I sensed something different in your voice. Something told me there was an answer here. I know this is my last stop. I can't take life like this anymore."

Crohn's disease is an inflammation of the intestinal tract that causes intense abdominal pain, and weight loss and other symptoms. I assured her that she would get well if she was willing to make the commitment. I ran the diagnostic tests, laid out her treatment plan, and over time, I watched her go through extremely tough detoxification symptoms. She had amazing tenacity and perseverance. She followed the recommended Anti-Inflammatory Diet (discussed in chapter 13) perfectly and actually gained back healthy weight. She is now thriving in life. She realized that to attain total health, all three areas of the triangle must be addressed. Once she realized this, she was able to take responsibility for her own health, just as you can.

THE PATIENT MATTERS

A few seconds. That is the typical amount of time it takes before most doctors interrupt a patient who is describing his or her history and current symptoms. In that brief period of time, many doctors have already decided the likely diagnosis and the best course of treatment. Decisions made in this abrupt manner may be correct, but they can also be wrong. We are simply not listening. In life, the only way to truly know someone and to learn about that person is to listen. True friends, the ones who know who we really are, don't just hear us— they listen. The same is true with doctors and their patients.

Dr. James Andrews, a renowned orthopedic surgeon in Birmingham, Alabama, taught me this lesson. Dr. Andrews has been the surgeon for some of the greatest sports figures in the world, from Walter Payton to Shaquille O'Neal and Pete Rose. When I went to him with a severe tear in my ACL (anterior cruciate ligament) in my knee, I figured I would get three minutes of this prominent doctor's time at best. I assumed he would be too busy to spend time with a regular patient, even though I was also a doctor. Dr. Andrews walked into the exam room, sat down, propped his feet up on a trash can, and settled in. "So, Doc," he began. "You tore up your knee. How did you do it?"

As I began to talk, he did something no other doctor I had seen had done before. He listened, and he never interrupted me. He performed surgeries like mine multiple times a week on multimillion dollar athletes, but I left that day feeling like my knees mattered just as much as any pro athlete's. My time with him taught me to listen to every patient, no matter what. A patient's health condition may not be unique, but that person certainly is. Everyone's situation, no matter how similar in some respects to another, is different, and must be treated with this mind-set.

Natural Medicine takes this approach with every patient. I don't assume to know anything about a patient when they walk in the door, whether that person is dealing with diabetes, cancer, heart disease, or a toe injury. All patients receive my undivided and unbiased attention. Doctors can hypothesize about what *might* be wrong, but why not let the tests *show* us what is wrong? And they will almost every time. There is a reason that you were healthy and living well ten years ago, but find yourself struggling today. Something in your body stopped working correctly, and if doctors ask the right questions, listen, and perform the proper diagnostic tests, we will all be able find out what that is so you can discover how to once again achieve balance in all three areas of your health.

HERE WE GO

Let's look at some nuts and bolts of Natural Medicine and the Health Triangle. This system of health care focuses on restoring the body to optimal health. As you read, remember that you must address all three sides of the Health Triangle and balance all sides equally to attain extraordinary health. Don't stay on the referral merry-go-round, bouncing from doctor to doctor, and hoping that you will get well. You might, but your prognosis will be much better if you are willing to focus on restoring and balancing all three sides of your Health Triangle.

The mental side of the triangle is addressed first. It is important to start there, because we live in a world where there is a pill for everything, but it takes more than a pill to bring health to the body. We'll discuss traditional medicine's approach to health. If helping people thrive is the goal, modern medicine often misses the point. Traditional medicine is effective in treating the symptoms and sustaining life, but has been content with helping people survive rather than thrive. Many are barely surviving. My hope is that through Natural Medicine they will find balance for their lives and their health.

The sides of the Health Triangle are listed in no particular order because one side is not more important than the other two. Get ready—your perspective on how the body works is about to change. Are you willing to move from the ordinary to the extraordinary? I promise that you will discover that great health is simple and really involves nothing more than common sense.

COMMITMENT PAGE

DO YOU WANT TO GET WELL?

NATURAL MEDICINE

I, _____, want to get well. I am committed to do whatever it takes, regardless of how hard it may be, because I am determined to live an extraordinary life for myself, my family, and the world, which needs me and all I have to contribute. I realize that God believes in me, and by signing this, so do I. I will not complain, make any more excuses, or settle for what my personal lifestyle choices have brought me. I realize that my past is gone, today is a gift, and by making new choices, I can have renewed health and renewed life. My best days are still ahead, and I am pursuing life with passion, persistence, and enthusiasm.

Today is the first day of the rest of my life.

PART II:

MENTAL HEALTH

NATURAL MEDICINE®
HEALTH TRIANGLE

4

ATTITUDE
We Are What We Think About

You treat a disease, you win, you lose. You treat a person,
you win every time.

—PATCH ADAMS, MD

Most health books—and there are some great ones out there—begin by talking about diet, exercise, weight loss, or another mainstream health idea. The road to health is traveled in many ways, and you must find the road that fits you best. But the place to begin your health journey—wherever it takes you—is in your mind. The way we think determines everything in life. We must learn the benefits of controlling our thoughts.

Too often, we seek to change the world around us, look to correct circumstances and situations, and try to get others to see things our way. We typically see problems and challenges as happening *to* us, and caused by someone else. We may say to ourselves, "What's their problem?" or "Why don't good things happen to me?" We tend to be more focused on what is going on around us rather than focused on what is going on *within* us. Instead, we must consider both worlds—the world around us, which is the external world of responsibilities, family, job, circumstances, and situations, and the world within us, which consists of our thoughts, emotions, habits, actions, hopes, and dreams. Many things in this world are beyond our control, but only *you* can control the world within you.

I hope to help you understand a concept that is neither new nor groundbreaking, but it is something that we all too often ignore or forget altogether. Simply put: If we will control the world within us, we can affect the world around us. We can't control the situations and circumstances that come our

41

way; however, we can control our thoughts and our reactions. The way we handle and perceive the world within us profoundly affects our attitudes toward our outward lives.

Your attitude is more important than your aptitude or skill in life. Having a good positive mental attitude will allow you to see things differently and will help you encourage others. Don't constantly tell people about your problems or challenges in life—it won't help them, and it usually won't help you. Instead of saying something negative, find something positive to say. Believe it or not, every thought, situation, or circumstance has a positive side.

THOUGHTS ARE POWERFUL

My mother is one of the most positive people I have ever known, and I have learned so much from her throughout my life. No matter the situation or how bad things appeared, she always looked on the bright side. Her entire world might be caving in, but it was still a "great day." Have you ever been around people like that? I call it *active hope*. That kind of relentless hope is contagious. She was always happy—delighted that God had given her a brand new day—and she knew tomorrow was going to be even better.

Recently I was visiting my family, and my mother quietly said, "Mr. Thompson has passed away." Mr. Thompson was a close family friend and had died at the age of eighty-two. I began to sulk, and then I began to list all the sad aspects of his death—how tragic it was for his wife and family. I let negative comments pour out of my mouth while my mother just looked at me with an upbeat smile, the same one she has always had, and after I finished my pity party, she simply replied, "Well, he had a great life—eighty-two years. Wow, what a gift for any human being! He didn't die with any pain. He just went to sleep. Now he is in a better place." *What an amazing way of thinking!* No matter what circumstance comes along, that woman always has a great attitude.

Did she recognize the reality of harsh situations and struggles? Sure she did! What she chose to do about those situations was something else entirely. She chose to have hope that a better day was coming, and to believe that God always has everything under control. I realize now that I actually grew up in a household with a motivational speaker. She continuously saw the positive side to every difficult circumstance in life. Although her food and lifestyle choices have not always been the best, my mother is seventy years old and is still experiencing vibrant health. I believe much of that good health is due to her amazing ability to control her thought life. She tells herself what she is going to think, rather than allowing circumstances and problems in life to dictate her attitude.

As Zig Ziglar said in his book *Over the Top*, "A positive attitude won't give you everything in life, but it will bring you more than negative thinking will."[1] The way we think is a choice. So if you have the chance to choose one attitude or another, choose to be positive. Earl Nightingale, in his 1957 audio series, *The Strangest Secret*, said, "We become what we think about. A person is what they think about all day long."[2]

Our thoughts have tremendous power. If you sow a thought, you reap an action; if you sow an action, you reap a habit; if you sow a habit, you reap character; and if you sow character, you reap a destiny for a lifetime. What we continually think about today determines who we will become tomorrow. What does that mean to us? It's simple—we have to change the way we think! Controlling our thought life is extremely important to our overall health.

EMOTIONS ARE POWERFUL

Our attitude has a significant impact on the types of emotions we experience. When my mother gave me the news that an old friend had passed away, my negative attitude caused me to react with grief, sorrow, and self pity; but my mother's more positive outlook allowed her to focus on the good things about our friend's life. More than mere reactions based on our own mind-sets, our emotions can have a significant effect on our physical health. We experience various emotions throughout the day and encounter circumstances that cause us to respond with a wide array of reactions, both verbal and physical. For example, these physical reactions typically occur in your body when you become angry:

- Cortisol production increases in the adrenal glands, which raises blood pressure, raises blood sugar levels, may cause infertility in women, and suppresses the immune system.

- Fat storage increases.

- Brain cells are killed.

- Free radicals (unstable molecules that are believed to cause tissue damage at the cellular level) are overproduced.

Anger increases aging, causes wrinkles, and increases the risk of cancer. Anger may also cause disorders of the digestive system, circulatory system, nervous system, glandular system, and immune system, as well as inflammation and skin diseases. Researchers have discovered that a meal containing high amounts of refined carbohydrates, processed carbohydrates, and sugar suppresses the immune system for up to seven hours. Did you know that the same response happens when you become angry or bitter towards someone? Think about a traffic jam when you got angry with the driver who cut you off—everyday events like that can cause your immune system to become suppressed, just like a meal of processed sugar and carbohydrates.

Think about it this way: You're on your way to work and you get angry because someone just took your parking space. Then you get to work and eat a doughnut, drink a soda or heavily sugared coffee, and eat a bagel. Throughout the day, you are frequently upset with your coworkers and angry at your boss—mad, mad, mad. With all the processed food you've eaten, your immune system is suppressed on an ongoing basis. When you go to lunch, you eat a hamburger and French fries, and your immune system is depressed for another six or seven hours. Tired and frustrated, you go home and eat a TV dinner, and now your immune system is suppressed all through the night. So your immune system is shut down twenty-four hours a day—and we wonder why we get sick!

Kristen came into my office with severe back pain. As I shook her hand I noticed that spot above the brow line between the eyebrows had a stern wrinkle in it—and she was only twenty-six! She began to tell me about her back pain, chronic since her divorce three years ago. However, after performing the diagnostic tests and exams, I couldn't find a thing wrong. At each weekly session she complained about life, spoke negatively, and played the victim. I finally asked her, "Kristin, are you still angry about the divorce?"

She exclaimed, "Yes, I am! He should've never cheated on me!"

She was understandably hurt, and harboring unforgiveness, bitterness, and anger. Adding to her unhealthy mental state, her blood tests revealed an imbalance in her brain chemicals. But ultimately, getting her to understand the power of forgiveness helped her in the healing process. As soon as she began to forgive, her back pain began to go away. The mental component of health is extremely powerful.

FEAR IS HAZARDOUS TO YOUR HEALTH

One particularly powerful emotion is fear. Unfortunately, fear has been a part of traditional medicine for years. We physicians don't do this intentionally. We are taught to base every case on the facts and test results. However, many times, this leaves out the best medicine that anyone could ever have, and that's hope.

If we see a spot on an X-ray or film, we are predisposed to think that it's possibly cancer, or if a patient's cholesterol level is 350, we may think a heart attack is imminent. Then we place fear into the patient, which is one of the greatest deterrents to getting well. But as psychologist Denis Waitley points out, fear is usually *F*alse *E*ducation *A*ppearing *R*eal, or as I frequently encounter in the medical world—false *evidence* appearing real.[3]

Sam had been diagnosed with cancer and called my show looking for guidance, or at least some comfort. I was about to give my standard answer for dealing with a cancer diagnosis, but something held me back. I could hear the fear in Sam's voice. I stopped all doctor talk, because all the antioxidants and good lifestyle choices in the world would not help his health challenge at this point. He was filled with fear and it was paralyzing his progress.

"I have just been diagnosed with lymphoma," he told me. "They want me to undergo chemotherapy. What should I do?" I assured him that he first needed to face his reality and not be scared of the unknown. Instead, he should focus on the steps he could actively take, and determine the things over which he had no control. I told him that the body regenerates itself completely over the course of several years. Sam could get well, but he had to eliminate his fear. I told him to focus on the *prognosis* rather than the *diagnosis*. He had three children. I reminded Sam that those kids needed their father, so it was time for him to stop thinking of what he could lose and focus on what he could win.

Maybe you think that sounds like advice you might get lying on a couch being charged by the hour. Can you suggest a better option? Cry, live in terror, believe life is over, and wait to die? No, you can get well, and that is what

I told Sam. That was a monumental conversation for him that night. He received a new prescription for his life, and he soon e-mailed to thank me. Although chemotherapy was still necessary in Sam's case, he informed me that he was doing well and the doctors gave him a favorable report that his immune system had improved and he was getting better.

The power of fear is great, but the power to believe, have faith, and hope that a better day is coming, regardless of your current circumstances, is even greater.

GET OVER IT AND GET ON WITH IT

Controlling fear, our thought lives, and anger and bitterness, and letting go of unforgiveness are just as important as watching our diet, exercising, and taking care of our physical bodies. Think about your life and the way you've lived it, the mistakes you've made, and the times you acted before thinking. Any wrong that has been done to you, you have probably done to someone else. So is it really worth holding on to unforgiveness when someone has hurt you? When you don't forgive someone, you are essentially putting yourself in a mental prison. You are the one still angry and focused on that person or event. The person against whom you hold a grudge is most likely not dwelling on it; that person has probably moved on. You must get to the point where you can forgive and let go. Remember this regarding unforgiveness:

It is what it is; get over it, and get on with it.

What is it in your past that you just can't let go? You need to identify those things first, and realize that whatever has happened to you—that was yesterday. Are you the same today as you were yesterday? I hope not; I hope you are growing and changing. After you identify those things in your past you've been holding on to, it's crucial to avoid similar grudges in the future. Here is one suggestion for doing this—repeat the following phrase to yourself and believe it: *There is always something I don't know.*

Whenever you are treated badly or given poor service, there is always one more thing—one more fact or circumstance in your offender's life that may have caused him or her to be rude to you. Maybe her child was sick, maybe she didn't get her paycheck when she was supposed to, maybe she has a family member in trouble, or maybe she lost someone whom she loves very much. Always give those around you the benefit of the doubt. Maybe the waiter has had a rough day—maybe you won't leave him as much, but don't completely stiff him on his tip. The bank teller may not have even realized she was being rude to you; perhaps her mind was somewhere else. Maybe her son was ill or her divorce papers were just signed. We are not all experts at hiding the hardships that life brings our way.

Recently I spoke at a conference to share my health and wellness message. The host treated me poorly, and I was promised some things that my host did not deliver. Even financially I did not receive what was promised. When I returned to the office from the event, it would have been easy for me to get upset thinking about the situation. But then I thought about the fact that a lot of people's lives were touched at that conference. I could have chosen to sit around and dwell on what happened to me, but instead I chose to focus on what happened to others—the impact that was made in people's lives through my message. I chose to forgive, and I chose to not focus on the negative thoughts, actions, and words that I experienced.

It doesn't matter what's done to us; what matters is the impact that we can have on those around us. That is the most important thing in life. The moments of today will pass away, but things that you pour into the lives of others are the things that really matter.

Forgiveness releases real power, but there is no power and no health benefit in holding on to grudges and refusing to forgive and move on. If you will train yourself to forgive others regardless of what they've done to you or how they've hurt you, health and vitality will return to you. It always comes back to you in good measure. Negative thoughts, negative words, and negative actions will rob you of the health that the Creator destined for you. By harnessing your emotions and managing them—rather than allowing them to manage you—you will be able to live the abundant life for which you were created.

5

LIFESTYLE CHOICES
You Decide How Healthy You Will Be

"Health is not simply the absence of sickness."
—GEORGE DENNISON PRENTICE

We've been led to believe it's all in the genes—Grandma had it, Mom had it, now I will have it. And then you wait for a heart attack to come your way. *What are you thinking?* You weren't born with cancer, heart disease, diabetes, Crohn's disease, or leukemia. I realize there are some defects and issues that are out of our hands. But I want to focus on the health challenges that *are* in our control. You weren't born with doughnuts, fried foods, French fries, sugar, and processed bread in your mouth—you or your parents put them there. By consistently eating the wrong kinds of foods, not exercising, drinking unfiltered tap water, and neglecting sleep, many people are now facing disease and sickness.

For the most part, your health is determined by your choices. The mind plays a critical role in how your body reacts to certain stressors and life situations. The great thing is that you have control over your mind. Indeed, we all must deal with some genetic factors. However, knowing the past gives you power in the present to make the best choices for your future. All health challenges that you face have a mental component. You can control your thoughts every day, and that may be one of the greatest prescriptions ever given to you. You control what you think, eat, and drink; the amount of exercise you do; and how much rest you get. No one else can do this for you. When cancer, diabetes, heart disease, or arthritis develops, many people get frustrated and think, *Why me?* Did you ever stop to realize that these lifestyle-related diseases did not just show up out of nowhere?

STRESS—THE SILENT DISEASE

Stress—we can't escape it. It is as much a part of the American lifestyle as television or baseball. It doesn't matter if we are in our cars, on vacation, at home, at work, or at play; stress will find us. Psychologist Dr. Kevin Leman said the best definition for stress is this: "The wear and tear on our bodies produced by the very process of living." Stress *is* life. We have good stress; we have bad stress; we have stress that moves us forward in life; we have stress that holds us back. No matter what circumstances we face, stress will be there, but how we cope with that stress will determine whether it has toxic effects on our health. When we get stressed, several things occur in our bodies:

- Increased neural excitability (increased anxiety)

- Increased cardiovascular activity (increased heart rate and blood pressure)

- Decreased metabolism with muscle wasting (also known as muscle atrophy, a decrease in the size of skeletal muscle)

- Sodium retention (water retention or bloating)

- Reduced digestive activity (inability to properly digest and absorb food)

- Decreased immune function (increased susceptibility to bacteria and disease)

When the body is over-stressed, it simply cannot function properly, and our overall health suffers. In life, we deal daily with what I call "false reality." Many times, our perception of what life is and what life actually is are two different things. We often perceive things to be worse than they are. For example, let's say you just lost your job. In your mind you believe that you lost your job because of an inability on your part, when the reality may be that you and your boss simply could not see eye to eye. Another prime example is a child's mistaken belief that his parents' divorce was caused by something he did.

Ninety percent of the stress that we go through every day is perceived reality, and only 10 percent of it is reality.[1] So the majority of the time we tend to worry and be stressed over perceived reality. The basis for most people's stress is fear. One of the greatest ways to cope with stress in our lives is to turn the fear into faith. That is also one of the keys to controlling our thought lives. We must learn how to turn negatives into positives.

When you get in the habit of seeing the positive side of life, this attitude can help bring health to your body. The Bible says that human beings are not given "a spirit of fear, but of power, love, and a sound mind."[2] Faith produces strength, but fear will rob you of your energy. Every individual has what I refer to as a "stress savings account"—an energy reserve. We have a certain amount of energy that we can use when stress hits. Once we deplete that stress savings account, the body begins to break down, and the immune system begins to shut down. The body becomes incapable of fighting off illnesses. We only have a certain amount of reserve to use, so use it wisely. That is why managing stress is so important.

Here are seven ways to cope with stress that will truly benefit you and improve your health:

1. Get proper rest. I can't overemphasize the importance of this coping mechanism. The amount of rest your body needs is extremely important for your overall health. The body needs between seven to nine hours of sleep a night. You should also take time each week to rest or relax during waking hours. Get away from your responsibilities and activities and completely allow your body to achieve rest—take time off. Take at least one day out of every seven to simply relax and spend time alone or with your family. This is a great coping method for stress.

2. Recognize your challenges. Identify what is causing stress in your life so you can find ways to cope with it.

3. Ask for help. Whether it is a counselor or a friend, it is always better to get things off your chest and off your heart. This allows your body to de-stress and cope with the situation. Then you can come up with sound ways to correct the situation.

4. Avoid toxins. Toxins include refined foods, poor water, poor air, alcohol, drugs, cigarettes, caffeine, and sugar. We will discuss toxins in more detail in chapter 10. By avoiding dietary toxins you will increase the body's immune response, which will allow you to better cope with stress. When undergoing pressure, many people turn to junk food, cigarettes, caffeine, or alcohol to handle the stress they are experiencing. But the reality is that these substances are so toxic that they actually increase the stress response in your body.

5. Schedule your life. I am not a shining example of this. It's something that I have really struggled with throughout my life. I had always been one to be a little bit late and procrastinate whenever possible. I often try to squeeze too much into my schedule. I wait until the last minute and rush around trying to get everything done. I functioned that way for many years, and I felt the stress associated with this lifestyle. Finally, I was able to discipline myself to be on time for appointments.

I was also the poster child for bad driving, speeding down the interstate headed to an appointment—always running late. I drove on everyone's bumper; you would not have wanted to see me in your rearview mirror. My perpetual lateness created a lot of stress and anxiety and placed undue pressure on my life. When I began to be more punctual, I found I had plenty of time to listen to the radio or make phone calls. It took me a while to realize that eliminating this one bad habit removed a huge amount of stress in my life (and reduced the risks I caused myself and others by my bad driving). Always plan ahead—it's a great coping skill.

6. Exercise. Exercising thirty minutes a day doing something you enjoy—walking, jogging, weight training, or some other physical activity—is an ideal way to cope with stress. It relieves the pressures of the day by getting blood flowing through your body. It also allows you to take more oxygen into the body, the brain, the muscles, and the tissues. This allows your body to process the stress it has been through during the day.

7. Take supplements. Take vitamin and mineral supplements regularly to counteract stressful situations in your life. In addition, the primary stress fighting vitamins are the B vitamins, specifically vitamin B6 and B12. This is especially true when you are going through a high-pressure situation.

HEADACHES—SIGNALS TO MAKE LIFESTYLE CHANGES

Headaches are an excellent illustration of the ill effects of unhealthy lifestyle choices. All three sides of the Health Triangle affect headaches; however, headaches tend to have a strong mental component. When you have a headache, no matter how positive you may try to be, it can immobilize you and take the joy out of your day.

Headaches can also affect other lifestyle choices. Let's say you are a parent with a full-time job, and during the day you develop a severe headache. You are tired from the long day and suffering from the throbbing in your head. The thought of going home and preparing a healthy meal for the family is the last thing on your mind; instead, you stop by a fast food restaurant on your way home. Don't use headaches as an excuse to make poor lifestyle choices.

Headaches are a warning sign that something is wrong. They are like the red warning light in your car. If you disregard that red light, the car will eventually break down. If you disregard the cause of your headaches, you could become unhealthy and dependent on more and more drugs while never addressing the root of the problem. For many types of headaches, dehydration can be a key factor. When you develop a headache of any kind, drink sixteen ounces of pure, non-chlorinated water and see if the symptoms go away. If not, then you must look farther to find the underlying source of the headache.

Headaches are not caused by a lack of aspirin in the diet. They are caused by lifestyle choices. But finding the cause of headaches and not just fighting the symptoms is not an easy task. Changing your eating patterns and getting exercise will help curtail most headaches. These habits are difficult to procure and require mental preparation and stamina. You have to choose to get well and be willing to do anything that it takes. Like a runner preparing for a marathon, you can't give up and you can't cheat on your preparation. We will talk about the specific chemical deficiencies that cause headaches and how to align your chemical makeup to avoid them in Chapter 9.

THE BEST THINGS IN LIFE ARE FREE

We truly were given a great gift—we are in control of our lifestyle choices, which in turn gives us control over our health. Some of the greatest treasures in our lives—our mind, hopes, dreams, soul, body, ambition, intellect, health, and love for family and friends—are free. Ironically, those are the areas where we tend to spend the least amount of time in today's fast-paced lifestyle.

Perhaps you or someone you know spent a lot of money for a shiny new car. You've been saving for it, and now the day has finally come. You drive it to the grocery store and park it on the farthest end of the parking lot so it will not get a single scratch or ding. You carefully get the oil changed at regular intervals, keep the tires at the correct pressure, and have your coolant levels checked. Interesting, isn't it? We take better care of our cars then we do ourselves. For most people, health comes as standard equipment at birth, but it is up to us how we take care of that equipment. Eat the right foods, exercise, avoid stress, and maintain the right mental attitude. *We do have a choice*— the choice to do what is best for our health every day. Remember, no one can do it for you.

We try to "keep up with the Joneses," get the kids through college, earn more money, find a better job, and after all this effort, many of us will lose our most valuable possession of all—our health. We are constantly reaching for happiness. We get married, and in five to seven years, we are ready to get a divorce and move on. We live in a society focused on instant gratification— we want it all, and we want it now. Everything in life reflects this trend—high-speed Internet connections, cell phones, giant supermarkets and department stores, fast food, twenty-four-hour-a-day constant streaming news channels, fast sports cars—and we are never satisfied.

When you finally realize that your health is your wealth, you will be ready to live the abundant life you desire.

THE BE-DO-HAVE PRINCIPLE

Be before you do, then do before you have. Sound confusing? It isn't. Life teaches us lessons over and over until we finally learn them. Sometimes it's painful and other times it's fun, but it's always life.

Have you ever wondered why some people have everything they want and others never seem to have what they need or want? It's called the Midas Touch—it seems as though whatever some people touch turns to gold. In actuality, what they have is an innate ability to define what they want, and then they go after it. What does this entail? Here are the steps to making correct lifestyle choices and decisions. They are applicable for life in general, and especially in regard to your health:

1. Decide what you want.

2. Define it with clarity—in one clear and concise sentence.

3. Become it and live it.

4. Then, and only then, will you have it.

Most of us think: *I really would like to have a better job, a bigger house, or a different husband* (don't tell him that). We are dissatisfied and live in a dream world that never comes to fruition. We all have our *need to* lists . . . I need to lose weight, start exercising, stop smoking, or quit drinking. But rarely do we turn our *need tos* into *have tos*. We wait for life to simply hand us things, especially our health. We must understand the BE-DO-HAVE principle.

When we were young, most of us felt invincible. We thought we could take on the world and no one could stop us. I once bought into that same ideology. I used to think, "I've got my whole life ahead of me with plenty of time to make decisions and move forward in life." But the reality is that life moves fast. Life is but a vapor—it's here for a moment and then gone. When we were young, we were full of energy, vitality, and purpose, and we envisioned all the great things still to come. The exciting thing is that by making healthy choices, you can have a life filled with that kind of vibrancy, not just experience it in your younger years.

To get well, you can't just desire it; you have to BE well first in your mind. You have to see yourself being well, living, and thriving the way you want. See yourself exercising every day, living without insulin, without doughnuts, without statin drugs, without chemotherapy. You have to BE . . .

Then you have to DO it. Nike said it best with its slogan, *Just Do It!* That is what you have to do. Make it happen. If you have already decided to become someone who is healthy, competent, wise, and living the way you want, then your body will start doing what you already have become in your mind.

By making the decision to become the person you desire to be in your mind, doing it will not be that hard. The body will always follow the mind. I was talking with a well-known NASCAR driver who was telling me about the mechanics of driving. He said when you are going over two hundred miles per hour, you don't have much time to react. The secret is looking down the track to where you want to go. If you can set your eyes on the track, the car will follow.

Set your vision on who you want to become: a person full of health and achieving all you want in life, and then DO the work it takes to become that person. Then you will HAVE the results, life, and outcome that you originally desired. Don't wait for it to come to you . . . it will never happen if you are just waiting for it.

Become it.

Do it.

Have it.

6

THE SUBCONSCIOUS MIND
The Mind-Body Connection

"Health is a state of complete physical, mental, and social well-being, and not merely the absence of disease or infirmity."

—WORLD HEALTH ORGANIZATION

Hope is the power in the mind that we can all harness. Whether your hope is in a loving God, or simply hope for the sake of hope, hope represents an inherent notion that a better day is coming. How far does this biological hope reach? Researchers have found that an active change in mind-set has the power to alter body chemistry.

Expectation, belief, and faith are the key elements of hope. They can literally block pain in the body by releasing "feel-good" brain chemicals called endorphins and enkephalins, which mimic the effects of drugs such as morphine. In many cases, hope and this mind-set shift can cause physiological changes in circulation, respiration, and neurological motor function. During the course of any disease or illness, hope can act like a chain reaction that creates improvement and healing in body, mind, and spirit. Hope is powerful. It is the new medicine that helps people take responsibility for their own health and their lives.

NEUROTRANSMITTERS—MIND-BODY CONNECTION

Hope is indeed a powerful force. But even the most hopeful of us can still experience feelings of sadness or despair. Do you ever feel depressed but don't know why? Your life is great, but for some unexplainable reason you are frequently unhappy. The bottom line is you just don't feel balanced, but you choose to be positive and not pay attention to it, shrugging it off as a passing mood.

There is another more likely reason. Our brain chemistry and mental function go hand in hand. Our brain performs its functions through chemicals called neurotransmitters, and often, these brain chemicals are not balanced correctly. The four most common neurotransmitters are:

- Acetylcholine

- Serotonin

- GABA (gamma-amino butyric acid)

- Dopamine

Emotion, attitude, and mental function are largely dependent on these chemicals working correctly in the brain. The neurotransmitters are affected by diet, lifestyle choices, exercise, and even our personal lives. We have control over our own thought processes, but we must be aware of the chemistry that can, if left unchecked, radically change our ways of thinking. We see clearly here how the Health Triangle is at work again; the chemical side of the triangle is affecting the mental side.

Remember that the health triangle is connected—each side affects the other two. For this reason, it is important to discuss the chemicals that most directly influence the mental aspect of our health. As we discuss the brain chemicals, be aware that these are technically also a part of chemical health, which is the next section of this book. Neurotransmitters like GABA and serotonin play significant roles in our moods, reactions, emotions, and ability to handle stress.

Rita was my first patient of the day. As I came in the room to greet her, she was smiling and crying at the same time. I smiled back and asked her what was wrong. She replied, "Oh, I'm fine."

Obviously she wasn't "fine."

She explained, "I cry all the time. I feel sad and don't know why."

I asked Rita if anything traumatic or upsetting recently happened, and she told me her son was in drug rehab, and she felt like a failure as a mother.

During testing, I found her serotonin levels to be low. She had been on an antidepressant for about six months; this drug was designed to raise serotonin levels, which would lift her out of a depressed state. It wasn't working.

Rita's blood work results showed that she had a severe iron deficiency and was anemic. She also had a vitamin B6 deficiency. I placed her on heavy amounts of organic iron supplementation and activated B6 to bring her nutrient levels back to normal. She ate organic red meat and green vegetables each day to increase her natural iron intake, and ate red peppers to increase her vitamin B6. Within two months, her serotonin levels were back to normal and her depressive state subsided. We may never really know what depleted her body of the vitamins. We do know, however, that once they were corrected, she began to think clearly again and regained control of her own emotions.

Our brain chemicals become unbalanced in two different ways. The first is when too much of a neurotransmitter is circulating in the body. Constant stress and traumatic events can cause the body to begin overproducing these chemicals. This overload causes malfunctions in the brain and mental functions due to overstimulation from the excess brain chemical. The second is when there is a deficiency in a certain brain chemical to maintain proper mental function. This is typically caused by the lack of certain supplements in the diet.

A neurotransmitter is like a baseball, and receptors in the body act as the catcher's mitt to receive the messages. The brain is capable of automatically manufacturing the quantity of chemicals it needs if it is given the necessary raw materials—nutrients from foods. However, our diets do not always supply enough of the raw materials the brain needs to manufacture the correct amounts of neurotransmitters.

Additionally, stress, worry, emotional dips, drugs, alcohol, pollution, and other factors of modern life deplete neurotransmitter levels. Neurotransmitter deficiency and imbalance can affect your stress level, energy, appetite, sleep, mood, memory, sex drive, anger, addictions, and other functions of daily life.

In the following sections, I will show you certain patterns in a person's behavior that best exemplify an individual with an imbalance in each of the four brain chemicals. I will also recommend the supplements that would best help those suffering from excessive or deficient levels of each of the neurotransmitters. Achieving balance in our brain chemistry is just as important as what we choose to think about. Don't be surprised if these examples make you think about someone you know, or even yourself.

ACHIEVE BALANCE WITH ACETYLCHOLINE

Martha is the kind of person who likes things in life to be in balance. She doesn't like chaos; she prefers calm. When she is overstimulated from events of the day, she becomes angry and aggressive toward others without understanding her own reactions. It's becoming increasingly harder for her to cope with many of life's struggles, and she begins to wrestle with fear-based panic attacks. This slows her heart rate tremendously, which then throws her into a tailspin, and she is overcome by dizziness and vertigo. While she is feeling this dizziness, she begins to feel a "rumble" in her stomach and has a frequent need to visit the restroom. What Martha doesn't know is that she had better get this under control soon; her liver can only take so much overstimulation. She probably has several nutritional deficiencies, such as vitamins B2 and B3, manganese, zinc, and magnesium.

Acetylcholine Symptoms

Deficiency	Excessive Amounts
Rapid heart rate	Slow heart rate
High blood pressure	Low blood pressure
Dry mouth	Excessive salivation
Poor digestion	Anger
Constipation	Aggressive behavior
Farsightedness	Panic attacks
Urinary retention	Vertigo
Glaucoma	Diarrhea
Myesthenia gravis	Asthma due to excessive mucous
High cholesterol	Resting tremors
Short term memory loss	Liver toxicity
Confusion	
Delerium	
Hallucinations	
Alzheimer's	

Martha also finds herself regularly confused and feels out of sorts throughout much of the day. Her memory often fails, causing her to frequently ask herself questions such as, *Where did I park the car? Where did I put the car keys? Did I leave the stove on again? Did I lock the door?* This is starting to concern Martha because her grandfather had Alzheimer's, and she saw what he went through and definitely doesn't want to go down that road. Besides, she's only thirty-four. She also suffers from constant dry mouth, slow digestion, and extreme constipation. She used to urinate all the time, but now barely uses the restroom one or two times during the day. If Martha had her diagnostic blood work done, it would show dangerously high levels of cholesterol causing many of these issues. *Something needs to change.*

Martha loves balance in her external life, but what she really needs is to first get back into balance on the inside. She can achieve this by taking acetyl CoA (an important molecule in metabolism and energy production), pantothenic acid (vitamin B5), manganese (an essential trace nutrient in all forms of life), and omega-3 oils such as cod liver oil. Supplementing these nutritional deficiencies will accomplish much of the balance she seeks; however, her stubborn, subconscious mind has also caused the neurotransmitters to change. Martha struggles with feelings of pride, intermingled with guilt and scorn. She still feels responsible for her parents' divorce when she was only seven years old. She also blames herself for her family's financial crisis—her husband lost his job, but Martha's spending habits have skyrocketed out of control. She shops when she feels depressed, and this is becoming an almost daily ritual.

She needs to start reciting the affirmation that she *can* get well to unlock her subconscious mind. Martha must also make changes in her current lifestyle choices. Only then will she achieve a healthy balance, and her husband can stop wondering, *What in the world happened to the sweet woman I married?*

FIND STABILITY WITH DOPAMINE

Brent is known to be a little unstable. He has a tendency to be overly excited one day and virtually catatonic the next. A few of his family members think he might be bipolar. He is indecisive and has poor concentration. He has been known to fly off the handle and be totally irrational. Everything is "all about Brent," and he is constantly seeking whatever is most satisfying to him and him alone. Always bumping into things, he's a little clumsy. He tends to be photophobic as well, and a flash camera hurts his eyes. He sometimes deals with tremors and loses his sense of smell, which frustrates him even more. When these things occur, Brent's dopamine levels are extremely low. But what about the days that he suffers from severe anxiety and nightmares? Brent is suffering from excess dopamine at those points, also causing him to be prone to extreme irritability. Occasionally, he has even become physically aggressive.

What he needs more than anything is supplementation with folinic acid (active folic acid), pyridoxal-5-phosphate (active vitamin B6), NADPH (activated niacin), and iron. It would also benefit Brent to take adenosylcobalamin (active B12) and some magnesium and zinc as well. Brent may also need copper and iron, as there may be a lack of oxidation in his body. These supplements have been proven to increase or regulate the production of dopamine in the brain. With the help of these supplements, he can become a more stable person.

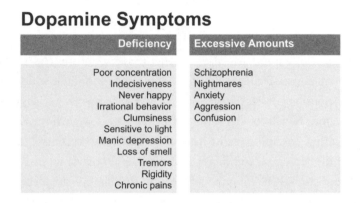

Dopamine Symptoms

Deficiency	Excessive Amounts
Poor concentration	Schizophrenia
Indecisiveness	Nightmares
Never happy	Anxiety
Irrational behavior	Aggression
Clumsiness	Confusion
Sensitive to light	
Manic depression	
Loss of smell	
Tremors	
Rigidity	
Chronic pains	

FIGHT DEPRESSION WITH SEROTONIN

As Michelle introduced herself she wore a smile, but it didn't mask the deep sadness in her eyes. She was the typical forty-something mother whose family was doing well, and yet she struggled with depression and despair. Like many mothers, she had given everything of herself for the last twenty years to be a great wife and parent. She took care of the kids and her husband, worked long hours, and handled the family's finances. Michelle lived in a three million dollar home, and both of her children were attending Ivy League schools and doing quite well. She was living the dream life—on the surface anyway.

"I just don't know what's wrong with me," she said. "For some reason, I wake up every day and feel sad. I'm tired all the time. I find myself eating large amounts of food and crying while I eat!" She continued, "When I start one task, like cleaning the house, I tend to do it compulsively, almost like I can't stop. I used to be a glass-half-full kind of woman and now life just seems empty."

Along with these compulsive behaviors, Michelle was experiencing sudden urges for alcohol. Her low body temperature kept her feeling cold all the time although her endocrinologist said her thyroid was working fine. Recently, she had been going to the bathroom every hour with the constant urge to urinate. She shamefully admitted, "Dr. Asa, I have really been struggling with the idea of taking myself out of this world."

Serotonin Symptoms

Deficiency	Excessive Amounts
Depression	Depression
Mood disturbances	Anxiety
Suicidal Tendencies	Aches and pains
Sleep disorders	Migraines
Impulsive aggression	Masked agression
Obsessive behavior	Obsessive compulsive
Rage	Shyness
Axorexia and Bulimia	Dehydration
Bladder issues	Kidney issues
Excessive weight gain	Fearfulness
Decreased sex drive	Low sex drive
Low blood pressure	High blood pressure
Low body temperature	High body temperature
Compulsive disorders	Lack of self confidence
Increased alcohol craving	

Michelle was like many people today—feeling hopeless. Michelle truly believed that such traits are genetic and she simply must learn to deal with them. That mind-set is an absolute misconception. Michelle and others like her suffer from a lack of serotonin, which is a major cause for much of the hopelessness and depression people feel.

Michelle was not getting certain vitamins and minerals vital to proper brain and chemical function, just as is the case with low levels of the other neurotransmitters. She needed 5-hydroxytryptophan (the naturally occurring amino acid needed to make serotonin), folinic acid (active folic acid), P-5-P (active vitamin B6), NADPH (activated niacin), iron, B12, magnesium, and zinc. A heavy dose of omega-3 oils was also essential.

COMBAT SEIZURES WITH GABA

Ryan was rapidly tapping his foot and cracking his knuckles when I walked in the room. As he began to tell me why he had come to my clinic, he grew increasingly nervous. Ryan was speaking as though he had just consumed a gallon of coffee—the words were flying out of his mouth at rapid speeds. He was pacing the small confines of the exam room and waving his arms around like a motivational speaker on a platform. Each health issue he brought up seemed to bring with it a new muscle twitch in his face or flick of his arm. Ryan also stuttered on select words and phrases.

GABA Symptoms

Deficiency	Excessive Amounts
Anxiety	Muscle relaxation
Convulsions	Stuttering
Epilepsy	Lung issues
Spastic disorders	
Balance disorders	
Peripheral vision disorders	
Large intestine issues such as parasites/ fungi	

He told me he had recently been diagnosed with epilepsy. About a year before, he had begun to experience occasional light seizures. He was exceedingly discouraged because life had changed drastically for him and his family. His wife, who sat quietly in the corner, sighed and added, "We just never know when the episodes are going to happen. Our kids are terrified when a seizure hits him." Both their faces showed deep worry and fear.

Ryan also told me that he frequently lost his balance and at times he struggled with the room spinning. What Ryan was suffering from was a GABA (gamma-aminobutyric acid) deficiency, one of the four major neurotransmitters. GABA deficiency is a real issue and is often missed in traditional medicine assessments. He was lacking in several key vitamins and minerals vital to brain health, and this was contributing to his lack of GABA production. He started taking P-5-P (active vitamin B6), magnesium, zinc, omega-3 oils, and an activated vitamin called thiamine pyrophosphate (a type of B vitamin). These supplements all help to balance neurotransmitter levels and may alleviate and even eliminate such ailments as seizures and epilepsy.

I am not claiming that simply by taking these supplements, the world will have no use for antidepressants and the pharmaceutical companies will all be bankrupt. I do believe, however, when you give the body what it needs, the body has a way of restoring itself to normalcy. Remember, everyone's body chemistry is different, which is why diagnostic testing is critical in the process.

WHAT'S REALLY MAKING US SAD?

Depression has affected people since the beginning of recorded time. What we now call depression can be found in numerous ancient documents. In the Bible, the Old Testament records the story of King Saul in a profound state of depression. In the *Iliad*, Homer tells of Ajax, whose depression led to his suicide. Around 400 BC, Hippocrates began to use the term *melancholy* to describe disturbances of mood.

Depression is not just sadness. Sadness is a feeling that is usually related to a specific event, such as personal loss. Depression, however, is an emotional state that dominates a person's outlook on life for a prolonged period of time.

Everyone feels depressed once in a while. Perhaps if it were not for episodic times of depressed moods, happy times would lose their value. But those who suffer from depression do not have transient depressed moods. A depressed person is down every single day, day after day, and week after week. Some sufferers are able to function through daily life in spite of feelings of anxiety, insecurity, and shame. These individuals are able to make it through the day, but are never really happy. Others are completely paralyzed in life and unable to function.

In many cases, depression is an appropriate reaction to a life event such as the death of a family member, bankruptcy, empty nest syndrome, divorce, or some other stressful experience, and specific medical treatment is not needed. In such cases, the patient may only require reassurance that the depression is not abnormal. For many people, depression comes and goes as an inevitable part of life.

When someone becomes depressed, it is typically linked to deficient neurotransmitter levels such as low serotonin. When some doctors see this, the first response is to place the patient on an antidepressant. Sounds normal, right? We then assume that this person will need to be on that drug indefinitely to keep things working. Forget that some antidepressants can cause liver damage and even erectile dysfunction. Thinking that living with a drug's side effects is just the price to pay for mental health is branch mentality thinking, and using antidepressants as the cure-all for depression is the wrong approach. In some cases they are necessary, but don't just put a Band-Aid on the problem. Instead, you must seek out the root of the chemical imbalance.

If you are not prone to states of depression, but recently have found yourself down for seemingly no reason, look at your diet and lifestyle to determine what could be causing this problem. Vitamin and mineral deficiencies are common culprits of imbalanced brain chemicals. One of the best ways to naturally raise serotonin levels is to take activated (more absorbable) vitamin B6 and B12. B6 is found in red peppers, and B12 is found in yellow and orange peppers. Don't forget omega-3 oils found in fish oil such as cod liver oil (one to three teaspoons daily). A lack of these oils in your diet can be a major contributor to low serotonin levels and depression.

Deficiencies in some vitamins may increase your chances of depression—here is a list, with the possible symptoms.

Vitamin	Deficiency May Cause
Vitamin B1 (thiamine)	Psychosis, mental depression, anxiety, irritability
Vitamin B5 (pantothenic acid)	Restlessness, irritability, depression, fatigue
Biotin and vitamin B12 (cobalamin)	Psychotic state, depression, irritability, memory loss, hallucinations, delusions, paranoia
Folic acid	Forgetfulness, insomnia, apathy, irritability, depression, psychosis, delirium, dementia
Vitamin C (ascorbic acid)	Hysteria, depression
Niacin (vitamin B3)	Apathy, anxiety, depression, hyperirritability.

Along with certain nutritional deficiencies, chemicals such as caffeine and nicotine that we place in our bodies every day may cause depression. Remember, depression is exactly what it sounds like—a depressed function in the body. Our mental, chemical, and structural sides of health can all be depressed, and regardless what area is affected, our mental state will usually be affected as well. Caffeine and nicotine are some of the most common chemicals that can actually trigger our body into a depressed state and should be avoided. It is commonly accepted that, unless you have a problem with alcohol, a few glasses of wine a week can be good for your health. If you do drink any alcohol, it should always be wine, but use common sense and moderation.

SUPPLEMENTS THAT WARD OFF DEPRESSION

It is helpful to think about deficiencies in terms of the levels of octane in your car's gas tank. Regular gas has an octane rating of about eighty-seven; premium has an octane rating of ninety-three. If you owned a finely tuned luxury automobile that required premium gasoline but continued to use regular gasoline, the car would run, but its performance would suffer. In the same manner, our bodies were created to be fine-tuned machines. Too often we do not give our bodies premium fuel—the nutrients needed to perform at peak levels—but instead provide fuel that is worse than the cheapest regular gasoline. By paying attention to the foods we put inside our body, the supplements we take, and our lifestyle choices, we can provide our body what it needs and prevent nutrient and vitamin deficiencies—and help prevent depression.

Here are my supplement recommendations for fighting or staving off depression:

Omega-3 fatty acids. One of the top nutrients to ward off or prevent depression is omega-3 fatty acids. Recent studies have shown that the majority of depression sufferers have low levels of omega-3 fatty acids in the blood.

Vitamin C. We have all heard about taking vitamin C to prevent the common cold, but vitamin C deficiencies are also associated with depression. In a 1983 study of 885 psychiatric patients, the average plasma level of vitamin C was 0.51 milligrams, compared to a level of 0.87 milligrams on 110 healthy, non-psychiatric patients—a 40 percent difference.[1] This study revealed that supplementation with vitamin C relieves symptoms of some disorders, including depression. In a study reported by the *British Journal of Psychiatry*, forty male psychiatric patients randomly received either vitamin C or a placebo. After three weeks, researchers noted a significant decrease in depression with those receiving vitamin C, but no change with those receiving the placebo. Numerous important studies demonstrate that many patients being treated for depression are deficient in vitamin C.[2]

Biotin. Biotin is one of the lesser-known B vitamins and is found in meat, dairy products, and whole-grain cereals. Biotin deficiency is also associated with states of depression. The *Journal of the American Medical Association* reported a study in which patients were deprived of biotin to determine the effect on the body. After ten weeks, subjects began to report symptoms of depression and fatigue. Placing biotin back into their diets relieved all symptoms.[3]

Folic acid and vitamin B12. Folic acid (a form of B vitamin) and vitamin B12 deficiencies are the most common nutrient deficiencies in the world, and depression is a common symptom of their shortages. In studies of psychiatric patients, as many as 30 percent have been shown to be deficient in folic acid, and in one study, 67 percent of patients admitted to a psycho-geriatric ward were folic acid deficient. In a study of forty-eight patients in a psychiatric hospital, it was found that the lower a patient's serum folic acid level, the more severe the patient's depression. Furthermore, research has demonstrated that serum folic acid or B12 levels are low in a substantial proportion of patients suffering from various psychiatric syndromes, especially depression.[4]

Niacin. Niacin is used during the metabolism of food, and a deficiency will result in significantly less energy being generated in the brain. Niacin supplementation can cause a rise in tryptophan, an amino acid used in brain functions responsible for processes such as perception and thought.

Vitamin B6 (pyridoxine). Vitamin B6 is an important coenzyme in the synthesis of compounds called monoamines in the central nervous system. Pyridoxine levels are typically quite low in depressed patients, especially in those using oral contraceptives. Studies have shown that depressed patients with low pyridoxine or vitamin B6 levels respond very well to supplementation.

Now that we have looked at the conditions that cause depression, let's look at some recommended treatment plans that I suggest to my patients:

- Adopt a regular exercise program with thirty minutes of aerobic activity three times per week.

- Eliminate smoking, oral contraceptives (they disrupt the natural hormone balance in the body), and caffeine.

- Use the food wheel approach to eating by consuming equal portions of fats, proteins, and carbohydrates. For more on this balanced food approach, see chapter 13.

- Use supplementation, including omega-3 oils such as cod liver oil.

The best programs are those designed specifically for you to help alleviate depression and other illnesses based on individual needs. However, I do make the following general recommendations as a daily anti-depression protocol:

- B vitamin complex: 100 milligrams two to three times per day
- Vitamin C: 1 gram, three times per day (3 grams/day)
- Folic acid: 400 milligrams per day
- Vitamin B12: 250 to 1,000 milligrams per day
- Magnesium: 500 milligrams per day—taken at night before bed as it relaxes the blood vessels and muscles, and will help you get a good night's sleep

As with all medical or dietary advice, consult with your physician, especially if you are taking medications, before eliminating any prescriptions or changing your diet.

PART III

CHEMICAL HEALTH

NATURAL MEDICINE®
HEALTH TRIANGLE

7

BUILDING A GREAT FOUNDATION
The Tree of Life

"Wisdom is a tree of life to those who embrace her."
—Proverbs 3:18 (NLT)

Think of the human body as a tree. The roots of a tree must be grounded in good soil—soil filled with the necessary vitamins and minerals so that the roots can gain the proper nutrients to grow a strong trunk and healthy branches. If your roots are well-grounded in a good environment that is free of excess toxins and bacteria, with plenty of nutrients available, and you get plenty of sunlight, clean air, and ample water, then you will flourish. However, if our sunlight is restricted, we receive inadequate water, are surrounded by dirty air, and our "soil" (nutrient base) is depleted of all its essential vitamins and minerals, we will eventually grow sick. Thus, building a great body is like growing a great tree. We must have all the necessary environmental factors to grow strong and healthy.

Some of the basic foundations for growing your own healthy Tree of Life were discussed in part I. Like the other two sides of the Health Triangle, having good mental health starts with giving your body the correct nutrients and replacing deficiencies, much like fertilizer does to a tree. In part I, we began to see just how connected each side of the Health Triangle is to the other two sides. For example, when the body is not producing adequate amounts of the brain chemicals serotonin, GABA, dopamine, and acetylcholine, this can adversely affect your mental state, make you depressed, and rob you of your vitality.

Additionally, part I discussed our lifestyle choices. Choices that you make every day have a profound effect on all three sides of the Health Triangle, and

73

thus determine the overall health of your foundation—your roots. Part II will delve even deeper into the more common nutritional deficiencies and uncover the root of many health challenges such as toxicity and improper food choices.

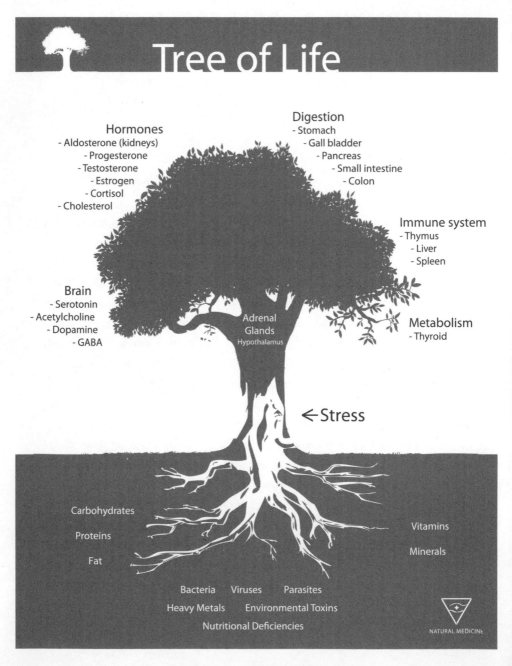

THE BRANCH MENTALITY

When we get sick, the first thing we do is run to the doctor's office. Let's say you are diagnosed with type 2 diabetes. Doctors run blood tests, check your sugar levels, and tell you that you "have diabetes." They slap a label on you—and no one appreciates that. Then they tell you that you will be on insulin or glucophage for the rest of your life. Gee, thanks for such an encouraging and hopeful response! These doctors are looking only at the "branches," chasing the symptoms rather than getting to the *root* of the cause. Some doctors have what I call a *branch mentality*.

The branches include most of the ailments we see today: high blood pressure, high cholesterol, diabetes, heart disease, cancer, fibromyalgia, colitis, headaches, and the like. These are all the symptoms and labels of conditions that are given to us. Many doctors only look at these symptoms. They focus on the fact that your blood sugar is high, rather than looking at what *made* your blood sugar high. The branches are nothing more than a result of the poor management of the soil and the roots around the tree. Don't be mad at medicine or doctors; that is how we are all taught in school, and most physicians genuinely want the best for you and your health. But getting to the root of the cause is the first step towards health restoration.

Susan was a new patient at my clinic. She had been suffering from heavy ulcerations on her leg for several years. The ulcerations reached all the way down to the bone. She had been to many specialists around the country and had moderate success using conventional therapies such as antibiotics and prednisone (cortisone) injections. These treatments slowed the inflammation and seeping of the ulcer, but nothing would stop it. She endured several surgeries to remove dead skin from the area, but the ulcer kept returning.

Susan came to me and said, "Dr. Asa, I heard you talk on the radio about how our bodies regenerate every year. I have gone to countless doctors and they keep looking and trying different methods; but I feel like we are missing something." I could see the desperation in her eyes; she just wanted to get well. She had dealt with the Branch Mentality long enough.

I explained to her that a skin issue such as a large ulcer is a result of something else going on in the body. Remember, the branches (symptoms) always reflect what is going on in the roots (real cause). You can't see the roots because they are in the ground, or inside our bodies. Conventional medicine's typical approach is to treat symptoms, and the roots continue to be ignored.

Blood tests and an examination showed that Susan had extreme dysfunction of the liver. Liver congestion usually leads to severe venous congestion and the symptoms are at their worst in the body's extremities—Susan's leg, for example. We changed her diet to reduce inflammation, eliminated and restored certain nutritional deficiencies, and implemented detoxification to eliminate toxic heavy metals and fungi. We took care of the roots first, and then waited to see what the body would do. After several months, the seeping stopped, the ulcer began to close, and the blood work began to show the liver enzymes at normal ranges. Her body responded because we looked at the roots and not the branches, and that is what it takes to get well.

Susan is living well now and has a renewed outlook on life. When she comes in for her checkups, I smile as I see the glow in her eyes: the glow of someone who is experiencing the health that she was designed to have. She is living extraordinarily, and you can see it.

Stop hanging out in the branches . . . get to the root!

GETTING TO THE ROOT

We know how traditional medicine handles illness—through the branches. Now let's look at the real reason behind any ailment you face today. The roots are the most critical components for any tree to grow. The roots are mainly built from what we consume in our diets (carbohydrates, fats, and proteins) and the additional vitamins and minerals we use to restore nutritional deficiencies. These strong roots produce a strong tree—and good fruit!

Then there are elements that attack and attempt to destroy a healthy root system. These elements include environmental toxins, viruses, parasites, and bacteria. In the next few pages, we are going to discuss each element so you can better understand how to build stronger and better roots.

The first roots are the "good" roots that produce healthy cells, and therefore healthy bodies. Your diet is of the utmost importance. The foundations of a well-balanced, "food wheel" diet include three elements: proteins, fats, and carbohydrates. These are the three types of food that the body requires in some combination every time we eat. These three foundations are called the three macronutrients, and they are the foundation of a healthy diet. (See The Food Wheel on page 168.)

Proteins. Proteins are large organic compounds made of amino acids arranged in a chain and joined together by bonds. They are the building blocks of all cells in the body. Proteins also work together to achieve a particular function, and they often associate to form stable complexes in the body. Proteins are essential components of all living cells and participate in every process within the body.

Protein is essential to sustain the life and health of body tissues. Good protein can be found in the following food sources:

- Organically raised meats (excluding pork, discussed in the next chapter)

- Fish (excluding shellfish, also discussed in the next chapter)

- Eggs

- Dairy (preferably from goat's milk rather than cow's milk)

- Nuts and seeds (excluding peanuts, which can contain a large amount of mold)

Carbohydrates. Carbohydrates are the energy source of the body. They fuel the muscles and the brain through a natural sugar, or glycogen, which is released in the "breaking down" process of carbohydrates. Our muscles and brain function primarily through the use of glycogen.

There are two types of carbohydrates: *low-glycemic,* which release slowly in the body, and *high-glycemic,* which are fast releasing. Carbohydrates cause a rise in blood sugar and in response, the pancreas secretes a hormone called insulin. Insulin helps keep the blood sugar in a balanced state. However, in the standard American diet, most carbohydrate consumption consists of the fast-release or high-glycemic carbohydrates, which cause a rapid spike in blood sugar levels. Soda, sugar, sweetened fruit juice, refined carbohydrates, pasta, white rice, potato chips, and French fries are examples of foods that cause the sugar levels in your body to become dangerously high.

When high-glycemic carbohydrates are eaten, large amounts of insulin must be delivered at a rapid pace to control blood sugar levels, and this is hard on the pancreas. This causes the body to overuse its supply of insulin and begins a breakdown of the pancreas, which leads to one of our major health concerns today—diabetes.

Let's look at an orange—an orange was created with fiber, pulp, and juice, and it was designed to be eaten in its whole state. The *glycemic index* is a scaling system that assigns a number to each carbohydrate source, and an orange has a glycemic index of twenty. The higher the number, the faster the release of blood sugar and the harder it is on your pancreas and body. The lower the number, the easier it is on your body. So while an orange has a rating of twenty, orange juice has a glycemic index of almost *sixty*—meaning your body has to work a lot harder to regulate blood sugar levels (plus you don't get the advantages of the fiber from eating the orange itself). It's best to avoid fruit juices, and eat whole pieces of fruit instead. If you feel you can't do without juice, limit it to four ounces a day—and avoid sweetened juice drinks, particularly those sweetened with high fructose corn syrup (in fact, you're going to want to start reading labels to avoid high fructose corn syrup entirely). A great resource for checking glycemic index is www.glycemicindex.com and click on the GI Database. You can type in the type of food to find out what the index is.

When you eat a carbohydrate, choose low-glycemic, or slow-release carbohydrates. These carbohydrate sources have fiber and nutrients that have not been altered:

- Whole fruits

- Sweet potatoes

- Milk sugars (like those found in plain yogurt)

- Most vegetables (especially leafy green vegetables)

Fat. Beginning in the early nineties, our country became low-fat *crazed*. We seem to have forgotten that fat is one of the foundational three macronutrients—it's essential to brain development in infants. After "nonfat mania" hit the nation, everything we ate was low in fat—low-fat cookies, low-fat ice cream, low-fat cheese, low-fat anything. Ironically, during this time obesity made a staggering statistical climb and cases of diabetes have reached an all-time high. How can this be with all the low-fat foods available? It is because we have removed one of the most crucial components from our American diet—one that our ancestors never left out—and that is fat. Fat does not make you fat. I will say it again—*fat does not make you fat*. In fact, it is crucial for the health of your body.

In the late eighties and early nineties, I was heavily involved in body-building and would not touch anything that contained fat because of all the articles I was reading and how the media portrayed its harmful effects. My fat consumption was 5 percent of my diet plan at best, and I was unhealthier during that period than during any other time in my entire life. My skin was dry and broken out, my hair was unhealthy, and my energy levels were low.

Fat is just as crucial to the body as proteins and carbohydrates. It is essential in the overall health of our body: our bodies need fat. But how much and what kind of fat we ingest makes a huge difference in how our bodies function, not to mention our appearance.

MORE ON FAT—DETERMINING THE GOOD FROM THE BAD

Proteins and carbohydrates are fairly clear-cut categories. Wise protein choices include lean meat and nuts, and the best carbohydrates are found in fruits and vegetables. However, determining good fats from bad fats can get complicated. There are major categories of fatty acids—saturated fat, unsaturated fat, partially saturated fat (commonly known on food labels as partially hydrogenated fat), and poly and monounsaturated fat. Another sub-categorization of fats designates them as omega-3, -6, or -9 fats. It can get a little difficult to decipher which of these are the healthy fats, and some people fail to understand the difference between the types. So we will briefly discuss each type of fat and its use it the body.

First, the amount of saturation of fat has to do with the absence or presence of hydrogen bonds in the fat. When fat is saturated (full of hydrogen), it changes the atomic arrangement of the elements in the cell. Hydrogenation converts liquid vegetable oils to solid or semi-solid fats, such as those in margarine. Altering the degree of saturation of the fat changes important physical properties such as the melting point.

Partially saturated fat. The reason that some fat is now considered unhealthy lies in the fact that most fat undergoes incomplete hydrogenation. When this partial conversion occurs, some molecules in the chain transform into *trans fats*, which have been implicated in many circulatory diseases.[1] Food manufacturers manipulate fat in this manner because partially hydrogenated vegetable oils are cheaper than animal source fats, are available in a wide range of consistencies, and have a longer shelf life. Nutrients are not meant to be manipulated for convenience's sake—they are meant to be consumed in the form in which they were designed.

Saturated fat. You have likely heard that saturated fat is bad, but it's not. It is when fat is partially hydrogenated (or partially saturated) that trans fats form that damage your body.

Saturated fat enhances numerous functions in the body. Some sources, however, are better than others. The best choices for saturated fat are organic butter (*not* margarine), coconut oil, and meat sources. Coconut oil and organic butter are the best oils for cooking. You may have been told that olive oil, canola oil, and safflower are the best oils for cooking, but those oils break down under heat and become trans fatty acids that harm the body. Trans fatty acids are some of the worst substances you can eat. If you are going to cook with oil, cook with coconut oil or butter.

We all need a reasonable amount of saturated fatty acids, but as with everything, it's all about moderation. Too much of a good thing can have adverse effects. In other words, keep your fat intake at the recommended level (one-third of your daily calories) and make sure all of your intake is a healthy mix of the different good fats.

Unsaturated Fat. In unsaturated forms of fat, double bonds (sharing of pairs of electrons between atoms) are formed in the fatty acid chains. When double bonds are made, this eliminates hydrogen atoms in the chain. That is where the term "nonhydrogenated" that appears on much of today's packaged foods comes from—it means *without hydrogen*. The body can more easily process this type of fat, and it is far healthier than consuming fats that have undergone partial hydrogenation. During the metabolism of food, hydrogen-carbon bonds are broken down to produce energy, so an unsaturated fat molecule contains somewhat less energy (fewer calories) than a comparably sized saturated fat. Most nuts, avocados, and olive oil contain unsaturated fats. As mentioned above, olive oil is not the best oil for cooking because of its tendency to break down under heat and form trans fats. However, salad dressings with an olive oil base, for example, are a good way to safely consume olive oil.

Monounsaturated and polyunsaturated fat. Poly and monounsaturated fats make more HDL (high-density lipoprotein), which is often referred to as the *good cholesterol.* HDL carries artery-clogging fat back to the liver so it can be processed for other uses, thereby clearing out the arteries. Polyunsaturated fats are the fats found in most vegetable oils and fish oils. Most omega-3 fats in fish and omega-6 fats such as those in evening primrose oil, flaxseed oil, and cod liver oil are considered polyunsaturated or monunsaturated.

Omegas. Omega fats are called *essential fatty acids* (EFAs) because our bodies can't make them on their own—we must get them from food.

Essential fatty acids are long-chain polyunsaturated fatty acids derived from linoleic and oleic acids. Omega-3 and omega-6 fatty acids are derived from linoleic acid, and Omega-9 from oleic acid. There are two groups of EFAs: omega-3 and omega-6, and omega-9. Omega-9 fat is essential to the body as well, but you don't need supplementation because your body can manufacture an adequate amount of this fat on its own (from eating vegetable oil and meat), provided the other EFAs are present. The number following the "omega" represents the position of the first double carbon bond, but for our purposes, it is more important to understand the purpose of the EFAs than their intricate molecular structures.

EFAs support the cardiovascular, reproductive, immune, and nervous systems. The human body needs EFAs to manufacture and repair cell membranes, enabling the cells to obtain optimum nutrition and expel harmful waste. As mentioned previously, a key function of EFAs is the production of prostaglandins, which regulate body functions such as heart rate and blood pressure, as well as playing a role in immune function by regulating inflammation and encouraging the body to fight infection.

Although some fats may be essential, some sources of fat are better than others. A healthy fat balance consists of a 4:1 ratio of omega-6 fatty acids to omega-3, or four times as much omega-6 as omega-3 . In most American diets, however, the average ratio ranges from 20:1 to 25:1; most of us eat too few omega-3 rich foods in proportion to omega-6 foods.[2] Cooking with vegetable oil is another reason for the imbalance; virtually every fried food is cooked in omega-6 and omega-9 oils. Most prepared salad dressings contain omega-6 rich oils rather than omega-9 or omega-3 oils. Not all omega-6 products are bad for you—it's simply that the ratio of omega-6 to omega-3 oils is out of balance. Omega-6 fatty acids have a longer shelf life, so most manufacturers use omega-6 oils to ensure their products' longevity.

The imbalance also stems from the fact that omega-3 rich foods such as eggs have fallen out of favor, with more people eating egg substitutes and egg whites. Fish such as salmon and trout used to provide high levels of omega-3 fats, but are no longer a good source because they are being raised on farms where they are fed omega-6 rich grains and grain byproducts. The majority of American meat consumption is beef, chicken, and pork that are fed primarily corn and corn oil diets, which are high in omega-6 essential fatty acids. We clog our arteries and accelerate aging by consuming the hydrogenated, oxidized trans fatty acids found in margarine, fast foods, and snack foods. Even though these foods also contain omega-3 fatty acids, their usefulness is diminished by modern food processing methods.

Some of the food sources that are highest in omega oils (specifically omega-3) are Atlantic salmon, albacore tuna, anchovies, halibut, Atlantic herring, lake trout, pink salmon, sardines, sockeye salmon, swordfish, rainbow trout, and whole organic eggs. Omega-6 sources include poultry, nuts and bread. The primary sources for omega-9 fat are animal fat and vegetable oils, and most of us get too much omega-9 fat because much food is cooked in vegetable oil, and we consume large amounts of meat.

The best source for omega-3 oils is cod liver oil. Flaxseed oil is highly beneficial to your health—but flaxseed oil requires an additional step in the liver to break it down to a usable form as an omega-3 fatty acid. The body uses only 15 percent of the omega-3 fat in flaxseed oil. However, the body uses up to 90 percent of the omega-3 in cod liver oil, because it goes straight into the body and is usable in its original form as an omega-3 fatty acid.

Making omega-3 fats a significant part of your diet has many benefits. Omega-3 fats are essential in proper hormone function. In men, they keep testosterone levels high, and in women, the keep estrogen and progesterone levels in balance.

In summary, here are some excellent sources of healthy fat, and remember to make your consumption of these fats approximately one-third of your daily caloric intake:

- Cod liver oil

- Most nuts (excluding peanuts due to their high mold content)

- Cold-water fish (not farm-raised) such as tuna, salmon, herring, and mackerel

- Flaxseed oil

- Organic coconut oil or organic butter (for use when cooking)

VITAMINS AND MINERALS—AT THE ROOT OF HEALTH

According to Joseph Mercola, D.O., author of the *Total Health Program,* about half the country takes nutritional supplements. He says this makes about as much sense as "building a boat with rotten wood and using the best screws in the world to fasten them together. The boat may hold together, but it will still leak."[3] The boards in this analogy are the macronutrients in our bodies such as proteins, carbohydrates, and fats. The fact is that most people don't make the best dietary choices. After all, that's how they have gotten into the nutritional mess we find ourselves in today. If we continue to make poor choices, it really doesn't matter what types of screws we use (or what supplements we take)—the boat will eventually break apart.

You could spend a fortune buying the multitude of supplements available today that all claim to have miraculous healing powers. However, I wouldn't recommend overdoing it in the area of supplementation. I recommend eliminating specific nutritional deficiencies in addition to taking the foundational four supplements (which will be covered in more detail in chapter 9). Here are the four nutrients everyone should take:

1. **Whole food multivitamins**—Whole food supplements come from whole, natural foods. This means that unlike synthetic vitamins, which base their ingredients on milligrams or specific amounts, a whole food multivitamin combines the correct balance of nutrients as they occur in nature.

2. **Digestive enzymes**—Digestive enzymes aid in the proper digestion of the food you eat to unlock the benefits of vitamins, minerals, proteins, and hormones and put them to work in the body.

3. **Probiotics**—Probiotics are good bacteria that assist the body's naturally occurring organisms in the digestive tract to allow for effective and healthy digestion and increased immune function.

4. **Omega-3 oils**—Fats are critical to overall bodily function. Because of improper diet and soil depletion, our bodies are lacking in omega-3

fats, which are responsible for proper hormone function, brain function, and skin, hair, and nail health. Cod liver oil is the best choice for absorption, plus it has a high concentration of vitamins A and D.

TOXINS—ROOT ATTACKERS

Toxins are everywhere! Pollutants in the air, chlorine in the water, chemicals in our skin care products, preservatives in our foods, pesticides and fertilizers—most people don't realize the potential harmful effects of these everyday substances. We live in a society filled with countless modern advances that make many aspects of life faster and more convenient. But as with most things in life and in nature, with the upside comes a significant downside. Along with all of the conveniences and advances that we have grown to depend on comes a variety of chemicals and other materials, largely from industrial carelessness that has saturated the water, food, and the air we breathe with toxins. Toxins are a serious concern that can cause serious health problems.

Many of these toxins can't be seen or even felt, at least not right away. That is what makes them so dangerous. They are often undetectable as we take them into our bodies. We don't realize that harmful toxins have affected us until we develop an illness caused by years of subtle exposure to these poisons.

Here are some alarming statistics:

- Close to 77,000 chemicals are produced in America.

- Over 3,000 chemicals are added to our food supply.

- More than 10,000 chemical solvents and preservatives are used in food processing.

- 1,000 new chemicals are introduced each year.

All these chemicals are absorbed into groundwater, rivers, lakes, and oceans; into our air; and into our food supply.

A study in the *British Medical Journal* estimated that as much as 70 percent of most cancers are caused by environmental and lifestyle factors, including exposure to chemicals.[4] Another report by the Columbia University School of Public Health estimated that 95 percent of cancer is caused by diet and environmental toxicity. Not surprising when you consider that estimates show most Americans have somewhere between 400 and 800 chemicals stored in their bodies, typically in fat cells.[5]

Toxins attack the body at our roots, and cause most of the problems and diseases (the branches) that modern medicine attempts to fix. But it's like putting a Band-Aid on a shark bite—branch-type treatment is grossly ineffective, and even the little that is accomplished will only cover up the problem for so long. Until we work to remove toxins from our personal environment, these problems will persist.

VIRUSES AND PARASITES—YOUR FOUNDATION AT RISK

Have you ever used anti-fungal cream for athlete's foot or ringworm? If you have, you may have noticed that the fungus returned after a few weeks or months. Perhaps you thought you simply caught the infection again, but the truth is that viruses and parasites living in your system cause those fungal infections and many other common ailments.

If you develop an "unexplained" condition, whether serious or not, it very well could be caused by viruses and parasites, and these substances can wreak havoc on a healthy foundation.

Health problems caused by a combined viral and parasitic attack can fool even the most experienced doctor. Viruses and parasites are often the culprits behind "mysterious" medical problems, and these viral and parasitic invasions can be painful and sometimes even deadly. Symptoms of a viral or parasitic attack are very similar to many commonly diagnosed diseases. These symptoms include headaches, strange forms of arthritis, all sorts of purulent skin problems and breakouts, immune deficiency and chronic colds, chronic dandruff, fungal infections, swollen glands, red eyes, prolonged unexplained pains in the body, chronic indigestion, ovarian and cervical problems, heart disease, hepatitis, shingles, and more. Viruses and parasites can also poison the blood. The parasites living in our bodies produce waste that can continue to build up and accumulate, exacerbating the harmful effects of these body invaders even further.

Changing your diet to include natural, whole foods and organic meats, fruits, and vegetables is a great way to start eliminating viruses and parasites from the body. Always be sure to drink the recommended amount of purified water during the day (one-half of your body weight in ounces) to help your body eliminate harmful substances. Fiber supplements also help to get rid of viruses and parasites, but they are not enough. Oftentimes, you need to use specific herbal formulas to cleanse the body of these toxins. There are several excellent anti-virus and anti-parasite treatments available to flush the harmful substances from your body. The treatment available through my clinic is listed in the appendix.

Look for these natural herbal ingredients when selecting an anti-parasite treatment, as they are known to be effective substances in fighting parasites and viruses: black walnut hulls, wormwood, pau d'arco, garlic, yellow dock, pumpkin seed, fenugreek, grapefruit seed extract, and prickly ash bark. Additionally, consult with a doctor who supports herbal remedies (You can usually find such doctors by asking at your health food store or seeking the advice of a nutritionist—most of whom are listed in the phone book.) The treatments are typically only used for a brief period of time, usually no more than a three-month period, as this is the average amount of time it takes to remove the toxins from your body.

Sometimes you may experience a day or two of feeling down, when the viruses and parasites are being killed in the greatest amounts. Some side effects may include fatigue, headache, exhaustion, muscular weakness, and slight fever. Remember, these symptoms pass quickly, and they are signs that those body invaders are being killed, so don't be discouraged if you experience some of these side effects. Temporary fatigue or a headache is far better than a lifetime of sickness!

ASA'S QUICK COLD REMEDY

Take 1,000 milligrams of buffered vitamin C every hour until you reach the point where you have slightly loose stools. Record the total amount of milligrams taken up to that point, and that will be your daily dose throughout the duration of your cold. Take your personal dose spread throughout the day every day until the cold is gone. For example, if I had a slightly loose stool at 5,000 milligrams, then I would decrease that amount to 4,000 milligrams, and that would be my daily dose. I would then take 1,000 milligrams, four times per day, until the cold was gone. For children ten to fifteen, repeat with 500 milligram doses, and for children two to ten, repeat with 250 milligram doses. Do not use for children under two.

HARMFUL BACTERIA—LIKE ACID RAIN TO THE ROOTS

Maintaining proper amounts of the bacteria present in the gastrointestinal (GI) tract is extremely important to digestion and to keep your tree of life strong and thriving. Each day your body wages a silent battle as beneficial bacteria in your bowel attempt to protect you from the massive number of harmful bacteria that you have ingested while consuming food and water. When toxic invaders remain and are allowed to multiply unchecked, their presence causes severe local distress as they break through the protective barrier of the colon wall, enter the bloodstream, and trigger infections throughout the body. That is why 35 million people in this country suffer from irritable bowel syndrome (IBS) and millions more have related health problems such as ulcers, indigestion, recurring vaginal infections, chronic constipation, and diarrhea.

It is not currently possible to eliminate all the potential pathogenic bacteria from our environment, nor would it be advisable, but improving the environment of the GI tract can reduce many symptoms related to conditions of unchecked toxic invaders.

In the 1930s, Dr. Westin A. Price demonstrated just how dangerous the toxic metabolites, or pathogenic bacteria, are to the human body. He took an infected tooth extracted from a patient with a known health problem and surgically implanted the tooth just under the skin of a rabbit. Within a short time, the patient recovered from the problem, but the rabbit soon developed an infection. Once the source of bacteria from the tooth was removed from the rabbit, its health returned to normal. Dr. Price repeated the experiment hundreds of times with the same results. Whether the condition was heart disease, kidney infection, or rheumatoid arthritis, the toxic metabolites from the bacteria created the same problem in the rabbit.[6]

Dr. Price's experiment suggests that health problems can develop practically anywhere in the body, even without a complete systemic bacterial infection. Based on this, it would seem that the unbalanced growth of pathogenic bacteria in the colon could be responsible for circulating toxic metabolites throughout the entire body.

The term *pathogen* refers to any of the bacteria, viruses, fungi, or parasites that harm the human body. Pathogens can enter through only three routes: the skin, the respiratory passages, and the GI tract. The skin is generally a highly efficient barrier. The respiratory tract is less efficient and is the route through which we typically contract acute problems such as a cold or the flu. The GI tract is particularly vulnerable, and it has the same links to the outside environment as the respiratory tract. If pathogens such as salmonella (food-borne illness) and influenza (the common flu) can survive the journey through the acids and enzymes in the upper part of the GI tract, they may find a perfect permanent home in the colon—a warm, moist, nutrient-rich environment that lacks oxygen and strong digestive fluids.

When you consider the current habits in our society, it's easy to understand how pathogenic bacteria can gain a strong foothold in the colon. We now consume less fiber and more refined carbohydrates than at any other time in history. Both of these trends slow bowel transit time and fuel harmful bacterial strains. Another trend that disrupts the bacteria balance is the excessive and widespread use of antibiotics (which means "against life") as opposed to probiotics (meaning "for life.") Antibiotics indiscriminately destroy *all* forms of bacteria, good or bad, in the body, and most people who take antibiotics never repopulate their body with good bacteria after destroying them. Antibiotics can be lifesavers when used prudently and properly, or when nothing else will work. However, they are not meant for long-term use as preventive medicine. Serious problems can be associated with the overuse of antibiotics. For example, the prolonged use of antibiotics begins to cause less harmful forms of bacteria to mutate into more potent drug-resistant forms—and the results can be severe, life-threatening infections.

Other drugs that affect bacterial balance within our system are nonsteroidal, anti-inflammatory drugs such as aspirin, ibuprofen, and naproxen. These drugs can cause stomach and intestinal bleeding, but even more alarming, they can affect the permeability of the entire gastrointestinal tract. When the GI tract becomes more permeable, the larger proteins, bacteria, and toxins are able to enter the bloodstream, resulting in allergic reactions, increased stress to the immune system, and the spread of toxins throughout the body.

Chlorinated water makes it almost impossible to maintain ideal bacterial flora in the GI tract. Chlorine kills bacteria—it doesn't matter if the bacteria are good, bad, or indifferent. If you drink chlorinated water, swim in a chlorinated pool, or shower in chlorinated water, it is absorbed into the bloodstream, and you would be wise to make a change. Chlorine intake must be eliminated, and this can best be achieved by using basic carbon filters on the water taps throughout your home. I recommend drinking genuine, tested spring water (such as Figi, Voss, Evian); distilled water has the potential to pull out minerals from the body that we are already lacking.

It is no wonder that most people have no energy and are constantly sick. Their imbalanced, infected colons support colonies of pathogenic bacteria that are spewing toxins into their systems. Their immune systems are constantly battling to keep things under control.

Sabrina heard me on the radio and brought her three-year-old daughter in to see me. The little girl had chronic ear infections and recurring skin rashes. The child was chronically constipated and Sabrina didn't know what else to do. I asked her if the child had been on antibiotics. She exclaimed, "Yes! She took them nonstop for about a year to try and get rid of these ear infections."

Well, that made total sense. Antibiotics are useful in emergency situations and they have their place; however, for this child's health challenge, it was a different case. When you use antibiotics, you are stripping away all of the bacteria in the digestive tract. We need certain bacteria in our digestive systems for proper immune function (so we don't get sick) and for proper digestion. When all bacteria are removed, it creates a breeding ground for illness, our immune system weakens, and we lose our ability to digest, assimilate, and absorb our food. We need fermented foods and probiotic supplements to get the "good" bacteria (probiotics) back into our digestive tracts.

In just two weeks after putting the child on a probiotic supplement, all of her symptoms were gone, including her constipation and skin rashes. It all starts in the digestive tract, and it's all about getting the bacteria in balance.

We are all exposed to pathogens every day, and yet some people get sick and some don't. Why is that? A strong immune system response determines who can or cannot fend off premature aging, sickness, and disease. Maintaining and nurturing the proper bacterial flora in the bowel is one of the most important tools for protecting yourself from a long list of pathogens, without any of the ill effects associated with antibiotic use. A great way to maintain this balance is to use probiotics every day, which are supplements that replace the good bacteria in the bowel. In addition, eat fermented foods such as plain goat's milk yogurt and goat and sheep cheeses, available in most health food stores.

HEALTHY GUT PROTOCOL:

Fast one day per week, drinking half your body weight in ounces of non-chlorinated water. (Consult with your physician before fasting.)

Take two to four probiotics (In capsule form, take 1 to 2 in the morning and 1 to 2 in the evening. For powdered forms, follow the directions on the bottle.) on an empty stomach two times per day.

Avoid chlorinated water, for drinking or bathing.

Avoid refined carbohydrates such as white flour and sugar.

Use digestive enzymes with every meal.

REBUILD YOUR ROOTS WITH FERMENTED FOODS

Now that you understand the importance of probiotics and maintaining proper bacteria in your GI tract, there are other foods you can consume to increase the amount of good bacteria in your digestive tract. Fermented foods—such as yogurt and sauerkraut—bring good bacteria back into your GI tract. Our immune system, much of which is concentrated in the GI tract, is being assaulted daily by unfamiliar microbes on the foods we eat. At the same time, our ability to effectively ward off these microbes has become compromised. Irritable bowel syndrome is on the rise worldwide and seems to be more prevalent in America. In less industrialized areas where fermented foods are still diet staples, the incidence of irritable bowel syndrome and other related gastrointestinal problems are about one-tenth of that in Western societies.

Here are the benefits of lactic acid and fermented foods:

1. Beneficial to the stomach. Fermented foods balance the production of acid in the stomach. As we age, the production of both digestive juices (hydrochloric acid) and the enzymes required for proper digestion decrease. The consumption of fermented foods helps increase the acidity of the gastric juices, and protect the stomach and intestinal lining when there is an overproduction of acid. Foods such as sauerkraut, buttermilk, and pickled vegetables can help make up for the loss of essential acids and enzymes. The key is to have two small portions daily and avoid large helpings.

2. Beneficial to nerves. Fermented foods produce acetylcholine, which facilitates the transmission of nerve impulses and is extremely effective in bowel mobility.

3. Beneficial for diabetics. The carbohydrates in lactic acid—found primarily in fermented milk products such as yogurt—and fermented foods have been broken down to a predigested state. As a result, and unlike most ordinary carbohydrates, they do not place an extra burden on the pancreas.

4. Beneficial for fighting cancer. Vegetables such as cabbage, broccoli, cauliflower, and brussels sprouts contain numerous compounds that produce high levels of anticancer activity.

5. Beneficial for killing microbes. Finally, fermented foods inhibit and destroy pathogenic bacteria. Many pathogenic forms of bacteria are sensitive to acidic environments—this is true of both cholera and typhoid. During a European epidemic of typhoid fever in the early 1950s, reports emerged that fresh sauerkraut was an effective agent for killing the bacteria. More recently, German scientists working with a strain of lactic acid bacteria in sourdough bread found it to be much more effective than past strands used for killing microbes. Dr. H. H. Booker believed that over 90 percent of diseases are caused by unhealthy foods not properly broken down, which create toxins in the GI tract.[7]

SLOWLY KILLING THE ROOTS—HEAVY METALS

Metal poisoning is a toxic accumulation of heavy metals in the soft tissues of the body. Heavy metal poisoning is much more common than most people realize. Because metals build up in your body over time, symptoms are often attributed to other causes and people often don't realize that metals have affected them until it's too late. And once they build up in your body, they can cause irreversible damage. Prevention is the best defense when it comes to metal poisoning. Here is a list of the five most common toxic metals:

Mercury. Mercury is one of the most toxic substances on earth and one of the most problematic of all toxic metals because, despite its dangers and known role as a neurotoxin, many people have it implanted in their mouth, injected into their bloodstream, or are consuming it daily in fish such as canned tuna.

Fillings. Silver amalgam fillings should be removed. Find a good biological dentist who is knowledgeable on how to remove these fillings. If a dentist wants to put silver mercury-loaded fillings in your children, refuse them. The porcelain ones will be a little more costly, but will pay off for your health in the long run.

Fish. Our oceans are largely contaminated with industrial pollutants such as mercury. Ocean and farm-raised fish pick up these toxic chemical residues, which accumulate in their flesh. People who regularly eat fish have higher levels of mercury than those who don't. Eat fish—but choose fresh wild fish over farm-raised and canned fish, as fresh catches have lower levels of mercury.

Lead. Humans can be exposed to lead in many ways. Among the major sources are lead-based paint, leaded gasoline, lead-contaminated water, manufacturing of lead batteries, rubber products, glass and other lead-containing products, and lead oxide fumes from demolishing industrial buildings. While some of these sources, such as lead-based paint and leaded gasoline, have been discontinued over the past few decades, it is estimated that millions of homes in the United States still contain lead paint (and products, such as children's toys, imported from other countries have been found to have lead paint). Merely breathing the air in a room painted with lead-based paint may be dangerous to your health.

Aluminum. Aluminum in the body has been linked to serious illnesses, including osteoporosis, extreme nervousness, anemia, headaches, decreased liver and kidney function, forgetfulness, speech disturbances, and memory loss. Aluminum has also been widely associated with Alzheimer's disease. People who have died from Alzheimer's disease have been found to have up to four times the average amount of aluminum accumulated in the brain's nerve cells. Antiperspirants contain aluminum that is absorbed by your body and should be avoided altogether. Instead, read the labels carefully and choose deodorants that are free of aluminum.

Arsenic. Organic arsenic compounds are mainly used as pesticides, primarily on cotton plants, while inorganic arsenic is mostly used to preserve wood. It will be one of the top heavy metals to contend with in the decades to come. Once arsenic is released in the environment it cannot be destroyed, and many arsenic compounds dissolve in water. The primary route of exposure to high levels of arsenic is typically through occupational hazards, or near hazardous waste sites or areas with high natural levels.[8] Arsenic has been detected in drinking water, especially well water, and long-term exposure to arsenic in drinking water has been linked to cancer of the bladder, lungs, skin, kidney, nasal passages, liver, and prostate. Lessen your arsenic intake by drinking purified water and eating organic foods or foods raised without the use of pesticides.

Cadmium. Cadmium is a naturally occurring metal that can be found in food, water, and tobacco smoke. It is a known carcinogen (cancer-causing agent) that harms DNA and disturbs the DNA repair system that helps to prevent cancer. Cadmium stays in the body for a long time and accumulates after long-term exposure to even low levels. Cadmium is released into the air from mining, industry, and burning coal and household wastes, where it then binds to soil particles and dissolves in water. Fish, plants, and animals accumulate cadmium from the environment, with the highest levels found in shellfish, liver, and kidney meats. Some signs of cadmium exposure are irritation of the lungs and the stomach, fever, cough, headaches, abdominal pain, vomiting, and diarrhea. Symptoms of higher doses include kidney damage, anemia, liver injury (jaundice) and aneurisms.[9] Avoid shellfish, drink purified water, and if you are a smoker, please quit. Your lungs will thank you, and your cadmium level will decrease as well.

STRESS REACTIONS—PULLING ON THE ROOTS

Everyone is familiar with stress, but in health care, the term is often misunderstood and misused. Stress is the reaction of the body to adversity, and it plays a major role in the health of our "trunks." Everyday life has many elements that cause stress; in fact, we can't avoid them. They can be physical, such as excessive work, or muscular imbalances, which cause joint strain. Chemical stressors include toxins, poor nutrition, and reactions to medications. Mental stressors are events such as interactions between people and worrying about health and financial problems.

While a medical student in the 1930s, Hans Selye noticed that people suffering from diverse diseases shared many of the same signs and symptoms. He spent decades researching stress and its effects on the body and defined these effects as the General Adaptation Syndrome (G.A.S.). As stress intensifies, the body experiences increasingly more serious ramifications. Simply put, your body breaks down as levels of stress increase. When the body undergoes constant stress and is unable to withstand the effects of this constant stress, then the general adaptation syndrome (G.A.S.) begins. This process occurs in three stages. The first stage is the alarm reaction, which is a "call to arms" of the body's defense mechanisms against a stressor. This includes normal activation of the adrenal glands to provide hormones for adapting to the adversities of the stressor. The second stage is resistance, which occurs if the effects of the stressor are prolonged. The adrenal glands grow in size to meet the prolonged stressor. Third is the exhaustion stage, during which the adrenal glands become depleted and can no longer meet the body's demand to respond to the stressor.

With prolonged stress, no matter what the cause, it is possible to "stress" yourself to death. In every case of death from stress, these organs are affected: the stomach develops inflammation and ulcers, the thymus gland stops working, the adrenal glands enlarge and malfunction.[10] Depending on the stressor, other organs can also be affected.

There are two main types of stress: eustress and distress. Eustress is the good form of stress that provides us with the ability to meet our demands and handle emergencies. Lifting a car off a child in an emergency is an extreme example; meeting a deadline with the sense of accomplishment that follows is a normal eustress. Eustress does not cause the body to go into the exhaustion phase. Distress is the type of stress that can have harmful effects on the body if prolonged.

Muscle function serves to indicate the state of the G.A.S. in the body. A weak muscle may be due to the G.A.S. moving toward the exhaustion stage. Hypertonic muscles may indicate the resistance stage. This is common in people who are highly competitive. It is important to have a balance between eustress and distress. Learn to recognize the body's reaction to both, and recognize the need for more rest or change of activities.

ADRENAL FATIGUE—A RED FLAG FOR UNHEALTHY ROOTS

Our adrenal glands control most of the energy balance within the body. They are the glands that help the body adapt to stress. When we get stressed, overworked, and full of anxiety, we overwork the adrenals. Statistics show that over 90 percent of Americans suffer from a condition known as hypoadrenia. That means your adrenal glands are exhausted and unable to adapt the body to the stressful demands placed upon it. They produce a powerful hormone called cortisol, which helps protect various systems such as the heart and brain during times of extreme stress. It is a helpful hormone in brief moments of use.

Many of us unknowingly suffer from adrenal dysfunction. Does this sound familiar to you? The alarm clock goes off. You are exhausted. You really don't want to get out of bed, but you know there's an office desk waiting for you. Maybe five more minutes of sleep will help, so you hit the snooze button. The alarm goes off again, and now you're annoyed. The kids aren't out of bed yet. You have to get them up. The dog needs to be let out, and now you have just thirty minutes to get ready. On the news, you hear there is a wreck on the interstate. Hurrying through the room, you suddenly jam your pinkie toe. It might be broken. And *where's the coffee?*

We all know what these mornings are like. We struggle to find enough energy to get our day going. We are overworked, overstressed, overcommitted, and under-rested. We finish our days completely exhausted and hoping that an extra thirty minutes of sleep will help. How do we correct this? We have to look at more than just chronic fatigue. We have to look at the cause and the failures within the body. God did not make us deficient in coffee and caffeine. He made us with all the energy we need.

You were made with an energy system that will allow you to make a difference and an impact in this world. You were made in His image; always keep that truth in mind. You have an amazing system called the endocrine system, which controls your hormones, and much of your energy. We have a multitude of different hormones throughout the body that control various mechanisms, but the "powerhouse" of energy resides in the adrenal glands.

However, we live in a constant state of stress. Our lifestyles, diets, and inability to slow down keep our adrenals running at an overloaded capacity. And the more caffeine, lack of sleep, sugar, and other stimulants we ingest every day, the more our adrenals shut down from exhaustion. Some cortisol is helpful, yet the amounts we produce daily destroy muscle tissue, lower blood sugar, cause hormone imbalance and rapid fat gain, and the list goes on.

What can be done to end this cycle and rebuild your tree of life with strong roots and a strong trunk? Instead of continuing to tear down the adrenal glands, we need to build them up. The most important remedy is to put things in our body that will combat our hectic lifestyles. Here are some ways to reset and restore your adrenal glands:

- Take 500 milligrams of panothenic acid daily (Vitamin B5).

- Take 1,000 to 3,000 milligrams of buffered vitamin C daily.

- Use a whole food stress supplement (B complex).

- Eat plenty of celery.

- Salt your food liberally with sea salt.

- Avoid milk chocolate, white flour, processed sugar, and caffeine.

- Drink one-half your body weight in ounces of water daily (i.e., if you weigh 100 pounds, drink 50 ounces of water per day.)

By building up your adrenal glands, you will experience a dramatic increase in your energy level.

THE THYROID GLAND—BRANCHING OUT

The thyroid is one of the larger endocrine (the group of systems that produce and control hormone levels) glands in the body. This gland is found in the neck just below the Adam's apple. The thyroid controls how quickly the body burns energy and makes proteins and how sensitive the body should be to other hormones.

The adrenal and thyroid glands are the primary hormone regulators essential for proper health and overall bodily function. They are the foundations that allow the branches to function well and be healthy. Any mental, chemical, or structural stress that we endure each day is regulated by our adrenal glands. We will learn more about this critical gland and how to protect it in the pages ahead.

Ultimately, remember that keeping the roots healthy will ensure that the entire tree is healthy. Good roots produce a solid foundation from which a tree can grow strong and live a long and fruitful life. A solid trunk will always yield a solid tree, but the roots and trunk are usually neglected because traditional medicine tends to focus on the branches. Typically, the branches can always be cut off, and the tree will keep growing. However, if you cut a tree close to its roots at the trunk, the tree will surely die. By building a healthy foundation that keeps your "trunk" healthy, you will experience a fuller life with greater energy and less disease.

8

FOOD CHOICES
You Are What You Eat

"Tell me what you eat, and I will tell you what you are."
—ANTHELME BRILLAT-SAVARIN

Eat those vegetables! You are what you eat!" I've heard that statement all my life and always rolled my eyes when I heard it. I used to think, *I eat French fries all the time . . . does that mean I'm a potato?* We tend to discredit things we heard growing up, but that statement is one of the truest I've heard. We are literally the sum total of what we eat. Our bodies are made up of the food choices we make every single day. When we eat, the body takes the food and makes either good cells or bad cells. In a way it can't tell the difference between a fast food hamburger and fries or baked chicken and broccoli; it will produce cells regardless of the source. But the quality of our food determines the quality of our cells.

I receive many types of calls on my radio show—lighthearted, funny, interesting, and sad. But Stephen was desperate and at his wit's end. He was fifty-six years old and had been diagnosed with rheumatoid arthritis several years ago, and it was getting progressively worse. He could not move throughout the day due to severe pain. The disease was affecting Stephen's entire body: his shoulders, hips, knees, wrists, and most recently his back. The doctors had him on eight different medications trying to make his pain manageable. He asked if I could help him.

I asked Stephen what he ate for breakfast, lunch, and dinner. He began to recount his standard American diet (or a S.A.D. diet, as I call it) of sugary cereal, orange juice, and a doughnut or two for breakfast. For lunch, he would eat a ham sandwich and chips with a soda, and for dinner a bowl of spaghetti and a soda. He said he was a soft drink addict. He also told me that after most of his meals he would be extremely bloated and felt gassy. I then asked him the question that I ask everyone: "Stephen, do you want to get well?" That's when he began to break down. He said he had grandchildren, and it was too painful to hold them and play with them. He began to cry. "Dr. Asa, I can't go on living like this." I repeated the question, "Do you want to get well," and he replied, "Yes, I do."

I told Stephen that first he had to radically change the way he eats because food is the greatest drug that we have. Most arthritis and inflammatory health challenges are due to excessive inflammation in the digestive system. He needed to eliminate all dairy and wheat products from his diet. He stopped me and protested, "Wait, Asa! I can't give up my sodas, my bread, and my milk! Please don't make me do that."

This was his real challenge. His arthritis was not going to be his greatest battle—*he* was his greatest battle. He was telling me what he couldn't do. Stephen had the "I can't" mentality.

I asked him, "Do you love your wife?"

"Yes," he quickly replied.

"Do you love your kids?" I asked.

"Of course!" he answered.

I then asked, "Do you love your grandkids?"

He got frustrated, raised his voice, and said, "Yes, I do! Why is that important?"

I replied, "If you love them more than you love yourself, then giving up sodas, doughnuts, and wheat products should be easy."

Stephen got quiet—extremely quiet. After a moment, he admitted, "You're right."

About five months later I walked into my new patient exam room at the office. There was a man who introduced himself as Jason. I said, "Hello, I'm Asa. How can I help you today?" I reached out to shake his hand and to my surprise, he pulled me in and gave me a big bear hug and said, "Doc, I came to thank you!"

I was confused and asked him why as I unwrinkled myself after the big hug. He replied, "You gave me my life back!"

"What do you mean?" I asked him.

He said that he had called into my show about five months earlier. "You really challenged me," he said. "I didn't like it at the time, but I was desperate. I used the name Stephen. I just wanted you to know that I've lost forty-five pounds since we spoke, I don't take any more medication for the arthritis, and the doctors say they believe it's gone—and it's a miracle."

I was so excited for him. Jason/Stephen had his life back and was able to enjoy his family with the kind of energy and vitality we all deserve.

We really are what we eat. Every single day our bodies take the food that we give it and turn it into good cells or bad cells, and only we can determine which type they will be.

THE BODY'S FUEL PUMP

The process of digestion is one of the cornerstones to overall health—it is, after all, how the body uses the food we give it to fuel our many intricate systems. The definition of *digestion* is "the process of metabolism where the body breaks down a substance, which is made up of complex organic molecules, into smaller molecules that the body can absorb and use for maintenance and growth."[1] Remember when your mother told you to eat your vegetables so you'd grow up to be big and strong? If it weren't for digestion, your muscles and bones would have no means of receiving the nutrients they need from those vegetables to grow "big and strong." Just as gasoline is dispersed to various engine parts through the fuel pump, the gastrointestinal tract (GI tract) takes food—our fuel—and breaks it down so that it can be sent throughout the body. If the digestive tract is not working properly, that means the food we consume cannot be properly broken down and dispersed. When your digestive system is dysfunctional, every other part of your body suffers the consequences.

WE'RE STILL TREATING ONLY THE BRANCHES

Many people today are unaware of the importance of the digestive system in our overall health and may have gone to the doctor for help. If you've paid attention to your most recent diagnosis at your family doctor, it was may have been some kind of "itis." Words that are associated with inflammation usually have the suffix "itis," such as arthritis, osteoarthritis, rheumatoid arthritis, colitis, and on and on. I am often asked, "How are inflammatory diseases like arthritis corrected?" With most of these conditions, the symptoms are usually treated with topical creams, lotions, gels, or some form of oral medication such as antibiotics or corticosteroids—and usually with little result. Arthritis medications, from over-the-counter to prescription drugs, have little or no effect because they only treat the symptoms. If there is any relief, it's only temporary. We must stop treating the symptoms and start treating the root of the problem.

Were you created to have joint problems that cause you constant discomfort and inconvenience, making you unable to fulfill your purpose in this life? No, you were created *with* more and *for* more. There is more in life for you— you were not created with an aspirin deficiency; you were not created with a lack of Advil; you were designed and created to function at optimal levels. We were created to *thrive*, and not merely survive.

The root of most inflammatory conditions originates in the gastrointestinal tract, with the skin and joints acting as the outlets for the toxic inflammation. That is why we experience so much joint pain and skin eruptions such as acne, psoriasis, and eczema. The creams and gels prescribed for these ailments do not help cure the problem; they only relieve the symptoms—temporarily. The real answers rest in the digestive system. If you fix the inside first, you'll fix the outside.

When treating my patients with such inflammation conditions, most of their joint and arthritic pain and acne cleared up when their digestive process improved. When an ailment is completely eliminated at the root, it is removed systemically (from the entire body), and not merely in one area. By reducing inflammation, patients also tend to lose weight and body fat, which results in increased energy levels. With healthy food consumption you will have increased energy levels, lose body fat, enjoy proper digestion, and feel better than you ever have. Does that sound like something you'd be interested in? Does eating processed cereals, processed breads, processed carbohydrates, and sugar really seem worth the cost? It sounds like a fair trade-off to me—I'll gladly give up sugary cereal and doughnuts for a healthy body.

REDEFINING "FOOD"

What we eat remains the common denominator in our overall health. Unfortunately, many people's everyday food choices actually damage their health.

In fact, some people may think of the sugary cereal and doughnuts as *food*. Maybe they are, in the strictest sense of the word, but food is meant to be fuel for the body. The foods that provide real fuel and lasting health are whole foods eaten in the unaltered state in which they were designed. Examples are hormone-free beef, lamb, chicken, and turkey; whole eggs; organic fruits, vegetables, lentils, nuts, seeds, properly prepared whole grains; and select fermented dairy products. These all bring health to the body. Foods that damage health are foods that have been altered from their original design and made into something else.

In its natural state, a potato comes from the ground and has numerous health benefits. When a potato is cooked in hydrogenated oils to make a French fry or sliced thin and deep fried to make a potato chip, the alteration that this once natural food undergoes makes it something that is no longer beneficial to the body. When you eat a potato, there are healthy ways to prepare it so that it retains its nutrients. Instead of eating fries or potato chips, try a baked or steamed potato. Even add a little organic butter if you want! The key is to stay away from foods that have been prepared with unnecessary fats and additives.

A banana in its original natural state is a whole piece of fruit, full of fiber, vitamins, minerals, and nutrients. A banana was meant to be a banana—not to be mixed with sugar, hydrogenated fat, and other ingredients to become banana pudding. I know it tastes wonderful, but a banana was not meant to be on the menu in this sugary state. A natural banana has certain nutrients in it that the body needs. When it is altered from its original state and made it into something else for consumption, this new "non-food" damages your health.

It isn't just adding fat to an item that places it in the non-food category. If that were true, then we could all simply eat fat-free potato chips and reduced-fat frozen dinners and be healthy. Don't be fooled by the label "fat free" or "low fat." When fat is removed from a product, a myriad of chemicals and additives have likely been added to make up for the taste and consistency the fat provides. It is best to avoid foods touted as "healthy" simply because they have less fat in their products than similar items.

Here is a short list of refined, prepackaged, genetically altered non-foods that rob your body of its health:

- TV dinners and microwaveable foods

- Processed bread you buy in most grocery stores

- French fries and potato chips

- White rice and pasta

- White flour

- Processed fruit juices (those sweetened with high fructose corn syrup)

- Sodas (especially those loaded with phosphoric acid and sugar)

- Diet sodas (those containing aspartame and sucralose)

- Any processed foods labeled 'fat-free'

- Prepackaged processed desserts such as Twinkies, brownies, cupcakes, and cookies

This is not a complete list, but it contains the majority of the foods in the Standard American Diet. Stay away from them!

NOT ALL BREAD IS EVIL

Bread—it's one of the staples of the S.A.D. diet—but real whole-grain, sprouted grain bread is extremely good for you. Most bread we see today, however, such as the breads that fill the shelves of the grocery stores, have a long shelf life and could probably sit there for several weeks before molding. This type of bread doesn't even have to be refrigerated. The processed flour has been taken out of its original state and combined with chemicals, and this wreaks havoc on your body.

No matter how many diets claim that all carbohydrates are bad, bread is *not* bad for you. Grains are the staff of life, and if they are made properly and kept close to their natural state, they are healthy for you because they are filled with fiber, vitamins, and minerals. I am often asked, "Can I ever eat bread again?" Of course you can eat bread—the key is choosing the right kind of bread. The breads that sit at room temperature on a grocery store shelf for a month and have an expiration date of a month from today are not good for the body. Real sprouted whole-grain bread is the wise bread choice.

Sprouted breads have to stay frozen or refrigerated, and they won't last much longer than a week. Stay away from the breads available in most grocery stores that require no refrigeration. Those breads will increase your blood sugar levels to a highly toxic level and impair digestion. Due to the lack of fiber in most store brands, the bread is broken down rapidly and can cause blockages in your intestinal tract. There is a wonderful alternative to the toxic grocery store breads called "Ezekiel" bread. Encourage your local health food store to carry it, and others like it.

Here is a good rule of thumb: If the bread will stay on the shelf, it will stay on yourself! Choose sprouted whole-grain breads that digest properly and nourish the body. And make sure to toast your bread to destroy most of the gluten, which causes allergies.

SOY IS NOT HEALTH FOOD

Soy is promoted as a health product, but soy is actually extremely hard on your body systems, especially your hormonal system. The popularity of soy and its widespread use is amazing, when less than a hundred years ago, the soybean was considered unfit to eat. While the soybean was named one of the five sacred grains (the other four were barley, wheat, millet, and rice) centuries ago in China, it was considered sacred solely because of its usefulness in crop rotation. The roots of the soybean plant were recognized to correct nitrogen levels in the soil, but the soybean was not eaten until fermentation was discovered, at which point soy was used to make fermented foods such as miso and soy sauce.[2]

The reason soy was not consumed is simple: The Chinese found that unfermented soybeans contained large quantities of natural toxins, strong inhibitors that block digestive enzymes from doing their job. These toxins are deeply imbedded proteins that cannot be destroyed during conventional cooking. They are known to produce serious gastric disorders, lessen protein digestion, and block the absorption of essential amino acids. Additionally, a large percentage of soy foods come from genetically engineered plants. Soy also contains goitrogens, which are compounds that depress thyroid function.[3]

Arguably, one of the greatest dangers of soy consumption is the phytoestrogen soy contains. Phytoestrogens are plant compounds that mimic estrogen in the body and are touted by some as miracle agents that may help fight diseases such as cancer, coronary heart disease, and osteoporosis. But there is a dark side to these compounds. Recent studies found that these compounds may actually increase the risk of breast cancer and cause thyroid disease. Some women say soy's high level of phytoestrogens and plant-based estrogens offer hot flash relief. However, some suggest soy could do more harm than good, particularly for menopausal women. A related concern is that soy supplements may interfere with tamoxifen, an anti-estrogen drug taken by women to help prevent breast cancer. Soy has also been loosely associated with reduced testosterone levels in men.

Researchers are still searching for a conclusive connection between breast cancer, testosterone levels, and the high hormone levels found in soy. While it is true that many still claim soy is a health food, there is simply too much emerging evidence to the contrary to be ignored. If soy is a significant part of your diet, and especially if you use soy milk as infant formula, educate yourself on this product and avoid its use as much as possible. Soy has crept into almost all of our foods, so read labels carefully and protect yourself.

TWINKIES WILL OUTLIVE US ALL

I heard a story about a man who attended a health food convention. As he looked at the latest samples and displays, he noticed one booth in particular. A man was sitting at the booth with an unwrapped Twinkie placed on a plate. The passerby found this interesting, and thought, *Wow, maybe this is some sort of organic super Twinkie.*

He approached the man at the booth and inquired about his unusual display. The man at the booth answered, "Well, I'm kind of doing a case study."

"What kind of case study?" the attendee asked.

He replied, "I am trying to determine the shelf life of a Twinkie."

Keep in mind that a Twinkie is nothing more than processed flour, sugar, and hydrogenated oil combined together in one little snack. The attendee was surprised by his answer and asked, "You are doing a case study on the shelf life of a Twinkie? So did you just pull it out of the wrapper?"

The man at the booth grinned and responded, "No, this Twinkie has been on a plate for eleven years."

The passerby looked at it, touched it, and found to his shock that it was just as soft as the day it was first unwrapped. It's a horrifying thing when bacteria are so scared of something that they won't even eat it! Still, we continue to put things such as Twinkies inside our bodies. You must consider what types of foods will bring health to your body and what will take your health away from you.

Twinkies are made of the same white flour as white bread, pastas, and processed foods. If it can sit on the shelf for long periods of time, imagine how long it can sit in you! Remember in elementary school when you made paper mache? What would you use? White flour and water. What would it make? A concrete-like substance that was hard as a rock. When we eat white flour and it goes into our digestive system, it will create the same hardening effect and block the absorbability of our foods. It creates a barrier in the intestinal wall. So the next time you eat a chicken sandwich, throw away the bread if it was not made from whole, sprouted grains; otherwise the gluten in the processed bread will block many protein in that meal from getting used.

ARTIFICIAL SWEETENERS—NOT SO SWEET

Artificial sweeteners have been a staple in American lifestyles. Diet sodas and foods sweetened with artificial sweeteners are consumed by countless people in an attempt to avoid sugar, cut calories, and lose weight. However, a recent study revealed that eating artificially sweetened foods and drinking sweetened beverages might actually hinder your body's ability to estimate calorie intake, which in turn boosts the tendency to overindulge. The study, which was performed on rats, found that the rats given artificially sweetened drinks consumed three times more calories than rats that didn't receive any sweeteners in their liquids.

The conclusion was that an inability to distinguish calorie intake is brought on by artificial sweeteners. The sweetener industry said that the results of the study were questionable because of the fact that animals were used for the study. They also stated that sweeteners played an effective part in weight management and were an important tool for weight control.[4]

Saccharin. For years, there was a warning label on saccharin, more commonly known to consumers as Sweet'N Low. We were led to believe that it is toxic to the body and warned by experts to avoid its use. However, unlike other sweeteners, it is derived from a whole plant source in South America. Despite its portrayal in the media, the safety of saccharin is supported by multitudes of studies about its effects on humans, has experienced a century of safe use, and has the approval of the World Health Organization as well as leading health groups.[5] Bernard Oser, Ph.D., a toxicologist and former president of the Food and Drug Research Laboratories, states that, "No chemical additive for food has been tested in as many laboratories, for as long a period, in as many species of animals (including man) and in successive generations, and yet has been found to be as innocuous as saccharin." In other words, it is acceptable to use saccharin as an alternative to sugar. Just remember, as with everything in life, use it in moderation.

Aspartame. Aspartame, on the other hand, is not derived from a whole food source like saccharin. Two amino acids in aspartame—phenylalanine and aspartic acid—have been proven to cause neurotoxic effects such as brain damage. During pregnancy, high levels of blood phenylalanine can be transferred to the fetus and produce serious adverse effects on brain development. The FDA requires all products containing aspartame to be labeled for phenylalanine so consumers will be aware of the substance's presence and can avoid or restrict it. Still other reports link aspartame to seizures and birth defects.[6]

Sucralose. Sucralose is a chlorocarbon, which is a chlorine-containing compound. Testing of sucralose, which is sold as Splenda, revealed damage to organs, genes and respiratory function. In tests lab rats displayed 40 percent shrinkage of the thymus gland, which is the very foundation of our immune system.[7]

PORK—THE DEADLY WHITE MEAT

It is easy for you to understand how to empower your health. Some plants and animals were designed for food, and some were not. Let's take a look at one animal in particular—the pig. The pig is a scavenger, created for one reason: to clean up the scraps and the bacteria on the ground. Four hours after a pig eats the worst imaginable things, that food becomes part of its system.

A pig's stomach is like an iron tank, and that stomach allows it to eat all the junk and bacteria that pollutes the ground that other animals need for healthy grazing. That is why cow's meat is considered healthy food, both technically and scientifically—the pigs clean the ground for the cows. However, a pig's meat is infested with bacteria and parasites such as trichinosis. Pork also contains a carcinogenic (cancer causing) substance called dioxin, which has become more well-known following a report issued by the Environmental Protection Agency (EPA) on the risk of dioxin as a human carcinogen. You may think you can cook these substances out—but you can't. Most people who eat pork regularly suffer more illness and disease than those who avoid pork products.[8]

SHELLFISH—THE PORK OF THE SEA

The oceans, rivers, lakes, and large bodies of water all have creatures living in them that were placed there for a reason. Shellfish such as lobster, clam, and shrimp are essentially the "pigs" of the sea, created as scavengers to suck the toxins out so the other fish could swim in clean and healthy water. When you eat shellfish, you are eating all the toxins in the water, but when you eat fish, you are eating clean food. Think about why these creatures were created as you make better decisions regarding your food choices.

When scientists check the mercury levels or the toxicity of the water, they don't just put an expensive instrument in the water. They gather samples of shrimp, clams, and oysters and place a probe inside their flesh to measure the toxicity levels. If that is how toxicity is measured, then logically you must know the reason these creatures were created—they are tiny toxic waste dumps.

When we eat scavengers, we are eating toxins—it's that simple. Our bodies can only make new healthy cells from the food that we give it. The choice is yours. Do you want good healthy cells from eating a nice piece of mercury-free tuna or bad cells from eating toxic-ridden shrimp and scallops? Does the shrimp taste better? Maybe. But I assure you, the cancer won't feel better. We all need you to make the right choice—and God does too.

THE INCREDIBLE EDIBLE EGG?

Another food source that has been under a lot of scrutiny in highly publicized studies is the egg. My favorite "heart supporter" is the egg—I eat four to six organic eggs every day, which means I consume thirty to forty eggs a week. However, because of the media's portrayal of egg yolks as being laden with cholesterol, many people consume only the egg whites or even egg substitutes.

The "egg scare" started in the 1950s during a promotional campaign that condemned cholesterol. Patients and doctors held fast to the idea that eggs should be avoided because of their high cholesterol content, despite the fact that hundreds of studies show that the amount of cholesterol we eat has little influence on our blood cholesterol levels. A study in the *British Medical Journal* showed that seven eggs per week combined with low-glycemic carbohydrates and high fiber did not raise cholesterol levels at all.[9]

The cholesterol level inside the yolk *is* high, but egg yolks are also high in two key components: choline and lecithin. Choline dissolves cholesterol in our arteries, so when the whole egg is eaten and digested, its healing properties are sent throughout the bloodstream. After digestion, the choline inside egg yolk dissolves the cholesterol already in the arteries, and lecithin actually takes fat and cholesterol and melts it so that it can be passed through the body and not attach to artery walls.

Throughout my years in athletics, I was constantly trying to maintain high levels of protein in order to stay at peak performance. I knew eggs were a quick and easy way to load up on protein, but I was convinced that yolks were unhealthy, so I would take twelve whole eggs, throw out the yolks, and just eat the whites. I did this to avoid all the fat and cholesterol that the media said was so harmful. In reality, I was throwing away the most important part of the egg. God knew what he was doing when he made the whole egg. He makes things whole—he doesn't make incomplete things. He didn't make *you* halfway or substandard. He made you wonderful and perfect just the way you are, and the way he made the foods we eat is no different.

If you are concerned about your cholesterol, here are some useful ways to lower your cholesterol levels without giving up the health benefits of whole eggs:

- Take one or two tablespoons of omega-3 oils (preferably cod liver oil).

- Eat two or three whole organic eggs daily cooked in coconut oil or organic butter.

- Consume two or three tablespoons of coconut oil daily.

- Consume 40 grams of fiber daily.

- Do a liver/gall bladder cleanse several times a year for proper liver function (see chapter 9 in the protocols for alleviating headaches section for cleanse instructions).

- Use red yeast rice daily.

Empowering your health is not a debate over high carbohydrate vs. low carbohydrate, high protein vs. low protein, or low fat vs. high fat. It's not about whether high or low is better—it's all about quality. The quality of our food is the most important factor to consider. Hormone-free, toxin-free, preservative-free, and chemical-free foods are the best. The quality of our food determines the quality of our health.

WATER—IT MATTERS WHAT YOU DRINK

The quality of our water matters too. Water is one of the few substances that we put in our bodies every single day. Despite the efforts made to clean our nation's water, the contamination problems seem to be getting worse. Even water that is approved by the Environmental Protection Agency can still have trace elements of lead, arsenic, mercury, radioactive particles, and other harmful contaminants. All of these have been found to accumulate in body tissue over time, leading to illness and premature death. Here are a few alarming facts:

- More than 75,000 chemical compounds are used by industry and agriculture, with thousands more added each year. Many of these are unregulated.

- 80 percent of these chemicals have never been tested for long-term chronic toxicity.

- As much as 20 billion tons of chemicals, radioactive waste, and pollutants are spewed into the environment each year, and most of these toxic chemicals will reach our water supply.

Thousands of chemicals, pesticides, herbicides, hormones, medications, and toxins are flushed into sewage systems every day. The city and state water suppliers only perform partial tests for contaminants, with their main focus on pathogenic bacteria.

BPA. One of the most frequently found contaminants is a substance called bisphenol (BPA), a chemical used in the making of plastic bottles. This chemical is also used to line the insides of thousands of cans and dental sealants. BPA is one of the most commonly produced chemicals in the world, and we are exposed to it far more often than we realize.

BPA mimics estrogen and can have a harmful impact on the body's hormone levels. In a study performed on animals, it was found that even a single low dose of BPA caused a rapid increase in insulin levels. Results showed that the animals developed an insulin resistance in just four days.[10] Certain levels of BPA also have been linked to prostate tumors, adverse effect on prostate and breast tissue development, decreased sperm count, and even the development of abdominal fat.[11]

Bottled water is another concern. Just because a company puts water in a bottle doesn't make it any safer than the water from your unfiltered tap at home. Although advertisements can make bottled water look clean and appealing, because of lax regulations on bottled water, it is often similar to tap water. In fact, sometimes it may be worse. Unlike tap water, the FDA tests the water that goes into bottles for drinking only once a year, while tap water is tested more frequently. Because the majority of toxins cannot be removed by municipal water treatment facilities, and bottled water is often not properly tested, it is better to simply take advantage of water treatment and filtration technologies available for your own home.

SMART FOOD RECOMMENDATIONS

Here are five recommendations to help avoid non-foods and aid your body in making healthy cells:

1. **Eat whole foods.** They are crucial to restoring proper digestion. Eating non-whole foods will cause gastric inflammation. (See chapter 13 for more information on the anti-inflammatory diet.) Avoid all starchy carbohydrates such as potatoes, rice, and most grains until the inflammation is eliminated; you can then put select carbohydrates back into your diet such as sweet potatoes and brown rice.

2. **Avoid all processed foods or foods with refined flour and sugar.** I have said this several times because it is *so* important! You must not eat these foods.

God made strawberries, not strawberry-flavored candies.

3. Consume omega-3 oils or cod liver oil. Cod liver oil contains omega-3 fatty acids, which are an excellent fat source and do not have to be broken down by the body. I recommend one tablespoon a day during the winter months when there is less sunlight, and half a tablespoon daily in the spring and summer months. Because of the high concentration of vitamin D in cod liver oil, you need less during times of increased sunlight due to the naturally occurring vitamin D that you receive from sun exposure.

4. Fast a partial day. A partial fast is easier to do than a traditional twenty-four-hour fast. Eat dinner the night before as normal, and fast the next day until dinner that night. It is still technically a twenty-four-hour fast, but you are asleep for part of the time, so it is a little easier to handle. We will cover fasting in more detail in chapter 10 when discussing ways to eliminate toxins. You should consult your physician before undertaking any type of fast.

5. Eliminate food allergies. When you think of allergies, you probably think of pollen and sneezing in the springtime. However, foods that you eat can cause allergic reactions. Most of the time, wheat is the culprit. Many people are allergic to wheat, so when you are attempting to lower inflammation, lessen swelling, or lose weight, avoid all wheat products. Other foods to consider eliminating are cow's milk, cheese, sour cream, and cow's yogurt. Substitute goat dairy products for these items (goat's dairy is discussed further in chapter 18).

A NATION OF CONVENIENCE

The majority of the decline in our health truly can be attributed to our food choices. With our fast-paced lifestyle, we frequently eat large quantities of food based solely on convenience. The entire fast food and "TV dinner" industries flourish in this hectic lifestyle. We are a "microwave-impatient" nation—we want it quick and we want it now. That's the way many people live and unfortunately, our bodies were not designed to operate at optimal levels on processed food, refined food, fast food, and prepackaged food.

The laws of human nature bring consequences when they are violated. Just like the law of gravity, the laws of health cannot be changed. If you jump off a building, you are going to fall and hit the ground—it's the law of gravity. No matter how much I may not want to fall, if I jump off a building, I *will* fall. Likewise, we cannot eat processed food without experiencing consequences. In the fast food industry, foods are created in quantity, with little regard to quality. We cannot eat junk foods, processed foods, and prepackaged foods that are taken out of their original states, pumped with chemicals, toxins, and preservatives, and expect a healthy body. It is not logical to believe that we can continually put junk food into our bodies and still live a long, fruitful life.

I was at the country club with some friends when a man who had been a long-time friend of my father came up to say hello. He mentioned his struggle with fibromyalgia (inflammation in the muscles) and that he had been to multiple specialists searching for answers. No one could help him. I asked him if anyone had addressed the issue of inflammation in his digestive system. He answered no, and I knew what to do. I recommended that he follow the Anti-Inflammatory Diet (detailed in chapter 13) made up of natural foods and ask that he avoid the specific non-foods discussed previously in this chapter. By doing so, his fibromyalgia disappeared through the elimination of inflammation in his digestive tract and the restoration of proper absorption. Get to the root of the illness, give your body quality fuel, and in most cases, the problem will be alleviated. It's a foundational principal to good health.

9

SUPPLEMENTS
The Foundational Four and Other Essentials

"Health is worth more than learning."
—THOMAS JEFFERSON

A hundred years ago, all soil was organic. Farmers practiced crop rotation (letting the soil rest every few years to replenish itself), natural pest and insect control (without the use of chemicals), and developed healthy, nutrient-rich soil through natural composting. Sadly, today our soil is in a perpetual state of depletion. Few people grow their own food anymore, and most of us simply assume the soil is healthy. But is it?

GOING ORGANIC—IT'S ALL ABOUT QUALITY

When a commercial farmer finds a disease or infestation in his crops, the immediate response is to dump chemicals on the entire crop to treat the plants. These harsh chemicals stay in the soil for years, which is why I stress organic eating throughout this book. Crops can't be certified as organic by the USDA National Organic Program unless they have been grown in soil that has been chemical-free for at least three years.

The term "organic" refers to environmentally friendly methods of farming. No chemicals are used, and the soil in which the food is grown is more nutrient rich than most commercial soil because it is naturally replenished with rich compost such as manure and fish emulsions. Natural compost helps build up the soil and create the correct balance of nutrients that God intended for our food.

I'm frequently asked: *Does everything have to be organic?* The answer is "no." First make the choice to eat baked chicken over fried chicken, switch from fried catfish to baked salmon, and begin eating apples instead of caramel apples. You should care more about choosing the right types of food than anything else. Going organic is simply the next step after you've begun to rid your diet of the most harmful foods.

People often use the excuse that it's more expensive to eat organic foods—and they are right. But if we all started eating organically, the prices would go down because of the basic laws of supply and demand. Second, it's typically only a few dollars more for eggs and meats that are organic. Is an extra dollar or two worth the difference between your body making healthy cells or cancerous ones? Of course it is!

You have likely seen these labels on many foods available today. But what do they mean?

Organic. Produce and other ingredients that are certified organic are grown without the use of pesticides, synthetic fertilizers, sewage sludge, genetically modified organisms, or ionizing radiation. Organically raised animals that produce meat, poultry, eggs, and dairy products do not take antibiotics or growth hormones.

Grass-Fed or Free Range. A great number of commercial farmers feed animals high-grain diets. However, these animals are designed to eat fibrous grasses, plants, and shrubs. When they are switched from pasture grazing to grain diets, they can become afflicted with a number of disorders. To prevent more serious and even fatal diseases, the animals are given chemical additives along with a constant, low-level dose of antibiotics. Feeding the animals grains also compromises the nutritional value of their meat and dairy products. The result is that the food has more of the things you don't want in your diet and fewer of the nutrients that are good for you. When livestock are grass fed, they are raised on pasture and live low-stress lives. As a result of their superb nutrition and lack of stress, they are extremely healthy. When you choose products from pastured animals, you are eating food as nature intended.

Cage Free. Many large commercial livestock and poultry farmers raise their animals in confinement. Tightly packed into cages, sheds, or pens, they cannot practice their normal behaviors, such as rooting, grazing, and roosting. Laying hens are crowded into cages that are so small that there is not enough room for all of the birds to sit down at one time. They cannot even escape their own waste. Meat and eggs from these animals are lower in a number of key vitamins and omega-3 fatty acids. Cage free means that these animals are allowed to exist in a more natural environment. Thus, they are healthier, and so are the foods we receive from them.

THE FOUNDATIONAL FOUR

Nutritional supplementation has become a standard in Natural Medicine. The reason is simple—we must supplement our diets with essential nutrients because of the lack of nutrients in our soil and food supply. Even the most organic sources of food do not contain all of the critical nutrients for optimal health. There are four supplements that everyone needs, regardless of specific deficiencies. I call them the foundational four. These are the four basic nutrients that are critical to optimal health, and are no longer in our food supply. You should continue taking these four supplements for the rest of your life, using the brands of your choice. A word of caution: Bargain supplements are not always a good idea. Don't compromise quality for price. It is not apt to be a health bargain and could harm you more than help you if it lacks purity and adequate antioxidants essential to preserve freshness. Consider it an investment in your good health! Here are the foundational four supplements:

1. **Whole food multivitamin.** Commercial brands of multivitamins (the ones you find in most drug stores and even some health food stores) are synthetic. Synthetic supplements do not come from food, which means that while they may contain the same molecular formula as the organic versions, they do not contain the "co-factors"—the naturally occurring enzymes—required for your body to properly use the nutrients. In essence, if you are taking a synthetic multivitamin, your body can use virtually none of it. But they don't just pass through the body. Your body has to process anything you consume, so it must process these synthetic supplements, which are man-made and often toxic. In short, synthetic supplements can actually do more harm than good and may even have adverse side effects, some as severe as sterility.

115

On the other hand, whole food multivitamins are whole foods with only the water and fiber removed. They are, in essence, compressed, dried food. One of the most noticeable differences between these and synthetic supplements is their limited shelf life. This is because the naturally occurring enzymes, the "co-factors" I mentioned previously that are necessary to properly use the nutrients in the body, are still alive and active in the supplements. Start taking whole food multivitamins and you will literally feel the difference as your body begins to regain balance with the right amounts of vitamins and minerals. Whole food multivitamins are generally clearly labeled as such. Look for brands that state that its ingredients are "whole plant derived" or from a "whole food source." If you are unsure whether or not your multivitamin is from a whole food source, it would be best to switch to a brand that is clearly labeled to avoid the synthetic varieties.

2. Digestive enzymes. Enzymes help break down the food that we eat. They help you assimilate all your nutrients. Past generations had ideal amounts of enzymes in their food because the soil was fertile and free of toxins. Today scientists say our soil is not even one-tenth of the quality it was years ago due to the heavy amounts of chemical pesticides used and the lack of proper crop rotation, which is necessary to give the soil time to replenish itself. The enzymes that you take with food will help break down protein, fat, sugar, starch, and carbohydrates. The body contains (or is supposed to contain) most of the enzymes it needs, but with the lifestyle choices of our fast-paced society and the depleted state of our soil, we have lost a lot of our enzymes' beneficial processes.

The lack of proper enzymes in the body creates a two-fold problem: It impairs the functioning of the immune system, and it results in illness and disease. We get sick so often because we do not have the enzymes to break down our food and we don't have the proper digestion to function and support this process. Take enzyme supplements with every meal—one to two per meal will help break down food and help assimilate it for proper digestion. Enzymes will also transform nutrients to become the new healthy cells that your body desperately needs to be well. Enzymes are most commonly found and easily taken in pill form. Look for brands that contain chlorella, chlorophyllase, and pepsin, as these are excellent enzymes; and avoid brands that say they have been freeze-dried or frozen, as this process takes away much of the enzymes' potency.

3. Probiotics. Our digestive system contains both good and bad bacteria.

Good bacteria are essential for proper digestion, increased immune function, and reduced inflammation. Because of our personal overuse of antibiotics and harmful bacteria in our food supply, we constantly need to manage our "gut health." Probiotics are dietary supplements containing beneficial bacteria. The bacteria used in probiotic formulas are able to convert sugars and other carbohydrates into lactic acid. That is what provides the characteristic sour taste of fermented dairy foods such as yogurt; it also acts as a preservative by lowering pH levels and creating fewer opportunities for harmful pathogens to grow. Probiotic bacterial cultures help the body's naturally occurring organisms in the digestive tract reestablish themselves and allow for effective and healthy digestion.

Choose brands that contain healthy strands of bacteria and are made from quality ingredients. Most probiotics need to be refrigerated to maintain effectiveness even if they promote having a long shelf life.

4. Omega-3 oils. Fats are critical to overall bodily function. Most people get enough omega-6 and -9 fats from foods like animal fats and butter. But many of us are shockingly deficient in omega-3 fats, those found in sources like cod liver oil, most nuts, salmon, tuna, and flaxseeds. Omega-3 fat is called an essential amino acid because it is truly *essential* that you consume it. Our bodies do not produce essential amino acids on their own, but they are necessary for a multitude of functions in the body such as proper hormone function, brain function, and skin, hair, and nail health. Cod liver oil is the best choice for absorption, plus it has a high concentration of vitamins A and D.

Beware of rancid oil. Here is a word of caution about taking oil capsules. Would you eat fish if it were rancid? Of course not. Unfortunately, if you take oil capsules such as cod liver oil or fish oil, you have no way of knowing whether or not the oil inside those capsules is rancid. Fish oil is unstable and it starts to oxidize as soon as it is extracted from the fish and exposed to oxygen, metals, light, and heat. Fish oil can go rancid within days, although labels often say it's safe to use it for three or four years. Here is how you can protect yourself against this:

- Test fish oil capsules by biting into one. It should taste fresh and mildly fishy. If it tastes bad or excessively strong, throw them away and avoid that brand.

Foundational Four Chart

	Upon Rising	Breakfast	Lunch	Dinner	Bedtime
Ages 17 and up					
Whole Food Multivitamin		2 caps.		2 caps.	
Digestive Enzymes		2 caps.	2 caps.	2 caps.	
Probiotics	2-4 caps.				2-4 caps.
Omega-3 Oil (cod liver oil)				1 tbsp.	
Ages 10 to 16					
Whole Food Multivitamin		1 caps.		1 caps.	
Digestive Enzymes		1 caps.	1 caps.	1 caps.	
Probiotics	2 caps.				2 caps.
Omega-3 Oil (cod liver oil)				1/2 tbsp.	
Ages 2 to 9					
Whole Food Multivitamin		1 caps.			
Digestive Enzymes		1/2 caps.	1/2 caps.	1/2 caps.	
Probiotics	1 caps.				1 caps.
Omega-3 Oil (cod liver oil)				1 tsp.	
Ages 2 and under					
Whole Food Multivitamin		1/2 caps.			
Digestive Enzymes		1/4 caps.	1/4 caps.	1/4 caps.	
Probiotics	1/2 caps.				1/2 caps.
Omega-3 Oil (cod liver oil)				1/4 tsp.	

- Choose brands that include d-gamma and d-delta forms of tocopherols (vitamin E) to prevent harmful oxidation and rancidity.

OTHER COMMON DEFICIENCIES

Here is a list of the most commonly deficient supplements in our diet today. Unfortunately, the depletion of the soil makes it necessary for us to take these supplements in pill or liquid form. The most effective way to ensure that you receive these vital vitamins and minerals is to find a good whole food multivitamin, as mentioned in the foundational four supplements. A good multivitamin will contain:

Calcium. Long-term calcium deficiency can lead to osteoporosis and affect bone and tooth formation, while too much of it can lead to kidney stones.

Magnesium. Magnesium works to support your bones, helps in the production of cholesterol, helps to activate many vitamins, aids in relaxing muscles, and is an essential factor in protein synthesis.

Potassium. Considered an electrolyte, Potassium makes our bodies capable of conducting electricity. Symptoms of severe potassium deficiency are fatigue, muscle weakness and cramps, and intestinal issues such bloating, constipation, and abdominal pain.

Vitamin K. Vitamin K's primarily role is to serve as a coenzyme that aids certain amino acids in the body in calcium binding. Vitamin K deficiency results in impaired blood clotting, and symptoms include easy bruising and bleeding

Folic acid. Necessary for the production and maintenance of new cells, a deficiency in folic acid delays DNA synthesis and cell division, which why it is especially important during infancy and pregnancy, when there is rapid cell division and growth.

Vitamin B12. The primary functions of this vitamin are the formation of red blood cells and the maintenance of a healthy nervous system. B12 is necessary for the rapid synthesis of DNA during cell division. Symptoms of deficiency include excessive tiredness, breathlessness, listlessness, and low resistance to infections.

Vitamin B6. The nervous and immune systems need vitamin B6 to function efficiently. Vitamin B6 also helps maintain your blood sugar levels. Vitamin B6 deficiency symptoms only occur during severe stages of deficiency and include skin inflammation, a sore tongue, depression, confusion, and convulsions.

Iodine. Iodine is an essential trace element that is necessary for proper production of thyroid hormones. Iodine deficiency can lead to hypothyroidism with symptoms of extreme fatigue, mental slowness, depression, weight gain, and low resting body temperatures.

Zinc. Zinc is an essential element and is an activator of certain enzymes. Proper eye function, taste, smell, and memory are all connected with zinc intake. Signs of zinc deficiency include hair loss, skin lesions, diarrhea, and wasting of body tissues.

Iron. Iron is an essential component of proteins involved in oxygen transport and is essential for the regulation of cell growth. A deficiency of iron limits oxygen delivery to cells, resulting in fatigue, poor work performance, and decreased immune function.

Antioxidants (Vitamins C and E, Co-Q-10, lipoic acid). Antioxidants counteract the damage of oxidation in our tissue caused by harmful molecules called free radicals. There is a constant need to replenish our antioxidant resources.

As you can see, many of the vitamins and minerals share common symptoms of deficiency. It is important to have a physician evaluate your symptoms so that appropriate medical care can be given and you can find the proper balance of the essential vitamins and minerals that is unique to your body's chemistry. Most of the time, a quality whole food multivitamin will provide you with the proper amounts of each of these vitamins and minerals. However, some people may require more of a certain nutrient depending on their specific bodily needs and deficiencies. The proper blood work will reveal where your own body needs additional supplementation. You can have your blood examined at most hospitals and through the majority of doctors. Blood work is a form of testing that most physicians utilize, regardless of their specialty, because of the extensive and revealing results obtained from this testing. You will learn more about the importance of blood work in chapter 14.

THE POWER OF PHYTONUTRIENTS

The term "phyto" originates from a Greek word meaning plant. Phytonutrients are organic components of plants that are believed to promote health. Fruits, vegetables, grains, nuts, and teas are rich sources of phytonutrients. Unlike the traditional nutrients (protein, fat, vitamins, and minerals), phytonutrients are not essential for life, so some experts prefer to use the term "phytochemical." Although these phytonutrients are not essential, they are beneficial for a variety of reasons:

- Serve as antioxidants (molecules that cancel out the damaging effects of free radicals, which are linked to cancer and other diseases).

- Enhance immune response.

- Enhance cell-to-cell communication.

- Can cause some cancer cells to die (apoptosis) and detoxify carcinogens (cancer-causing agents).

- Repair DNA damage caused by smoking and other toxic exposures.

Carotenoids. There are several classifications of phytonutrients. Of all the phytonutrients, we are probably most familiar with carotenoids. These are the red, orange, and yellow pigments in fruits and vegetables. Fruits and vegetables high in carotenoids may protect us against cancers, heart disease, and other health conditions. The carotenoids most commonly found in our foods are listed below along with their most common sources:[1]

Carotenoid	Source
alpha-carotene	carrots
beta-carotene	leafy green and yellow vegetables such as broccoli, sweet potato, pumpkin, carrots
beta-cryptoxanthin	citrus, peaches, apricots
lutein	leafy greens such as kale, spinach, turnip greens
lycopene	tomato products, pink grapefruit, watermelon, guava
zeaxanthin	green vegetables, eggs, citrus

Polyphenols. Another type of phytonutrient, these compounds are natural components of a wide variety of fruits and vegetables. Recent studies show that polyphenols can be used to prevent the spread of a number of degenerative conditions, including cancer and cardiovascular and neurodegenerative diseases. However, the positive effects of polyphenols depend on the amount you consume, and the method of food preparation can affect the polyphenol content of food. Polyphenols are found in higher concentrations in the outer parts of fruits and vegetables, so peeling can eliminate a significant portion of its beneficial value.

Also, cooking may cause fruits and vegetables to lose much of their polyphenol content. When a food containing polyphenols is fried, there is a 30 percent loss. When cooked in the microwave, polyphenol content drops by 65 percent. The boiling process results in a 75 to 80 percent loss. Does this mean you should never cook your food and only consume raw produce? No. Just be aware of the loss incurred by the various methods of food preparation and eat a few more raw fruits and vegetables during the day.

Fruits such as the ones listed in the following chart and beverages such as black and green teas are the main sources of polyphenols.

Polyphenol	Source
ellagic acid	strawberries, blueberries, raspberries
anthocyanins	fruits
catechins	tea, wine
flavanones	citrus
flavones	fruits and vegetables
flavonols	fruits, vegetables, tea, wine
isoflavones	soybeans

HEADACHES MAY SIGNAL DEFICIENCIES

As stated earlier, headaches are often caused by dehydration. More often, however, headaches are triggered by a deficiency in the body of a specific supplement or several supplements. Determining the type of headache you suffer from will help you find treatments that will normalize body chemistry imbalances and deficiencies that cause the headaches. The following is a list of the most common types of headaches and how to rid yourself of them with the supplementation and lifestyle changes.

Adrenal. Also known as fatigue headaches, these come on later in the day as fatigue sets in. Often your blood pressure will be low at this time. A good test to indicate the general health of the adrenal glands is called Ragland's test. In a person with adequately functioning adrenal glands, the systolic blood pressure (the top number in the blood pressure reading) is about 10 mm. higher when standing than when lying down. So here is the procedure for testing:

1. Lie down and take your blood pressure.

2. Stand and take your blood pressure.

3. Rest for six minutes lying down.

4. Stand up and immediately take the blood pressure.

If the systolic blood pressure is 10 mm. lower after standing, suspect adrenal gland weakness. The greater the drop in blood pressure the greater the degree of adrenal dysfunction. This is a sign of adrenal exhaustion and steps must be taken to normalize the imbalance in the body chemistry. Here are the protocols for an adrenal headache:

• Eat smaller meals.

• Get plenty of mild exercise.

• Take buffered Vitamin C. (Buffered forms of vitamins are combined with minerals such as calcium, magnesium, or potassium. Buffered vitamin C may be helpful for people with stomach sensitivity, or who are taking high doses of the supplement. Take as much as you can according to bowel tolerance).

• Use an adrenal support formula (multivitamin and mineral supplement designed specifically for the adrenals).

• Take panthenate (active vitamin B5)—500 milligrams per day.

• Avoid processed flour, sugar, and cow's milk. Organic cow's milk is not harmful; however, it is the most common food allergy (accounts for 60 percent of all food allergies).

Low blood sugar. The low blood sugar sufferer will get a headache with a skipped or delayed meal, which allows the blood sugar to drop. Eating the wrong foods is the primary cause of this kind of headache. Consume the right amount of healthy fats and proteins and avoid refined carbohydrates (avoid anything in a package). Adrenal weakness and vitamin B deficiency accompany this type of headache. Snacks should be fresh foods, and eating a good breakfast is a must. Here are the protocols for a low blood sugar headache:

- If eating at night, eat only protein close to bedtime.

- Eat balanced portions of proteins, fats, and carbohydrates.

- Take chromium picolinate—200 mcg per day (chromium picolinate enhances your metabolism by improving impaired insulin function—therefore, it supports healthy blood sugar).

- Take a pyridoxal-5-phosphate supplement (P-5-P or active B6)— 500 milligrams per day.

- Get plenty of omega-3 fats (cod liver oil is an excellent source).

Depression. When you're depressed, you're susceptible to chronic headaches because of physical or emotional lethargy. One of the listed side effects of psychotropic drugs such as Paxil and Prozac are headaches. Eat a diet of whole, organic foods and start an exercise program that includes aerobic exercise and weight lifting if you can, although it is not always easy to exercise if you are depressed. Here are the protocols for a depression headache:

- Get your neurotransmitters (brain chemicals) checked for deficiencies.

- Consume high amounts of omega-3 fats such as cod liver oil.

- Take a pyridoxal-5-phosphate supplement (P-5-P or active) —500 milligrams per day.

- Get thirty minutes of exercise per day.

- Use replacement therapy when depressive feelings come on such as doing an activity that you like.

Heart weakness. Heart weakness headaches are accompanied by difficulty breathing, weakness upon exertion, chest pain, fatigue soon after awakening, and low blood pressure. These headaches will usually occur after exertion of some type. Such people are often diagnosed with congestive heart failure (CHF). This weakness leads to a lack of oxygen and excessive carbon dioxide buildup in the cells. Here are the protocols for a headache associated with heart weakness:

- Increase omega-3 intake.

- Increase exercise to four to five days per week for thirty minutes per day.

- Through diagnostic blood work, have your levels of homocysteine (an amino acid that is thought to be one of the causes of heart disease) checked and reduce its level. Dietary supplementation with folic acid can help reduce elevated homocysteine levels in most patients. (1 mg per day is the usual prescribed dose, but may differ slightly for each individual). When this is not effective, vitamins B6 and B12 can be added.

Structural. This is a term for headaches caused by misalignment of the spinal vertebrae. These types of headaches are often out of our direct control, and the best protocol is proper structural care by an osteopathic or chiropractic physician.

Liver toxicity. Nausea and a metallic taste in the mouth typically accompany a liver toxicity headache. Body aches, nightmares, or insomnia are also frequent. Intolerance to fats and oils is common. Eliminate all junk food, fried foods, refined oils, soft drinks, margarines, and commercial salad dressings from your diet. Eat fresh (preferably organic) fruits and vegetables, and use organic butter and extra virgin coconut oil for cooking. In some cases, several liver detoxification sessions combined with a proper detoxification regimen will resolve these headaches. Here are the protocols for a headache caused by a toxic liver:

- Do a liver flush:

  For three days, drink nothing but freshly juiced organic apples and water.

  On the night of day 3, drink a mixture of four ounces of extra virgin olive oil, mixed with four ounces of freshly squeezed lemon juice. Drink this mixture right before bed. You may experience some slight discomfort in your abdominal region during the night as the mixture cleans your liver and begins the process of eliminating excess bile and gall or liver stones. As with any treatment, consult with your physician before performing a liver flush to ensure that you can safely do so.

- Incorporate a partial fast (skip one or two meals during the day) or a 24-hour fast into your diet. Eat dinner one night, and eat nothing until dinner the following night. This gives your body a full 24 hours to rest from the digestion process. You should consult your physician before deciding what type of fasting works best for you.

ASA'S SUPER CLEANSE

Use this cleanse for five to ten days in a row, at least four times per year (consult with your doctor before using this cleanse). Do not eat with this cleanse. Mix together the following ingredients and drink up to twelve times per day:

    2 tablespoons lemon juice or ½ lemon
    2 tablespoons pure maple syrup
    Pinch of cayenne pepper
    10 ounces of non-chlorinated water

Food allergies. Offending foods consistently produce headaches. The most common are cow's milk, wheat, chocolate, and pork. One cause of food allergies or sensitivities can be weakened adrenals, but usually the main problems are digestion and malabsorption. Here are the protocols for a food allergy headache:

- Follow the Anti-Inflammatory Diet (see chapter 13).

- Eliminate all wheat, grains, and cow's milk dairy products.

- Fast for one day per week. You may drink water during the day. For those with blood sugar issues, you may want to include sipping on broth to keep your blood sugar levels regulated. Be sure to consult your physician before undertaking a fast.

Environmental allergies. Many headaches can be traced to man-made chemicals. Pesticides, fertilizers, perfumes, and products found in new houses such as glues, carpets, paints, and thinners can overwhelm the lymphatic, circulatory, and nervous systems, producing toxic headaches. Here are the protocols for a headache brought on by environmental allergies:

- Eliminate heavy metals through some type of detoxification program such as ionic therapy (for more ways to detoxify, see chapter 10).

- Use air purifiers in each room in the house or workplace.

- Breathe fresh air for at least thirty minutes per day.

- Use a mini trampoline for increased lymphatic flow.

- Avoid mainstream, chemically laced personal care products such as shampoo and deodorant.

Gallbladder. This is similar to liver toxicity headaches; problems occur when eating fats and oils, and the headache is usually accompanied by nausea. There is often pain over the liver and gallbladder area. Even if the gallbladder has been removed, the problems and headache may still be present because removal of the gallbladder treated the symptoms and not the cause. Here are the protocols for a gallbladder headache:

- Reduce fat intake for three days to see if symptoms go away. If so, the headache is gallbladder related.

- Follow the Anti-Inflammatory Diet (see chapter 13).

- Do a gallbladder flush. This flush takes twenty-one days and is gentle on the body:
    1. Avoid all foods high in fat, meats, dairy, and eggs. Eat unrefined grains, vegetables, fruits and legumes to help clear the gallbladder.

2. For every 160 pounds of body weight, use five teaspoons of cold-pressed flaxseed oil. Pour the flax oil over your food during one meal of the day or divide into half and use on two meals.

3. Radishes also help remove stones, so, for the entire twenty-one days, eat one to two raw or cooked radishes a day between meals.

Ovarian. These headaches usually occur during ovulation or menstruation. Due to hormonal involvement, they often come with emotional reactions and mood swings. Because of imbalances in estrogen and progesterone levels, acne can occur during this time, and many women take birth control pills to control these problems. Try to normalize the body chemistry and hormone production by getting your blood thoroughly checked annually to detect deficiencies or abnormalities. Supplements are often needed to balance body chemistry and bring hormone stability. Here are the protocols for an ovarian headache:

- Have your hormones checked regularly.

- Avoid soy products (for more on soy see chapter 8 on non-foods).

- Exercise five to six times per week for thirty minutes per day.

- Increase omega-3 fat intake (cod liver oil).

- Check for low iron levels.

- Find alternative means of contraceptives to eliminate birth control pills if possible.

- Avoid mainstream beauty creams and lotions because of hidden hormones and chemicals, and instead use organic products made from non-toxic ingredients. For a list of companies who offer organic and natural beauty products, please see the appendix.

Thyroid. This type of headache usually shows up first thing in the morning. As the thyroid gets fired up later in the day, the headache usually subsides. Sufferers should consider liver toxicity as a contributing cause of their headaches. Exercise is a must, and meal portion sizes should be kept small. Here are the protocols for a thyroid headache:

- Eat two to three tablespoons of organic coconut oil daily (best way is to use for cooking).

- Check underarm temperature to make sure it is above 97.6 degrees.

- Check iodine levels regularly and take an organic iodine supplement if deficient (this can be obtained from your physician).

- Have TSH (thyroid stimulating hormone) levels checked on thyroid blood tests to ensure proper hormone function.

- Avoid the cabbage family (cabbage, brussels sprouts, etc.), which lower thyroid function.

Capillary fragility. These can be crushing headaches caused by blood leaking from weak and fragile capillaries. People suffering from this problem may have chronic bruising, bleeding gums, ulcers, and cuts that heal slowly. No amount of ascorbic acid will resolve this problem because it is caused by deficiency in the bioflavonoid portion of the whole vitamin C complex. Remember that prescription drugs can contribute to the problems, and pain-killers, arthritis drugs, and NSAIDS are notorious for causing these problems. Here are the protocols for a headache caused by weakened capillaries:

- Omega-3 fats such as cod liver oil are important for strengthening capillaries.

- In most cases, supplements are needed and you should seek the advice of your physician.

WHICH SUPPLEMENTS ARE RIGHT FOR YOU?

I was stunned at what I saw when I entered the exam room. Kristen sat there with four grocery bags full of vitamins beside her. She had never been diagnosed with any major disease, but she wanted to make sure she was not missing any of her vitamins!

She had an herb, pill, or cream for every ailment imaginable. However, she was giving her body far more than was necessary or effective. Heavy supplementation is only needed in short intervals until nutritional deficiencies are replenished. Once you have corrected major deficiencies, you can maintain with the foundational four, and perhaps two or three other supplements for specific ongoing needs. The bottom line is that you have to find which supplements are right for you. Taking every pill you can, hoping to cure or prevent all health concerns is not the answer.

There is a term called *biological individuality*, and it means that everyone is different. The vitamins and minerals my body needs might not be the same that yours requires. That is why it is important to have your body evaluated yearly using extensive diagnostic blood work. This yearly checkup is a great way to ensure that you are giving your body what it needs.

It is true that our soil is in a perpetual state of depletion, and because of this, much of our food is grown without the necessary amounts of the vitamins and minerals our bodies need to flourish in abundant health. For example, you may eat a healthy amount of green vegetables and red meat, which are both natural sources of iron. However, it may still be possible to develop a lack of iron in the body, or an iron deficiency. The lack of iron can create a breeding ground for a host of diseases including chronic fatigue, but by replacing nutritional deficiencies through supplementing your diet with organic iron, you can reverse disease processes and eliminate many health conditions.

Have your blood tested to find what vitamins and minerals your body lacks, and begin to give your body the supplements to rid itself of these deficiencies. You can feel better! You simply have to give your body the right tools to do its job.

Continue to take medications that your doctor has prescribed even if you plan on taking the foundational four. Ultimately, the way to empower your health is to find the right balance of specific nutrients to effectively manage your deficiencies and toxicity internally. You also need to manage the toxins that surround us outside our bodies, as we will see in the next chapter.

10

ELIMINATING TOXINS
Restoring Our Internal Environment

"In minds crammed with thoughts, organs clogged with toxins, and bodies stiffened with neglect, there is just no space for anything else."

—ALISON ROSE LEVY

When most people think of the "environment," they think of rain forests, global warming, and pollution. These things make up your external environment: the factors outside your direct control. It is difficult to control your surroundings once you step outside your home, but you do have power over one environment—your personal environment. This includes the air you breathe in your home or car, the water in which you drink and bathe, and the lotions and cosmetics that you put on your skin. Your personal environment consists of the multitude of products used in your home and on your body every single day—even the toothpaste you put on your toothbrush.

In school, I learned the importance of controlling the use of toxic personal products and environmental toxins, but I viewed these warnings more as suggestions rather than necessities. I ate well, exercised, rested, took care of myself, and worked hard to practice everything I learned in school—surely that would be enough. I was determined not to be one of those "health nuts" or overboard extremists I heard about. Who cares about what kind of toothpaste or shampoo I use, what kind of water I drink, or what personal care products I put on my body? My mentality was: *We are all going to die of something—I can't live in a bubble.*

The cliché, "If you knew better, you would do better," was not entirely accurate for me—I knew better. That is why it is important to be aware of the difference between simply knowing something and truly *believing* it. You only find true understanding when knowledge goes from mere fact to becoming a part of your heart and lifestyle. It was foolish not to apply good, sound principles to my life, but that is what I was doing. It was lazy to shirk the responsibility of actively controlling my personal environment; I know better now, but I see this mentality every day in others. People may not always have problems eating well, exercising, getting proper rest, or taking general care of their bodies, but they have such resistance toward taking control over what they put into their personal environments.

No one makes a complete lifestyle transformation without understanding the reasons that make this change necessary; to discover exactly how to control your personal environment, you must first have a clear understanding of what that term "personal environment" means. By fully grasping the concept, you will begin to understand what you can change to make your life healthier and achieve the optimal health you desire.

THE MOST COMMON TOXINS

Thousands of toxins are circulating in the air around us and in our water. Many of these toxins are commonly found in products you use every day, the water you drink, and the air you breathe, both outside and inside the home.

PCBs. Polychlorinated biphenyls (PCBs) are industrial chemicals that have been banned in the United States for decades, and yet these persistent organic pollutants are still present in our environment.[1] PCBs were developed in the 1930s for making products such as paints, inks, dyes, hydraulic fluids, and electrical transformers, and have been shown to cause cancer and impair fetal brain development. Despite a worldwide ban of PCBs in the late 1970s, high concentrations of them continue to be found in the fatty tissues of land animals and fish. Today most farm-raised salmon are raised on pellets of ground-up fish that have absorbed PCBs from the environment, which is why I recommend eating cold-water salmon rather than farm raised.

Chloride dioxins. Organic compounds called dioxins are commonly found in consumer products and are also present in a large majority of commercially raised animals. These compounds contain carbon, oxygen, and hydrogen, and can be created naturally from volcanoes and forest fires, or through the manufacturing of PVC products such as plastic piping. Chloride dioxins have been linked to cancer, reproductive and developmental disorders, chloracne (a severe skin disease with lesions), skin rashes, skin discoloration, excessive body hair, and mild liver damage. Over 95 percent of exposure comes from eating commercial animal fats, so you can greatly reduce your exposure by consuming organically raised livestock.

Heavy metals. Metals are frequently found in a surprising number of everyday items. Metallic particles of mercury, lead, arsenic, aluminum, and cadmium accumulate in the soft tissue of the body, which can lower IQ, cause developmental delays, and incite behavioral disorders. Mercury is especially prevalent in canned tuna, and arsenic can often be found in tap water and treated wood. Use a water filter and limit your consumption of canned fish to help lessen your intake of heavy metals.

Asbestos. Schools and office buildings constructed in the 1950s through the early 1970s were insulated with a cancer-causing material called asbestos. Asbestos can also cause scarring of the lung tissue and mesothelioma, a rare form of cancer. It was discovered that asbestos is highly toxic, so many asbestos-infested buildings have been carefully torn down. However, problems persist in buildings that are still standing because the insulation in ceilings and in heating and cooling ducts crumbles and releases asbestos particles into the air. If you live or work in a building constructed during this time period, you might want to consider having the structure tested by an accredited asbestos testing lab. For more information, go to the Environmental Protection Agency's Web site at www.epa.gov/asbestos.

Talates. Talates are chemicals used to soften plastic and lengthen the shelf life of cosmetics, hairsprays, mousses, and fragrances. Talates harm the developing testes of males and damage the lungs, liver, and kidneys of both sexes as well as causing damage to the endrocrine system. Check the labels of your personal care products and discontinue use if the words "talate" or "phthalate" are listed in the ingredients.

Chlorine. This toxic gas is one of the most heavily used chemicals. Anyone who has ever gone swimming knows about chlorine. Chlorine is a chemical compound used as a disinfectant to kill, destroy, or control bacteria and algae. Chlorine is commonly used in municipal water supplies and is found in many household cleaners. Its many side effects include sore throat, coughing, eye and skin irritation, rapid breathing, wheezing, accumulation of fluid in the lungs, pain in the lung region, unexplained eye and skin burns, lung collapse, and a type of asthma called reactive airways dysfunction syndrome. The best way to begin eliminating this harmful substance is to use a water filter in your home and drink purified or spring water rather than water from the tap.

Pesticides. According to the Environmental Protection Agency, 60 percent of herbicides, 90 percent of fungicides, and 30 percent of insecticides are known to be carcinogenic. Pesticide residues have been detected in up to 95 percent of U.S. foods. Symptoms of prolonged pesticide exposure are severe and can include cancer, Parkinson's disease, miscarriage, nerve damage, birth defects, and blocking of the absorption of food nutrients. Buying organic produce and discontinuing the use of bug sprays around your home are excellent ways to limit your exposure.

Mold and fungi. It is suggested that one in three people has had an allergic reaction to mold. Fungal toxins can cause a range of health problems such as cancer, heart disease, asthma, multiple sclerosis, and diabetes with exposure to only a small amount over long periods of time. Avoid peanuts, as they contain a high amount of mold, and check for mold in or around your home.

VOCs. VOCs (volatile organic compounds) are a major contributing factor to air pollution. They have been linked to eye and respiratory tract irritation, headaches, dizziness, visual disorders, and memory loss. The most common sources of VOCs are tap water, chemically treated carpets, deodorants with antiperspirant, most commercial cleaning fluids, dry cleaned clothing, and air fresheners. VOCs tend to be even higher in indoor air than outdoor air because they are present in so many household products. Do not treat your furniture or carpet with chemicals, and buy only natural cleaning products, such as the cleaning product line by Seventh Generation, which is free of chemicals.

Chloroform. This colorless liquid has a nonirritating odor and a sweet taste, and is used to make other chemicals. It's also formed when chlorine is added to water. Common side effects and possible complications from overexposure to chloroform include cancer, potential reproductive damage, birth defects, dizziness, fatigue, headache, and liver and kidney damage. It is found in both indoor and outdoor air, as well as in tap water. Therefore, use only filtered, purified, and spring water, and keep an air filter in your home and office.

Although our bodies are designed to eliminate toxins, our immune systems have become overloaded to the point that they are waging perpetual uphill battles. The body absorbs and excretes water-soluble chemical toxins, but fat-soluble chemicals such as dioxins, talates, and chlorine are stored in fatty tissues; it takes months or even years for these toxins to be eliminated from the system.[2]

HUMAN SKIN—A GIANT SPONGE

We think of the skin as a perfect barrier, but it is actually a sponge. If you don't believe that, take off your shoes and rub a clove of garlic on the bottom of your foot. In about thirty minutes, you will taste the garlic. This happens because whatever you put on your skin is absorbed directly into the bloodstream.

The skin is a large semipermeable membrane, which means that it serves as an excellent first line of defense, preventing harmful things from entering the body. The skin absorbs some substances while blocking others. As mentioned above, tap water contains many deadly toxins such as chlorine, chloroform, heavy metals, and VOCs. And despite the skin's amazing abilities, here is an alarming fact: Because of the high toxicity of the unfiltered water found in most homes, you absorb as much poison through the lungs and skin in a hot shower as you would by drinking eight glasses of contaminated water.

Many medications today are available in cream or patch form. For example, look at the nicotine patch—you can place it anywhere on your body, and nicotine is slowly released into your system through the skin to alleviate cigarette withdrawal symptoms. Just like in creams and patches, the chemicals in personal care products are absorbed directly into the skin as well, and they go straight into the bloodstream.

The personal care product industry is a multi-billion dollar industry—these companies are not interested in your health; they are interested in your money. If you tell a woman she can reduce wrinkles and prevent aging by applying certain lotions and potions, she'll gladly do so, and cosmetic companies make billions of dollars a year as a result.

Many consumers buy products based on advertising or reputation. However, I suggest that you start reading the labels of your favorite beauty and personal care products. Here is a list of harmful chemicals found in the majority of mainstream personal care products:

- Any substance with the word phthalate or talate in the name
- Polyethylene glycol
- Propylene glycol
- Propane
- Polyoxyethylene
- Butane
- Sodium laurel sulfate
- DEA and TEA
- Isopropylene
- Fluoride
- Aluminum

If you see any of these ingredients listed, discontinue use of that product and switch to natural beauty product lines such as Jason's, Botanical Skin Works, Jenulence, Perfect Organics, or Tom's. These products are available online as well as in many health food stores, including Whole Foods, Trader Joe's, and the Staff of Life. If these chains do not have a location where you live, check your local health food store for their selection of personal care products.

THE DAILY POISONING ROUTINE

Let's look at a typical morning for many of us.

Water. The alarm buzzes—you sit up in bed, yawn and stretch, and then glance at the clock, wishing for a few more minutes of sleep. You know you can't stay in bed any longer, so you stagger into the bathroom to turn on the hot shower. Once you step into the shower, the water hits your face—water that is chlorinated, filled with poisons and toxins that remove the good bacteria inside your digestive tract and create cancer-causing chemicals in the body. The hot water soon opens up the pores and chlorine begins to pour into your bloodstream; but it doesn't seem to matter because it feels so refreshing. You are finally waking up, and you are happy—but your body is miserable.

Shampoo. Next, you take the shampoo, which also contains toxic chemicals, and rub it on your scalp. The pores on your scalp are already open from the hot, chlorinated water; and chemicals such as DEA, TEA, isopropylene, and sodium lauryl sulfates (substances that are toxic and cancerous) travel directly into the bloodstream.

Soap. Then, you grab a bar of soap—full of animal fat and processed lard—out of the tray where it has been sitting in a warm, moist environment for many days or weeks. Lard and dead skin cells cover you as you rub the soap over your body; but at least you smell good.

Lotion. You rinse off the soap and shampoo and get out of the shower. Now that you have toweled off, your skin feels dry; it's time to apply lotion, even though most dry skin is not really dry skin at all. That dry, filmy feeling on your skin is caused during the lathering process when you strip the natural oils off your body and replace them with dead skin cells and lard—sounds lovely, doesn't it?

Toothpaste. You then head over to the sink, pull out your toothbrush, apply the toothpaste, and begin brushing your teeth. You probably forgot to read the warning label on the back of the toothpaste that says, "Keep out of reach of children under the age of six. If accidentally swallowed, please contact a poison control center immediately." The FDA requires that label to be placed on the box and on the tube. It requires this frightening label because toothpaste contains fluoride, which is highly poisonous to the body, and like your skin, whatever you put inside your mouth goes directly into your body and bloodstream.

Mouthwash. After your teeth are brushed, its time to gargle with mouthwash. Studies have shown that a mouthwash that contains at least 25 percent alcohol content increases the chance for oral cancer. If you use the types of mouthwash that are typically found in a pharmacy or grocery store, those products produce up to a 60 percent increased cancer risk in men and up to a 90 percent increased risk in women.[3]

Deodorant. You are ready to get dressed, but first you apply your deodorant with antiperspirant. The truth is, however, antiperspirants were never meant for our bodies—we were made to sweat. When you repress the body's sweating mechanism, you prevent it from releasing natural toxins through the sweat glands. The active ingredient that prevents sweating in antiperspirants is aluminum, which has been linked to breast tissue lumps, Alzheimer's disease, and memory loss.

Many women shave their underarms and apply antiperspirants or deodorants immediately after they shower—even when they have nicked themselves. When you read the label on the back of antiperspirants and deodorants, you see a warning: "Do not apply on broken skin." If you place these products on broken skin, the toxin absorption increases two-fold, allowing even more chemicals into the bloodstream.[4] To avoid these toxins, look for deodorants that do not contain antiperspirants.

Cosmetics and toiletries. For many women, the next step in the morning process is makeup application. Numerous deadly diseases are contracted through the use of common cosmetics. Cosmetics include all makeup, foundation, face powder, lipstick, eye shadow, and blush used by millions of women (and some men). One of the more toxic substances used is an element called propylene glycol—a colorless, odorless alcohol compound found in most personal care products.[5] Examine the labels on your favorite cosmetics, lotions, and potions, and you'll notice that it is usually one of the first two ingredients listed. Propylene glycol can cause extreme dermatitis (more commonly known as eczema) and kidney and liver abnormalities, and restrict cell growth.

Sodium laurel sulfate is a substance also found in most cosmetics and toiletries. It is a foaming agent that causes permanent eye damage to animals, drying the mucous lining within the body much like an overabundance of acidic foods in the diet. In addition, sodium laurel sulfate increases cancer risks.[6]

Conventional toiletries such as shaving cream and gel, perfume, aftershave, and cologne normally contain propane, butane, and sodium laurel sulfate. This is especially true in shaving cream ingredients. Have you ever wondered why your blades rust and dull so quickly, and you are required to change blades sometimes as often as several times a week? The chemicals in your shaving cream are literally breaking down the razor blade—more than water damage or overuse. Switch to an organic, chemical-free shaving cream and discover how much longer your blade lasts, not to mention your skin! The corrosive abilities of these toxic chemicals are astounding; just imagine what these chemicals are doing when they enter through your skin and pollute your bloodstream, cells, and tissues.

Baby products. Those with young children have not just themselves to consider in their daily routines, but also their children. Some baby shampoos have one of the most harmful chemicals contained in any personal care product. Since 2002, The Campaign for Safe Cosmetics has performed numerous scientific studies on baby care products. The Campaign for Safe Cosmetics is a coalition of public health, educational, religious, labor, women's, environmental, and consumer groups whose goal is to protect the health of consumers by requiring the health and beauty industry to phase out the use of chemicals linked to cancer, birth defects, and other health problems, and replace them with safe alternatives. Laboratory tests performed in conjunction with the Campaign revealed the presence of 1,4-Dioxane in a number of the mainstream brands of baby products.[7] 1,4-Dioxane is a harmful and hidden ingredient that removes the mucous lining in the urinary tract. You'll never see it listed as an ingredient on the label because by law, companies do not have to list one-third of their products' ingredients; but it is in many baby shampoos and bath products. The best way to avoid this harmful substance is to recognize ingredients most likely to be contaminated with 1, 4-Dioxane. These ingredients include polyethylene, polyethylene glycol, and polyoxyethylene. It is critical to *stay away* from mainstream baby shampoos and bath products; you can purchase organic alternatives at your local health food store. Your children's bodies are developing and changing every day, and they deserve the chance to form good healthy cells.

By the time you complete your typical morning routine, you may have poisoned your body with untold amounts of harmful chemicals—and for many people, this exposure occurs from birth until death. As stated above, companies are only required to list two-thirds of the ingredients in a given product if it is considered a "proprietary formula." Proprietary formulas are privately owned formulas protected by law from being made public.[8] Companies say they want to protect their trade secrets and the millions of dollars they pour into formula research, but it also happens to be a convenient way to hide the use of poisonous substances from their customers. You must break this cycle now!

"GO GREEN" WITH YOUR BEAUTY ROUTINE

When it comes to personal care products, most ingredients are listed, but some of them are hidden. The only way to avoid potentially harmful substances is to make the switch to natural, organic products. I struggled with this change, thinking that organic products were inferior, or were going to have an unpleasant smell. I remember thinking *I don't want to use this stuff. It will make me smell like leaves. I bet these products will taste bad.* It has been quite the opposite experience. I discovered that I enjoy using organic personal care products even more than the conventional products. Recently, I ran out of toothpaste while speaking at an out-of-town conference. The hotel provided me with a commercial brand, and I could actually taste the fluoride and chemicals; it was so acrid that I could hardly stand to put it in my mouth. You will also notice how much better the natural alternatives taste once you make the switch to organic personal care products.

Eliminating dangerous personal care products is like choosing not to eat harmful or addictive foods such as pizza, fried foods, and sugar. In the same way the body processes food, it also processes the personal care products you use; and this has a significant impact on new cell growth. Changing your personal environment is one of the simplest ways to achieve healthier living—and the great news is that little to no will power is involved. The same cannot be said for dietary choices or exercise. By taking advantage of this simple switch, you can reduce the risk of cancer and ill health for both you and your family.

You have the choice to restore health to your body or continue to break it down. You can use toothpaste laced with poison, shampoo that is unfit for lab mice, and traditional toxic makeup—or you can use organic, chemical-free alternatives. Remember, yesterday's cells are not today's cells; the body you had yesterday is not the same body you have today or the body you will have tomorrow.

THE DAILY ROUTINE REVISITED

We have looked at the typical morning for many people. Now here is a typical morning for the health conscious person:

You wake up naturally with no alarm because you went to bed before 10 PM and your body's natural clock woke you at 6 AM, full of energy. You hydrate with twelve to sixteen ounces of pure, non-chlorinated water and take two probiotics to help start the digestive and immune processes for the day. You get in a shower equipped with a filter to remove any chlorine and toxic chemicals, and use organic shampoo containing no DEA or sodium laurel sulfate (such as Jason's Naturals or Trillium Organics) to prevent those toxic chemicals from entering your bloodstream. You lather up with chemical- and dye-free soap, and after the shower, apply a progesterone-free, hormone-free lotion.

You then brush your teeth with a non-fluoride, poison-free toothpaste, and you rest easy knowing that your children also brush two times a day with a substance that won't send them to a poison control center if swallowed. You skip the mouthwash because your intestinal flora is healthy, which will keep your breath clean and fresh. You apply an aluminum-free deodorant without antiperspirant. If you use makeup, you apply organic makeup that is free of toxins and hormones to keep your body in balance.

It's going be a great day; you can just feel it.

WAYS TO REMOVE TOXINS

Fasting. Fasting is something every person needs to do—and this has nothing to do with your religious beliefs. It is simply one of the oldest and most effective "pills" you could ever take for your health. Any time you abstain from food, you give your body a chance to rest. In America, we incessantly eat endless calories, and the body never has a real chance to rest, repair, and restore itself as it should. At night you may be sleeping, but your digestive system is working around the clock. When you eat, it takes that meal three to four hours to travel through the stomach, another five hours for the food to be processed by the small intestine, and an additional twelve to thirty-six hours for the food to go through the large intestine. That means that a sandwich you ate at 2:00 PM on Saturday is not fully processed by the body until some time Sunday afternoon!

I recommend fasting to everyone, and I incorporate it in my weekly routine. Some fasts you can do routinely and some of them are extreme. You should consult your physician before deciding what type of fasting works best for you. If you have been diagnosed with hypoglycemia or diabetes, or if you have any blood sugar related health challenges, you may drink chicken or beef broth on your fasting days if dizziness occurs.

The body was built with its own fasting mechanism. Whenever you get sick or contract a virus, the body begins to shut itself down. What's the last thing on your mind at that point? That's right—eating. Your body knows that it needs to stop the eating process so that it can "turn up the heat." That is why the body becomes feverish—to burn off the bacteria and rid your system of the invading germs. Your body needs this time to restore and repair itself, and the principle behind fasting is the same. In making a conscious decision to fast one day a week, you will actually give your body more chances to rid itself of abnormal cells, toxins, heavy metals, and chemicals that you have ingested. Simply put, *fasting cleans your system out.*

This is the fast that I incorporate into my own personal health plan. Eat dinner in the evening and do not eat anything until dinner the next evening. Essentially you are fasting for twenty-four hours, but part of that time you are sleeping, so that makes it easier. Eat dinner, then drink water and supplement drinks (green drinks and fiber drinks) throughout the day, and take your probiotics and supplements as usual. Be sure to drink plenty of non-chlorinated distilled or spring water throughout the day and then have dinner in the evening. In doing this, you allow your body to cleanse itself by giving your digestive tract a break. You will feel better and see your energy levels multiply exponentially.

Chelation. Chelation therapy is a process involving the use of chelating agents (substances that bind with toxic substances like heavy metals) to stabilize them so that they can be safely removed from the body. Chelation removes excess or toxic metals before they can cause damage to the body, and was used in the 1940s by the Navy to treat lead poisoning. For the most prevalent forms of heavy metal intoxication, those involving lead, arsenic, or mercury, the most common substance used is DMSA (dimercaptosuccinic acid). Other chelating agents include DMPS (2,3-Dimercapto-1-propanesulfonic acid), ALA (alpha lipoic acid), and an amino acid called EDTA (ethylenediamine tetraacetic acid). Chelation can be performed intravenously, where the chelating agent is added to the blood through a vein, or orally by taking certain amounts of the chelating agents. If you are interested in chelation therapy, ask your physician about safe and effective treatments.

Breathing. One of the most effective yet simplistic weapons to fight toxicity in the body is breathing. Breathing is an excellent way to remove toxins, cleanse, and purify the body. When we exhale, we breathe out toxins and carbon dioxide, which is a deadly poison that the body creates. The body has a great capacity and need for oxygen. The lack of oxygen in the blood makes us feel tired, and can cause headaches. A few deep breaths can lower anxiety, ease mild indigestion, and help us wake up and go to sleep. The more air you take in, the more vitality you create. Here is a breathing exercise that is easy and effective for energizing, relaxing, clearing the sinuses, and detoxifying the body.

1. Sit or lie in a comfortable position.

2. Breathe in through the left nostril (use a finger to keep your right nostril closed) and hold your breath for ten counts.

3. Exhale gently out of the right nostril.

4. Repeat this breathing in through your right nostril and exhaling out of the left.

5. Repeat the cycle for each nostril five times.

When considering any detoxification program, it is essential that you consult your physician or a natural health care practitioner to ensure that you gain the benefits of detoxification and not harm your body in any way. These detoxification techniques vary in levels of intensity and price. If you are unsure about chelation, or any other detoxification program, ask your doctor, or study them to learn more. However, almost anyone can practice the simple breathing exercise listed above to begin the process of detoxification. Start by breathing deeply every day for a few minutes and go from there. You've spent years absorbing these toxins, so now spend a little time flushing them out!

11

THE BODY'S BALANCING ACT
Hormone Systems

"As I see it, every day you do one of two things: build health or produce disease in yourself."

—ADELLE DAVIS

Our hormones are the powerhouses of the body. We can diet and exercise, but if our hormones aren't right, our bodies won't be right. Hormones are dependent on many factors in the body, and one of the primary factors is dietary fat. High quality fats in the form of nuts, seeds, nut butters, fish oils, and avocados are essential for our hormones to function at an optimal level. Whether it's our adrenals, our thyroid, or our male and female hormonal systems, we need quality fats to keep them running strong. For the most part, we are only as good as our hormones. When our hormones decline, all of our processes begin to decline. The body thrives on balance, and when hormones such as insulin, testosterone, and estrogen get out of balance, the body has difficulty properly processing nutrients, which leads to weight gain and disease. By keeping our dietary fat intake at an optimal level of around one-third, we will optimize how our body works, whether we are seven or ninety-seven.

THE ADRENAL SYSTEM—OUR STRESS MANAGER

People are always looking for the special pill or magical cure for weight loss. They visit nutritional shops and purchase diet pills and energy drinks, believing that these will help them lose body fat—but what they are really doing is overstimulating their adrenal systems. The adrenal system functions through the adrenal glands. Adrenal glands secrete epinephrine and norepinephrine throughout the body and are activated as the body's natural response to stress. High levels of stress and products such as caffeine supplements, coffee, soda, or tea often stimulate the adrenals. When the adrenals are overstimulated, they begin to wear down, which causes a condition called adrenal fatigue, or *hypoadrenia*. Close to 95 percent of Americans suffer from adrenal fatigue during their lifetimes.[1] Sufferers experience symptoms of exhaustion and must rely on compounds such as caffeine to get them through the day.

Years ago, I sought the advice of a leading authority in the endocrine system when I still didn't fully understand how the body's systems worked. I was searching for the best solutions for weight and fat loss after rapid weight gain. He told me the specific nutrients to give my body to rebuild the adrenal glands, and what I should remove from my diet that would help strengthen and rebuild them. When I followed his recommendations, I began to lose weight rapidly in a healthy way, and I saw my energy levels increase exponentially.

The protocol he gave me to strengthen my adrenal glands was

- Vitamin C ascorbate complex

- B5 (pantothenic acid)

- A substance called phosphatidyl serine, which lowers cortisol levels, decreases abdominal fat, and helps strengthen the adrenal glands

In addition, I avoided all refined foods, red meat, caffeine, and sugar.

THE THYROID SYSTEM—OUR METABOLISM REGULATOR

The thyroid is a gland that secretes hormones called T3, T4, and thyroxin, and is largely responsible for rates of metabolism. Countless people have their thyroid removed due to abnormalities. Removing the thyroid robs you of your vitality, metabolism, and energy, but the importance of this system is often overlooked in modern health care.

When thyroid hormones begin to decline, modern medicine's solution is to place you on moderate levels of Synthroid (synthetic form of thyroid hormones). Synthroid is needed in certain situations and is certainly a better alternative than thyroid removal; however, it will eventually cause the thyroid gland to shut down further because you are getting sufficient thyroid hormones from an outside source (the synthetic hormone). The better alternative is to get your thyroid to function on its own. And because the body regenerates itself a little each day, over time this can be a reality.

The problem with conventional medicine's solution is that the symptoms are treated rather than the root of the problem—the fact that the thyroid gland has become weak. It must be built back up so it can function properly and do what it was created and designed to do in the body. How can this be done?

Hypothyroidism, or inactive thyroid, is the failure of the body to produce adequate amounts of the thyroid hormone, thyroxine, which regulates many functions, including your metabolism and the conversion of food into energy. For centuries, the Japanese have maintained high levels of iodine in their diets (about 13.8 milligrams per day), taking in fifty times the amount of iodine that Americans consume. Interestingly, they have significantly fewer cases of hypothyroidism, obesity, metabolism disorders, and cancer. The need for iodine to keep our metabolism working well is great. In the fifties each slice of bread had 150 micrograms of iodine. In the sixties manufactures began using bromide (a halogen which actually reduces thyroid function). Since then, we have became one of the leading countries with cases of hypothyroidism.

Women today seem to suffer from lack of iodine the most. Women need at least 450 micrograms per day for the ovaries, thyroid gland, and the breast tissue. Men only need iodine for the thyroid. Since we don't have iodine in our diet anymore, we need daily iodine supplementation. When looking for an iodine supplement, make sure that it is organic and contains potassium for better absorption. Iodine must be administered under the supervision of a physician and is not typically sold in health food stores in its pure form.

When I began to shed pounds after my rapid weight gain, I noticed that my energy levels were not increasing as much as I thought they would, and I was having a hard time losing body fat. A physician and good friend introduced me to the benefits of taking iodine. I began to study it for myself, and then I began to take it. My energy levels, metabolism, and body fat levels changed radically. After six months of iodine supplementation, I noticed a vast improvement.

Don't be discouraged if you don't notice dramatic, instantaneous results once you introduce new minerals into your system; they have to restore the gland or system they support, and this process takes time—it will not happen in two or three weeks. After six months, I lost almost four inches in my waist although my body weight barely changed, indicating a loss of fat as my body stabilized itself and came into a balanced state where my thyroid once again functioned properly. If you are struggling to lose weight and seem to be resting on a plateau, your thyroid could be causing the standstill. An inactive or underactive thyroid causes millions of us to experience exhaustion and the piling on of unwanted pounds—even when eating habits have not changed.

IODINE PATCH TEST

Take liquid iodine (found in most drug stores) and put a drop on your forearm. The iodine will quickly dry, but will leave a discoloration on your skin. If the discoloration disappears within three hours, that indicates a deficiency in iodine. The quicker it disappears, the more deficient you are.

THE HYPOTHALAMUS—THE GOVERNING GLAND

In every system there has to be a leader. John Maxwell, author of *The 21 Indisputable Laws of Leadership*, says that everything rises and falls on leadership. Nothing could be truer, especially when it comes to our bodies and our health. The governing gland—the president and CEO of the body—is the hypothalamus gland. It is the center for controlling body functions, including our hormonal system. It is located above the pituitary gland and below the thalamus gland. It consists of several different sections (known as nuclei) that control different functions within the body. The hypothalamus is connected to the limbic system, which is responsible for our emotional lives and has to do with the formation of memories. The hypothalamus is mainly concerned with keeping balance within the body.

It works like a thermostat—when the room gets too cold, the thermostat conveys that information, and the body turns on. When the room heats up and the temperature gets beyond a certain point, it sends a signal that tells the furnace to turn off. The hypothalamus is responsible for regulating many body systems such as hunger, thirst, response to pain, levels of pleasure, sexual satisfaction, anger, and aggressive behavior. It also regulates all sides of the nervous system, which in turn means it governs things like pulse, blood pressure, breathing, and response to emotional circumstances. We must maintain a healthy hypothalamus gland to have the weight management we desire. Here are some ways to keep the hypothalamus regulated:

1. Eat a big breakfast—this breaks the fasting cycle and stops cortisol production, which stores body fat, destroys brain cells, and tears down muscle tissue.

2. Sleep between the hours of 10:00 PM and 6:00 AM. Your body does most of its repair between 11:00 PM and 2:00 AM. So don't miss it. Of course, those of you who work third shift are always up at these hours. This does not mean you are always going to be unhealthy. The body has a way of adjusting and retraining itself to new schedules. It is important in such cases to be consistent and go to bed as soon as your shift ends to allow your body to repair itself.

3. Avoid stress as much as possible. If you are a procrastinator, start doing things early or on time to eliminate unneeded stress.

4. Eat three regular meals per day (with one-third of your caloric intake from each meal coming from each of the three macronutrients—protein, carbohydrates, and fat) and two to three snacks per day. Eating regularly will stimulate metabolism and take your body out of starvation mode.

5. Drink half your body weight in ounces of pure, non-chlorinated water daily. For example, if you weigh 150 pounds, drink 75 ounces of water a day.

6. Eat two to three tablespoons of organic coconut oil per day.

Thyroid self-test. You can perform a self-test to check your thyroid for hypothyroidism. Place an oral thermometer by your bed at night. Shake it down until it reaches approximately ninety-six degrees. As soon as you wake up the next morning, place the thermometer under your armpit and leave it there for ten minutes before getting out of bed. Relax and remain still; then record the temperature. A reading between 97.6 and 98.6 degrees is considered normal. Temperatures below 97.6 indicate a thyroid imbalance. Men and postmenopausal women can do the test anytime during the month, but women in their menstrual years will get the most accurate reading on the second or third day after their menstrual flow starts.

Here are my recommended supplement protocols for returning your thyroid system to a healthy state:

- Iodine—2 to 4 drops of organic iodine two times per day as directed by a physician.

- Zinc—30 to 50 milligrams per day for females; 50 to 100 milligrams per day for males. Remember, this is a mineral and takes time to build in the system. It may take months for zinc and other supplements to improve a chronic thyroid condition.

- Copper—2 milligrams per day to avoid nutritional deficiency. This is necessary because high levels of zinc can create a copper deficiency.

- Selenium—70 to 200 micrograms a day. In addition to supplementation, you can eat selenium-rich foods such as tuna, herring, beef liver, eggs, sunflower, and sesame seeds.

HEALTHY HORMONE LEVELS

Females. Many women take oral contraceptives despite the studies that prove they increase a woman's chances of breast cancer. They also increase the risk of pregnancy complications. It is *critical* to use alternative methods for birth control. Oral contraceptives increase the levels of estrogen in the body, which affect the estrogen-progesterone balance. Estrogen and progesterone decline as women get older, and this decline triggers the onset of menopause. If you must take oral contraceptives, use a natural, non-synthetic progesterone cream that will help keep your hormones balanced.

Margie came in two weeks before surgery to help what were thought to be cysts on her ovaries, due to excessive bleeding. She was twenty-seven years old and had just had her second child only seven months prior. I found that she was severely anemic and her hormones were off balance. Her estrogen was extremely high and her progesterone was low. She was a vegetarian and relied heavily on soy protein, soy milk, and other soy products. I pleaded with her to give Natural Medicine a chance before she made any decisions about surgery, and she willingly agreed. I started her on activated ionic iron to begin increasing absorbable iron. I also made sure she had at least one serving of hormone-free red meat each day along with dark green vegetables such as spinach, kale, and broccoli to help increase iron reserves through food. By adding high doses of omega-3 fats, eliminating soy products, and stopping using personal care products such as lotions and beauty creams, her hormones regained balance. In less than two weeks, all the bleeding had ceased and her energy levels increased. Surgery wasn't necessary and Margie was able to thrive in her life rather than just survive.

Protocol for maintaining proper female hormone balance:

- Have your blood checked regularly, especially for all three types of estrogen (estriol, estridiol, and estrone).

- Avoid all soy products (see chapter 8 for more on soy).

- Maintain proper iron levels to avoid anemia.

- Eat one-third dietary fats, including high quality omega-3s (cod liver oil is an excellent source).

- Avoid most commercial beauty creams and personal care products for excess hidden progesterone.

Males. Testosterone is the chief male hormone, and it is extremely important in many processes of a man's body. Testosterone begins to slowly decline after men reach age twenty-five, and this decline causes decreased muscle mass, increased bone loss, and a decreased sexual drive. There is a traditional synthetic replacement therapy available, but men should avoid synthetic hormones. When you take synthetic hormones, it interrupts natural hormone regulation in the body, which causes levels of testosterone to drop below normal. Estrogen levels also increase when men take synthetic hormones.

A man can naturally increase testosterone levels by making sure that he takes in one-third of his daily caloric intake in the form of healthy dietary fat (omega-3, -6, and -9 fats, monounsaturated fats, and polyunsaturated fats). Men should also supplement their diets with 50 to 100 milligrams of zinc per day and 2 milligrams of copper.

Stan sat in my office with a frown as he said, "Things just aren't working like they used to."

His wife slowly nodded her head in agreement. I knew where this was going. He continued, "We haven't had 'relations' in over three months and things are going downhill, if you know what I mean." Stan was forty-two years old, a high pressure CEO executive for a Fortune 500 company, and successful in every way, except recently in the bedroom.

ED, or erectile dysfunction, is caused by several factors. Men go through a period of life similar to women and menopause in which their hormones begin to shift and change. This period is called andropause. Male testosterone normally begins to decline starting around age twenty-five. However, through lifestyle and dietary choices we can slow this process considerably.

Stan's test results revealed that his testosterone was in the 200 range (450 to 550 is a healthy range). He was also suffering from high blood pressure and low levels of HDL (the good cholesterol). High blood pressure can contribute to most vascular problems in the body, even ED. The low HDL cholesterol could lower his natural output of testosterone. The tests also indicated that he had potential problems with prostate function. This is usually affected when testosterone levels become lower.

I increased Stan's good fats to around one-third of his diet, gave him key supplements to repair his nutritional deficiencies and to restore his hormone balance to lower his blood pressure. After about two months, his system completely rebalanced. Now everything is working again. The body is amazing, and if we look deep enough and take the necessary steps, it will regenerate. Remember, through our lives, our choices got us into the wrong place, and our choices and actions can get us out.

Protocol for maintaining proper male hormone balance:

- Keep dietary fat to one-third of your daily intake, and be sure they are good fats, including omega-3s (again, cod liver oil is a good choice).

- Take 50 to 100 milligrams of ionic zinc per day and 1 to 2 milligrams of copper per day.

- Maintain thirty-minute high intensity workouts four to five days per week.

- Avoid all soy products (see chapter 8 for more on soy).

- Make one-third of your food intake lean protein (such as lean turkey, beef, chicken, tuna, or salmon).

- Take hormone-balancing supplements if blood work shows it to be necessary.

OVERCOMING HORMONE IMBALANCE AND DISEASE

Weight management is the most important element of controlling blood sugar levels and maintaining your hormonal balance. This requires a change in your diet as well as your exercise habits. Here are several recommendations for general health and for achieving hormone balance:

1. Eat three meals a day. The average person needs three balanced meals a day. If you get hungry throughout the day, eat a small handful of nuts (except peanuts) around ten o'clock in the morning or three o'clock in the afternoon to ease hunger pangs. Nuts are a great way to stabilize your blood sugar, stimulate your thyroid, and provide valuable nutrients.

2. Don't skip meals. Do not skip meals, especially breakfast. Skipping meals signals your body to go into starvation mode, and your body will automatically reduce its metabolic rate. Of course, I do recommend fasting one day per week in previous chapters. When I mention skipping meals, I am referring to the recurring or habitual tendency to skip breakfast every morning, for example. Your body needs energy to get you through your day, so if you aren't a "breakfast person," start by eating a piece of fruit on your way to work and see how much more energy you start to have after a few days of fueling your body in the morning.

3. Avoid artificial sweeteners. The sugary taste of sweeteners such as aspartame and Splenda in your mouth triggers the release of insulin even with no sugar present. Candies and gum have a similar effect. Instead, use alternative sweeteners such as stevia, honey, xylitol, and small amounts of saccharin.[2]

4. Avoid soft drinks and fruit juices. Carbonated beverages and fruit juices should be avoided, even if they have been sweetened naturally. Sweet drinks increase blood sugar, which causes increases in insulin production to regulate blood sugar back to a normal level, as well as causing a spike in hormone production.

5. Start exercising. Exercise provides four important benefits: It increases lean body tissue, burns fat, increases sensitivity to insulin (enabling the pancreas to rest), and raises your metabolic rate. Exercise for twenty to thirty minutes, six times a week; at a minimum, exercise three times a week. Brisk walking, jogging, swimming, and bicycling are all good choices. Add weight lifting to your exercise program—you don't have to become a bodybuilder, but some amount of weight training is beneficial. It helps increase muscle mass, decrease body fat, and increase your resting metabolic rate. Because muscle tissue uses 80 percent of the blood sugar produced after a meal, it is easy to understand why every bit of extra muscle helps.

Unlike fat tissue, muscle tissue constantly uses energy. The more muscle tissue you have, the higher your metabolic rate will be. You burn calories during exercise, and your muscle tissue will continue to burn calories for several more hours after you work out.

6. Eliminate processed foods. You must eliminate processed, refined, and prepackaged foods from the diet. They are loaded with sugars and preservatives. Processed sugar is taken from its original state and then chlorinated for preservation—and yet we consume it in pounds every year. People who consume the highest amounts of sugar also tend to absorb the lowest amounts of many important nutrients such as vitamins A, C, and B12, and folic acid, calcium, phosphorous, magnesium, zinc, and iron.

7. Eat lean meats and healthy fats. Eat a lean protein source with every meal—meat, fish, or eggs. Consume some form of healthy omega-3, -6, and -9 fats with every meal; this includes nuts, seeds, and omega-3 oils. When you eat fat with meals, it slows the release of sugar, and this helps lower the glycemic index of the foods that you eat.

8. Consume low-glycemic carbohydrates. If humans have altered it, it's probably no longer good for you. Eat carbohydrates from low-glycemic, whole food sources. Good examples are certain whole fruits (such as apples, cherries, grapefruits, and prunes), brown rice, sweet potatoes, and most vegetables. Eliminate sugar from your diet so you can regain control of your hormone levels, and you'll notice your weight begin to normalize and fat stores begin to decrease.

All of these recommendations are beneficial to your overall health, with one of those aspects being balanced hormone levels and proper function of the hormonal systems. Hormones really are the powerhouses of the body, and you want them working on your side! Remember that when hormone levels decline, so do the body's normal processes. You've lifestyled and eaten your way into hormone imbalance, but you can find that balance again!

Just as your hormones need to be in balance, so does your pH level. In the next chapter, we will learn more about pH, its important role in the body, and how to regulate it.

12

UNLIMITED ENERGY
The pH Scale

"I finally realized that being grateful to my body was key to giving more love to myself."

—OPRAH WINFREY

Stella came to see me because of her lack of energy. Although she was only twenty-four, she was chronically tired morning, noon, and night. She said the only way she could stay awake during the day was by drinking Red Bull. Red Bull energy drinks stimulate the adrenal glands (our energy glands) by using large amounts of caffeine, B vitamins, and an amino acid called l-taurine to stimulate you. You may be drinking them for more energy, but in reality you are stripping energy from the body.

I asked Stella to place a pH strip under her tongue and it read 5.0, an acidic reading, as I expected. This causes a multitude of health challenges from cancer to bone degeneration, to robbing your body of the energy that it needs.

To accomplish the millions of complex functions that occur during the day, your body has to be able to communicate with itself. And how does it accomplish this? Through pulses of electricity.

Your body operates on an electromagnetic current. All of the organs in your body emit fields of electrical current. In fact, nerve signals are nothing more than electrical charges. What creates this electrical power in your body is a very fine balance that exists in your biochemistry. All the systems in your body depend on this delicate, biochemical balance, and one of the most important is your bloodstream. This is where pH comes into play.

The pH scale measures how acidic or alkaline a substance is. The scale ranges from 1 to 14, with 1 being acid, 7 neutral, and 14 alkaline. The pH of your blood is extremely important; the ideal level is around 6.8 to 7.2, and your body goes to enormous lengths to maintain this level. If your blood pH were to vary too much in either direction for extended periods of time, the body would be in a constant struggle to find balance, but will be unable to do so; and in this lack of balance is when your body becomes more susceptible to sickness and disease. As you can see, maintaining the right pH level in your blood is important!

TOO ACID

Our bodies are always striving for balance. When we eat, the food choices we make cause our bodies to become either *acidic* or *alkaline*. Proper pH balance is important and is essential for good health. A good way to avoid upsetting this delicate biochemical balance would be to take a look at those things that can compromise the maintenance of the ideal pH level in your body. And what is the main culprit in this case? The creation of acid in your body.

Red blood cells are how oxygen is transported to all the cells in your body. As red blood cells move into the tiny capillaries, the space they have to move through gets extremely small. In fact, the diameter of the capillaries gets so small that the red blood cells sometimes have to pass through these capillaries one cell at a time. Because it's important for the red blood cells to be able to flow easily and quickly through your body, they have a mechanism that allows them to remain separate from each other—a negative charge on the outside of healthy red blood cells. Similar to pushing the negative ends of two magnets together, the negative charges in your blood cells resist each other and stay apart.

Unfortunately, acid interferes with this important mechanism in a frightening way. Acid actually strips away the negative charge from red blood cells. The result is that your red blood cells then tend to clump together and not flow as easily. This makes it much more difficult for them to travel through the bloodstream. It also makes it harder for them to move through those small capillaries. This means less oxygen gets to your cells. Acid also weakens the red blood cells and they begin to die. And guess what they release into your system when they die? More acid. Aside from the acid that is secreted into your stomach to aid digestion, acid in your body is harmful. Your body needs balance.

WHAT CAUSES ACIDITY

The primary cause of an acidic condition in your body is from what you put in your mouth. In other words, what you eat, and what you drink. And it isn't how acidic something may seem when you eat or drink it. It has to do with what is left over when you digest it.

Specifically, it depends on whether eating or drinking something leaves behind an acid or alkaline "ash." For example, when your body digests scallops, it leaves an extremely acid ash. In fact, scallops are one of the most acid foods you can eat. Unfortunately, a lot of the things most people put in their mouths create an acid ash. These include alcohol, coffee and a lot of flesh protein in your diet. Interestingly enough, stress also tends to create an acid condition in the body. Maintaining an ideal slightly alkaline state is a constant challenge.

The idea that various foods influence the pH of the body is not new. In the early 1900s, doctors began studying the pH-altering effects of various foods. They discovered that while a few foods were neutral, most were either alkaline or acid producing. They also discovered that changing the diet to include more alkaline foods brings the body pH closer to the normal range. However, the idea of adjusting the diet to influence the body's pH fell out of favor rather quickly—this is likely because most people don't understand just how critical proper pH is to their health.

Over the years, various food plans, formulas, and charts were invented in an attempt to outline exactly what amounts of particular foods need to be eaten to achieve the proper acid-alkaline balance. Unfortunately, most are so confusing that it seems to make the problem too difficult. In reality, the solution is quite simple. Look at societies where osteoporosis is not a significant problem, and you discover that 75 to 80 percent of their diets consist of alkaline-producing foods.

One of the primary health issues associated with maintaining acidic levels in the body is cancer. Cancer thrives in an acidic environment, but cancer cannot live, breath, or survive in an alkaline environment. An alkaline environment brings health to the body and creates energy. Make it your goal to include more alkaline foods than acidic foods in your diet. (You'll find a chart at the end of this chapter.)

I am not saying that all acid foods are bad, but they should be limited to about 20 to 25 percent of your total diet. One acid-producing product that you should especially avoid is soda—diet or regular. A major ingredient in all sodas is phosphoric acid, which wreaks havoc on your digestive system. It is so acidic that one twelve-ounce soda requires thirty-five glasses of clean purified, non-chlorinated water to reduce or neutralize the acidity it causes. It's not just the sugar or artificial sweeteners that should concern you; the phosphoric acid contained in sodas causes your body to exist in a perpetual acidic state.

OSTEOPOROSIS AND pH

According to Dr. Susan Brown, an osteoporosis nutritionist, osteoporosis can be seen as a hidden tax of our fast-paced modern society.[1] We pay this tax as a consequence of high acidity in the body, which robs us of our mineral reserves and impairs our bodies' attempt to rebuild bone density. In America, most acidity is brought on by three main factors: poor dietary choices (excess protein, trans fats, and phosphoric acid, which is found in sodas); maladaptation to stress, causing reduced function of the adrenal glands; and recurring allergic reactions, causing immune functions to decrease over time.

Here are some ways to avoid high acidity and therefore reduce your chances of getting osteoporosis:

1. Eat plenty of fruits and vegetables (see the pH food chart at the end of the chapter for the most alkalizing fruits and vegetables).

2. Maintain fat intake to around one-third of your daily caloric intake.

3. Drink half your body weight in ounces of high mineral content spring water daily.

4. Use alkalizing nutritional supplements such as ascorbate-buffered minerals, including calcium, magnesium, zinc, and potassium.

5. Take L-glutamine, an amino acid found in foods high in proteins, such as fish, red meat, and peas. It is also available in supplement form found in most health food and nutritional stores.

6. Take cesium, a naturally occurring alkaline element that has been shown to be an effective anti-cancer treatment. Cesium raises the cell pH to the range of 8.0, which is a deadly environment for cancer cells.

7. Supplement with rubidium, a trace mineral that helps maintain a balanced pH level. It is also available in most health food stores.

8. Consume sesame seeds (serving should fit in the palm of your hand) to keep proper pH between 6.5 and 7.5.

9. Reverse stress patterns by practicing relaxation techniques, participating in enjoyable activities, and including weight lifting exercises in your fitness routine.

STEPS TO IMPROVE PH

Fortunately, it is fairly easy to immediately change your pH for the better and make it more alkaline. The first step is to understand which of the foods you are eating and the drinks you are drinking are acid and which are alkaline. Then it's simply a matter of eliminating some of the more acid foods and adding more alkaline foods. However, before you start, it's important to get a baseline of what the pH is in your body so that you can see how you are improving or if you need to continue to eliminate more acid foods and add in more alkaline ones. You can do this by testing the pH of your saliva regularly.

The easiest and most inexpensive method to test your urine and saliva pH is using litmus paper. Be aware that holding the litmus paper in your urine or saliva longer than a few seconds can wash the indicator off the paper, and possibly result in an inaccurate reading. So first thing in the morning and last thing before bed, gently, but quickly, touch the pH test strip to a drop of urine or a bubble of saliva. Remove the strip once contact has been made, and look at the strip to make the color reading. You can purchase litmus paper at most health food and drug stores.

In addition to decreasing the amount of acid foods you eat and increasing the amount of alkaline foods you eat, one of the best ways to immediately begin changing your pH is to drink "green drinks," which are phytonutrient powders made from ground, organic vegetables. They are great supplements to diets seeking balance in pH. Depending on your urine and saliva pH readings, one of the best ways to bring the values back into balance is to change certain foods that you eat. Below are the different values and ranges and the foods that correlate with each.

The Effects of Common Foods on the Body's Acid-Alkaline Balance

Eat 50% alkaline foods and 50% acid foods for perfect pH balance

Acidic Value	Sweeteners	Fruits	Beans Vegetables Legumes	Nuts/ Seeds	Oils	Grains Cereals	Meats	Eggs Dairy	Beverages
Most Acid	Sweet 'N Low	Blueberries Cranberries Prunes	Carob	Peanuts Walnuts		Wheat White Flour Pastries Pasta	Pork Beef Shellfish	Cheese Homogen- ized Milk Organic Ice Cream	Beer Soft Drinks
Acid	White Sugar Brown Sugar	Sour Cherries Rhubarb	Potatoes Pinto Benas Navy Beans Lima Beans Soybeans	Pecans Cashews		Corn Buckwheat Oats Rye	Turkey Chicken Lamb	Raw Milk	Coffee
Lowest Acid	Processed Honey Molasses	Plums	Cooked Spinach Kidney Beans String Beans	Pumpkin Seeds Sunflower Seeds	Corn Oil Flax Oil	Sprouted Wheat Bread Spelt Brown Rice	Venison Cold Water Fish	Eggs Buter/ Yogurt Cottage Cheese	Tea
Lowest Alkaline	Raw Honey Raw Sugar	Oranges Bananas Cherries Pineapple Peaches	Carrots Tomatoes Fresh Corn Cabbage Peas	Chestnuts	Canola Oil	Amaranth Millet Wild Rice Quinoa		Goat Milk Goat Cheese Whey	Ginger Tea
Alkaline	Maple Syrup Rice Syrup	Melons Grapes Kiwi Berries Apples Pears Raisins	Okra Squash Green Beans Celery Lettuce Zucchini Sweet Potato	Almonds	Olive Oil			Breast Milk	Green Tea
Most Alkaline	Stevia	Lemons Watermelons Limes Grapefruit Mangoes Papaya	Asparagus Onions Vegetable Juices Raw Spinach Broccoli Garlic						Lemon Water Herb Teas

Food Effects on pH Balance

Ideal Normals: Salivary 7.4 and Urinary 6.4

If pH Values are:	Then increase these foods in your diet:
Salivary > 7.4 Urinary > 6.4	Vegetables, Potatoes, and Fruits
Salivary < 7.4 Urinary < 6.4	Meat, Fish, Eggs, and Cottage Cheese
Salivary > 7.4 Urinary < 6.4	Cereals, Breads, and Grains
Salivary < 7.4 Urinary > 6.4	Fats & Oils, Milk, Cheese, Butter, and Cream

The optimum pH value for both urine and saliva is between 6.4 and 6.6, with 6.8 being the ideal pH for the body's fluids. Note the pH reading for body fluids is different from the pH of blood, which averages 7.1 to 7.4.

An acidic body is a sickness magnet. What you eat and drink will affect where your body's pH level falls. Test your pH level regularly to ensure that your body is not a breeding ground for disease. Just remember that balance is the key!

13

HITTING THE RESET BUTTON
Food and The Anti-Inflammatory Diet

"The patient should be made to understand that he or she must take charge of his own life. Don't take your body to the doctor as if he were a repair shop."
—QUENTIN REGESTEIN, MD

When working with patients, I have found there to be one common denominator with their health—and that is digestion and bodily inflammation. Eating the wrong kinds of foods combined with poor lifestyle choices is how most of us have operated for years. These choices and the subsequent inflammation they cause are the foundations for most diseases we see today. Many people complain of having to take antacids, heartburn medication, or anti-gas relievers. They are bloated, uncomfortable, and constipated. Is this really something that we are all supposed to live with?

When we think of inflammation, we typically think of a sports injury or a twisted ankle. That *is* inflammation, but those conditions are more properly called injury inflammations. Another form of inflammation occurs in the gastrointestinal tract when the wrong foods continue to be ingested. Inflammation of the intestinal and digestive tract is one of the most common problems facing many of us today.

Inflammation is a process that typically happens in the body when something is wrong. It is the body's natural defense mechanism for repairing damage. If you ever sprained your ankle, it probably swelled up like a tennis ball and was difficult to walk on without intense pain. I was playing flag football in college and ran to catch a pass from the quarterback. As I leaped up for the reception, I landed on the defender's foot and rolled my ankle. It swelled to the size of a softball. I hobbled back to my room, put ice on it, and kept it elevated. The body knew the ligaments and tissues had been stretched and damaged and that's why it sent the fluid in to help repair the injury. I could walk on it, but it hurt tremendously. As time went on with proper rest and ice treatment, the swelling went away and I could walk normally again.

The same is true with any part of our bodies. Inflammation (swelling) is not just the body's response to a sports injury. If we eat the wrong kinds of foods, the body senses that something is wrong, and it will send fluid to try and repair the area. When we process high-inflammatory foods such as bagels for breakfast, microwaved pre-made sandwiches for lunch, and frozen dinners day after day, we develop chronic inflammation in our digestive systems, and that is how most disease starts. We experience chronic bloating and indigestion and wonder why we stay sick. Our stomachs are barely functioning. They are swollen, just like my ankle was. We need to get the inflammation out so we can healthily process our food again. We are only as healthy as the food we can digest, absorb, and assimilate.

Inflammation is brought on by the consumption of refined foods. Our country is built on a foundation of refined, prepackaged foods, marketed in the form of refined carbohydrates and sugar. When you look on the shelves at the supermarkets, you see box after box of refined foods such as macaroni and cheese, pasta, cereal, and bread. These foods are highly glycemic in nature, and when digested cause a rapid release of blood sugar. This rapid release of blood sugar causes your body to emulate a diabetic state.

More specifically, sugar is the cause of most of the inflammation in the body. In the 1700s, people consumed approximately four pounds of sugar per year; in the early 1900s, people consumed approximately five pounds of sugar per year; today, the average American consumes an astounding two to three pounds of sugar *per week*.

And still we wonder why obesity rates soar and diabetes is at an all-time high. The annual sugar consumption of the average person today is more than the weight of the average female in America. When we fill up on refined carbohydrates and processed foods, it creates inflammation within the body.[1]

THE SPARE TIRE—FAT IS MORE THAN JUST FAT

Many people think their extra weight or obesity is from fat alone, but much of what you see in the mirror is fluid retention and inflammation. Fluid retention occurs when you have too much sodium in your diet, which causes the body to retain water and swell. This swelling also occurs as a result of inflammation within the digestive tract from eating processed foods and experiencing excessive stress within our lives. That is why when people begin to consume an all-organic diet they often lose weight quite rapidly. I've heard patients say, "When I began to diet, I lost some weight, but it was all water," and that is partially true. The first response your body has is to eliminate the excess fluid due to inflammation. Once fluid is passed from the body, the inflammatory state subsides and enables proper digestion. That is one of the first steps to weight loss, but it is only a small step toward lasting weight loss and health.

The primary consequence of continually eating processed refined foods is a condition called malabsorption—the inability of the body to absorb the necessary nutrients from foods. Overeating non-foods such as processed sugar causes malabsorption. The condition causes an inflammatory response and few nutrients are absorbed. This leaves the body open to a host of inflammatory conditions such as fibromyalgia, cancer, heart disease, and arthritis.

THE MIND-DIGESTION CONNECTION

In his book, *The Second Brain*, Dr. Michael Gershon, professor of Anatomy and Cell Biology at Columbia Presbyterian Medical Center in New York, points out that two nervous systems develop early in fetal development. One becomes the central nervous system, which houses the brain, and the other becomes the enteric nervous system, which is the bowel. The vagus nerve is the large electric cord that connects these two systems. It winds from the brainstem through the neck down through the thorax and through the organs, ending in the abdomen. So when you experience nervousness or anxiety, or you feel butterflies in your stomach, and you can't eat, your body is experiencing a physical response to stress. This happens because the brain and stomach are connected. When this occurs, both areas become inflamed.

Dr. Gershon contends that "the brain is not the only organ full of neural transmitters. One hundred million neurotransmitters line the length of the intestines, and this is approximately the same number that is found in the brain."[2] The brain and the bowel must both function properly or you will not have the ability to think clearly. Sadly, due to the lack of essential nutrients caused by improper diets, many people do not give their bodies the chance to fully utilize this mind-digestion connection. As a result, many live in a continual state of inflammation, which only worsens over time if you don't address the root of the issue—your food choices.

A SOCIETY THAT LIVES TO EAT

Food has become a hobby for many of us. Many people today *live to eat.* Myriads of social gatherings in America revolve around eating. When we get together with friends or attend meetings, the events typically involve a meal. Church groups like to call it "fellowship." I call it "pigging out." Obesity rates have skyrocketed in the last twenty years. Sixty-five percent of Americans are overweight and 30 percent are classified as obese. According to the American Diabetes Association, if we don't change our eating habits, in the next few years, one out of three children under the age of ten will develop diabetes.

Look at the portion sizes of food in restaurants—often more than enough for two or three people. In fast food chains, everything is available in super, biggie, and mega sizes. Automobile companies are even making larger cup holders in new vehicles to accommodate extra-large drink cups. Extra-large cup holders are great; just put a big bottle of purified non-chlorinated water in them instead of a soda!

To better understand the effect of your food choices on your health, consider this. The food you eat is broken down by your body's digestive system. Once the food is metabolized, it is sent throughout the bloodstream to form new cells. Your body is made up of 60 trillion cells. Many of these cells die every day, and the nutrients we consume help to create and generate replacement cells. The food we eat today determines the body and the health we will have tomorrow. Fast food hamburgers and French fries are full of trans fats or hydrogenated fats, chemicals, and oils—all toxins that harm the body. If that is the only fuel your body has to work with, then that is what the body is forced to use to make new cells.

166

If you eat large amounts of junk food today, then that is the body you will have tomorrow. You have a choice: You can give your body what it needs to make new healthy cells for your heart, liver, lungs, pancreas, brain, skin, and hair cells by choosing healthy food, or you can feed your body junk food—and produce junk cells. "You are what you eat," is a cliché, but it's also true! I used to think this adage was just a scare tactic, and I kept eating what I wanted and never considered the impact that my food choices had on my future.

I may sound like a broken record, but some things are worth repeating—*what you eat today determines the body and the health you will have tomorrow.* We have the privilege and the power to choose. Every time you sit down to eat, that meal is either going to bring life to your body by creating new healthy cells, or it will bring disease to your body by creating bad cells that are likely to cause inflammation, cancer, heart disease, diabetes, and many other unwelcome health conditions. We are the only creatures on this earth who have the cognitive ability to make choices, so let's not waste that gift.

We as a nation have strayed from the whole foods that were meant to be our primary food source. We eat junk foods, processed foods, and prepackaged foods that make us overweight, undernourished, and unable to live the exciting lives that we are meant to live. We are eating ourselves into an early grave—not just metaphorically, but literally. In our society, we say yes to any and every indulgence that looks appetizing and appealing, and this results in a palate that causes weight gain, an increased desire for junk food, and the tendency to lead a sedentary and even lackluster life. It's time to make a change, so let's look at how you can find the right balance in your diet.

THE FOOD WHEEL—IT'S ABOUT BALANCE

Your body craves stability, and this becomes more apparent when stress levels in life reach extremes. One way to counteract this is to seek equilibrium when you eat. When you look at your plate, remember it too should be balanced. All three of your meals each day should be balanced in this manner. I call this eating guideline the "food wheel," which will give you the correct balance of the essential macronutrients and give you all the nutrition your body needs.

The three types of food that the body requires in some combination are proteins, carbohydrates, and fats. These three foundations are called the three macronutrients that we discussed previously. Understanding the basics of obtaining good protein, carbohydrate, and fat sources is fairly simple. Good protein sources are found in organic meat, fish, dairy and eggs. The best carbohydrate sources are low-glycemic, in the form of fruits and vegetables, and a limited amount of sprouted grains. Good quality fat sources are found in the form of omega-3, -6, and -9s, which can be found in such sources as nuts, seeds, nut butters, avocados, and high quality oils.

Our bodies need all three sources to achieve extraordinary health and to reproduce the healthy cells that we all need. One problem in our diets today is the popularity of fat-free foods. Even after I explain the vital role of fat in the diet, I often have a difficult time getting my patients to eat one-third of their daily caloric intake in healthy fat. They think it will cause heart attacks, make them fatter, and cause strokes. This is simply not true. Fat is truly essential, and we must make it an everyday part of our health plan. Just like the other two macronutrients, fat must make up one-third of your daily caloric intake. When selecting which fats to consume, consider the different types of fat discussed in chapter 7 and choose healthy, unprocessed fats from natural sources such as cod liver oil, other fish oils, coconut oil, avocados, organic butter, and nuts.

The Food Wheel

When you make choices about the way to combine food at each meal, here is what I suggest. Each meal should be composed of

- One-third of your daily caloric intake in lean high-quality protein.

- One-third of your daily caloric intake in low-glycemic carbohydrate (see chapter 7 for list of low-glycemic carbohydrates).

- One-third of your daily caloric intake in healthy fat.

THE ANTI-INFLAMMATORY DIET

We are what we eat, and especially what we can assimilate and digest. What we need is a fresh start. The Anti-Inflammatory Diet is designed to provide just that. When your computer freezes, it needs to re-boot. If the DVD player is malfunctioning, sometimes you must press the reset button on the back. This eating plan does exactly that to your body. It helps us hit the reset button on our bodies. This food plan, which lasts four weeks, will:

- Reduce insulin

- Eliminate toxins and food allergies

- Help break food addictions

- Regulate body composition

- Reduce body fat

- Create an increase in energy

- Reset body chemistry and function

It is also vital to watch portion size in addition to the combination of foods. When looking at the amount of food each time you eat, select portion sizes that will help keep your caloric intake under control. It's easy: All protein and carbohydrate portions should be about the size of your fist. Fats should be about half the size of your fist due to its caloric density (which for most people would be a small handful of nuts or half of an avocado). I also suggest eating three primary meals per day. This will allow for proper digestion time and allow your body to effectively digest and assimilate all the ingested nutrients.

169

Calorie Chart

1 gram of protein	=	4 calories
1 gram of carbohydrate	=	4 calories
1 gram of fat	=	9 calories

As far as the foods listed in the diet, just use some common sense. I found as many foods as possible that would be good for you to eat and would stay within the guidelines to reduce inflammation in the body. Did I miss some? Probably. The good news is that you have plenty to choose from. If it's on the approved list, you can eat it. If it would cause inflammation or be harmful to your health, then it's on the non-approved list.

The first week can be somewhat difficult for some people. In the beginning you will begin detoxifying and getting rid of food addictions. How bad you may feel reflects how sick you really were. Flu-like symptoms may occur such as headaches and fatigue, and you might be a little irritable. Make sure to warn the family that there may be a grouch in the house for a couple of days.

I had a patient call and beg me to let her have ice cream after only three days. "Of course," I said. "But do you want to get well?"

She was frustrated, but she said, "Yes."

You can do anything that you want, of course, but there is a price to pay on the road to getting well. You can do this. What is four weeks out of your life to have years of energy and extraordinary health? It's worth it. Follow the Anti-Inflammatory Diet faithfully and watch your health transform.

I'M FINISHED—WHAT'S NEXT?

Once you have finished reducing inflammation and hitting your body's reset button, you can add more foods back into your eating program. I still advise keeping wheat and cow's dairy to a minimum due to the food allergies they create. In addition, stay away from all processed flour, sugar, scavenger meat, and bottom feeders such as shrimp. Continue following the same guidelines in the food wheel by eating a combination of foods that bring health to the body. You will need to eat certain foods to keep your blood sugar and blood chemistry reset and stabilized. This is a great start and will get you on the right path toward the excellent health for which you are searching.

Ultimately, it's all about finding equilibrium—and it's all about moderation. I am often asked if I personally follow a high-protein diet, a low-fat diet, or a low-carbohydrate diet. My response is that everything was created in this world to balance something else, and the Anti-Inflammatory Diet is designed with the goal of achieving this balance in your body.

Approved Foods for
1 Protein source (33%) 1 Fat source (33%)

Protein Sources

Meats
(Hormone-free/organic is best, but non-organic is still permitted)

Beef
Lamb
Venison
Veal
Buffalo
Meat bone soup/stock
Liver
Beef hot dogs (No pork casing – organic and nitrite/nitrate free. Use sparingly.)

Fish
(Make sure it has fins and scales)

Salmon	Tuna
Scrod	Haddock
Pompano	Trout
Orange roughy	Snapper
Herring	Whitefish
Halibut	Cod
Grouper	Mahi-mahi
Wahoo	Tilapia
Sea bass	Mackerel
Sole	

Salmon (mercury –free, canned in spring water)
Tuna (mercury-free, canned in spring water)
Sardines (canned in water or olive oil only)

Poultry
(Pastured/organic is best, but non-organic is still permitted)

Chicken
Duck
Turkey
Chicken or turkey bacon (no pork casing – organic and nitrite/nitrate free)
Chicken or turkey sausage or hot dogs (no pork casing – organic and nitrite/nitrate free)
Liver
Canned chicken (all white meat, no nitrates)

Luncheon Meat

Turkey (preservative and nitrite free)

Eggs
(high omega-3/DHA)

Chicken eggs (whole with yolk)

Dairy

Goat's milk yogurt (plain)
Goat's milk kefir
Goat's milk cheese
Pecorino Cheese

Carbohydrates Sources

Vegetables
(organic fresh or frozen)

Broccoli
Asparagus
Cauliflower
Cabbage
Squash
Beets
Brussels sprouts
Carrots
Celery
Eggplant
Garlic
Okra
Spinach
Peas
String beans
Cucumber
Pumpkin
Onion
Leaf Lettuce (all kinds)
Mushrooms
Peppers
Tomatoes
Artichoke
Leafy greens (kale, collard, broccoli, mustard greens, etc.)
Sprouts (broccoli, sunflower, pea shoots, radish, etc.)

Fruits (organic fresh or frozen is best)

Blueberries
Strawberries
Apples
Blackberries
Raspberries
Cherries
Grapefruit
Lemon
Lime

the Anti-Inflammatory Diet
1 Carbohydrate source (33%)

Fat Sources

Fats and Oils (organic is best, but non-organic is still permitted

Avocado
Cow's milk butter, organic (BEST for cooking)
Extra-virgin coconut oil (BEST for cooking)
Extra-virgin olive oil (not best for cooking)
Flaxseed oil (not best for cooking)
Expeller-pressed sesame oil (not best for cooking)

Nuts and Seeds (non-roasted, organic, raw, or soaked is best, but non-organic is still permitted)

Almonds
Pumpkinseeds
Hempseed
Flaxseed (ground)
Sunflower seeds
Almond butter
Hempseed butter
Sunflower butter
Pumpkinseed butter
Sesame butter
Walnuts
Cashews

Miscellaneous Approved Items

Condiments, Spices, Seasonings (organic is best, but non-organic is still permitted)

Salsa (fresh or canned)
Tomato sauce (no sugar added)
Guacamole (fresh)
Apple cider vinegar
Celtic sea salt
Mustard
Omega-3 mayonnaise (Hain brand)
Herbs and spices (no added stabilizers)
Pickled ginger (preservative and color free)
Wasabe (preservative and color free)
Organic flavoring extracts (alcohol based, no sugar added), e.g., vanilla, almond, etc.
Any organic salad dressings (e.g., Annie's)
Whole commercial salad dressings without high fructose corn syrup (e.g., Newman's Own)
Whey protein powder
Goat milk protein powder

Beverages

Purified, non-chlorinated water
Natural sparkling water
Herbal teas (preferably organic) – unsweetened
Regular (preferably organic) Green Tea (Substitute for Coffee)
Wu-Yi, eleotin, and yerba matte teas
Raw vegetable juice (beet or carrot juice – small quantities)
Beef or chicken broth

Sweeteners

Unheated, raw honey
Stevia
Agave Nectar Sweetner
Sweet N Low (saccharin) in small quantities
Xylitol

173

Non-Approved Foods for

Protein Sources

Meats

Pork
Ham
Sausage (pork)
Veggie burgers
Imitation meat product (soy)
Bacon

Fish and Seafood

Fried, breaded fish
Catfish
Eel
Squid
Shark
Avoid all shellfish, including crab, clams, oyster,
mussels, lobster, shrimp, scallops and crawfish

Poultry

Chicken, fried and breaded

Luncheon Meat

Turkey
Roast beef
Ham
Corned beef

Eggs

Imitation eggs (such as Egg Beaters)
Egg whites only

Dairy

Soy milk
Rice milk
Almond milk
Avoid all dairy products other than those listed in
"Approved foods."

Carbohydrates Sources

Vegetables

Corn
Sweet potato
White potato

Fruits (organic fresh or frozen is best)

Avoid all fruits except berries, grapefruit, limes, and
lemons. This includes bananas, apricots, grapes,
melon, peaches, oranges, pears, dried fruit, and
canned fruit.

Beans and legumes

Soy beans
Tofu
Black beans
Kidney beans
Navy beans
White beans
Garbanzo beans
Lima beans
Pinto Beans

Grains and Starchy Carbohydrates

Avoid all grains and starchy foods, including bread,
pasta, cereal, rice, oatmeal, pastries, and baked
goods

the Anti-Inflammatory Diet

Fat Sources	Miscellaneous Non Approved Items

Fats and Oils	Condiments, Spices, Seasonings
Lard	All spices that contain added sugar
Margarine	Commercial ketchup with sugar
Shortening	Commercial barbecue sauce with sugar
Soy oil	Any fat-free or reduced-fat salad dressings
Safflower oil	
Canola oil	**Beverages**
Sunflower oil	Alcoholic beverages of any kind
Corn oil	Fruit juices
Cottonseed oil	Sodas
Any partially hydrogenated oil	Chlorinated tap water
Grains and Starchy Carbohydrates	Coffee
Honey-roasted nuts	**Sweeteners**
Macadamia nuts	Sugar
Pecans	Maple syrup
Hazelnuts	Heated honey
Brazil nuts	Fructose or corn syrup
Peanuts	Aspartame(Equal)
Peanut butter	Sucralose (Splenda)
*Any nuts or seeds dry or roasted in oil	Acesulfame K
	Sugar alcohol (including sorbitol and malitol)
	Miscellaneous
	Soy protein powder
	Rice protein powder

Sample Daily Meal Plan for the Anti-Inflammatory Diet

Awake	Upon waking: Take 2-4 probiotics with 8oz. non-chlorinated water
Morning	Wait 30 minutes before eating Breakfast: Protein Source - 1-3 organic eggs Fat Source - 1 tbsp. coconut oil or real butter for cooking Carbohydrate Source - 1 bowl of fresh berries Supplements: Whole Food Multivitamin Digestive enzymes
Mid-Morning	Snack if needed: Approved nuts or vegetables
Noon	Lunch: Protein Source - organic chicken breast (4-8oz.) Fat Source - approved salad dressing Carbohydrate Source -spinach, leafy lettuce, and assorted vegetables Supplements: Digestive enzymes
Afternoon	Snack if needed: Approved nuts or vegetables
Evening	Dinner: (Eat at least 3 hours before bedtime) Protein Source - wild salmon (4-8oz.) Fat Source - advocado Carbohydrate Source - steamed asparagus Supplements: Whole Food Multivitamin Digestive enzymes Omega-3 oil (such as cod liver oil)
Bedtime	Take 2-4 probiotics with 8oz. non-chlorinated water

14

THERE'S POWER IN THE BLOOD
Diagnostic Blood Work

"A wise man should consider that health is the greatest of human blessings, and learn how by his own thought to derive benefit from his illnesses."

—HIPPOCRATES

Diagnostic blood work has been the "gold standard" in medicine for years. In the 1800s, doctors realized that life was in the blood, and practiced a system called *bleeding*, draining substantial portions of a person's blood in an attempt to remove disease from the body. Unfortunately, many died from this practice. That idea seems ignorant to us today, but as misguided as it was, the concept behind it was sound. If the blood is clean, the body is clean. Diseased blood yields diseased bodies. Today's blood checks have advanced far beyond this antiquated method, and modern medicine has developed a powerful diagnostic evaluating system that can tell us anything we need to know about a person's health, where it's been, and where it's going. There's truly *power in the blood*.

Blood cells are constantly being created and destroyed, as well as undergoing chemical changes. Blood has three essential functions: transportation, regulation, and protection. Blood is the main transportation system of the body. As the blood travels throughout the veins, it carries nutrients, oxygen, hormones, and other substances to the tissues of the body and carries away waste such as carbon dioxide from the cells. The waste is then filtered through the liver and kidneys for removal from the body.

Life is in the blood, and that's why it is so critical to examine it regularly—which is one of the primary foundations of Natural Medicine. The blood regulates body temperature by the heating and cooling properties of the water elements in it. A body could be taking in all of the necessary nutrition, but without proper circulation, the body will never receive this nutrition and will waste away and die.

There are a multitude of factors, numbers, ranges, and references relating to your blood—it can get quite confusing. But knowing what those test results mean is important because blood testing is part of a good health routine.

THE MAKEUP OF YOUR BLOOD

Blood is made up of a number of key elements: white blood cells, red blood cells, plasma, platelets, and stem cells.

White blood cells. White blood cells are considered to be part of the immune system. When foreign matter (antigens or toxins) is detected, the white blood cells are drawn to it. They are the body's defense against these invaders as they engulf the foreign matter and destroy it.

Red blood cells. Red blood cells are linked to the respiratory system because their main function is to carry oxygen to the cells, and carry carbon dioxide away from them. This is accomplished by a molecule in the red blood cells called hemoglobin. When it passes through the lungs, hemoglobin picks up oxygen to dispense throughout the body, and picks up carbon dioxide to return back to the lungs.

Plasma. Plasma is the liquid that keeps the blood flowing continuously through the body. It contains nutrients such as protein, water, carbohydrates, and electrolytes.

Platelets. When there is damage to blood vessels, the platelets travel through the blood to prevent excessive blood loss. Coagulation occurs at a traumatized or injured area by combining specific proteins in the blood to form a clot. Platelets live for only nine to twelve days and are then removed by the spleen.

Stem cells. These are found in the bone marrow, and they manufacture red and white blood cells, platelets, and more stem cells. The stem cells check the conditions of the body, and regulate the manufacturing of various elements as needed. For example, if oxygen in the body is low, the stem cells produce more red blood cells. The presence of an infection produces more white blood cells, and blood loss produces a mass production of platelets.

In Natural Medicine, diagnostic blood work is part of our foundational analysis for determining what health challenges a person might be facing. Nutritional deficiencies are a major factor in skewing the values, causing certain clinical ranges to be unhealthy. I use a seventy-component, comprehensive panel designed to show you everything going on inside your body—from the health of your heart, to your liver, kidneys, pancreas, immune system, oxygen levels, and even hormone function. I also use specific tests to determine your genetic predispositions to some of the most common diseases such as cancer, diabetes, and heart disease. I've heard it said that "numbers don't lie," and this is exactly the case when it comes to evaluating blood work. Blood work is the standard, and I want you to understand the results so you don't have to simply take the doctor's word—and then you can begin to take responsibility for your own health.

HOME ON THE RANGE

Blood testing measures results according to several defined *clinical ranges*. These are the reference ranges that physicians use to determine the status of our health relative to our blood. I personally do not refer to the traditional ranges in my practice, because those ranges get us too close to the edge of the "health cliff." And as we all know, if we get too close to the edge of a cliff and there's a gust of wind or we lose our balance, we might fall off. It's much safer to be several feet from the edge—the view from there is usually the same anyway. Natural Medicine's goal is to prevent disease and keep you from ever getting too near the edge of the cliff where the test results become dangerous or of major concern.

If a physician is consulting someone with diabetes, he or she looks at a Hemoglobin A1C test, which is used as a test for diabetes. The edge of the clinical range for this particular test is 6.0. In traditional medicine, we were trained that if an individual is within that range, they are safe. If patients are at a level of 5.9, the physician will say, "All is well!" and send them home. But if that number hits 6.0, *Oh no!* See my point? My comfort level is found in what I call *optimal ranges* that keep a person from getting near the edge of the cliff. An optimal range in this scenario would be 1.5 to 4.5. Do your own research and take responsibility for your health. If you don't, no one else will.

Let's get into the blood panels that you have likely seen but never understood. There are some words in the pages that follow that you may have never heard before if you are not involved in the world of medicine. It's not crucial that you remember the names of tests or parts of the blood. What is most important is that you understand a little about the world of diagnostic blood work, which will empower both you and your health.

BASIC TESTS AND NUTRITIONAL DEFICIENCIES

Rather than overwhelming you with a seemingly endless battery of blood tests, let's examine three of the basic blood panels:

- Complete Blood Count (CBC)

- Lipid profile

- Comprehensive Metabolic Panel (CMP)

These are some of the most common tests run by most physicians and they help determine any nutritional deficiencies that might be causing specific health challenges. Nutritional deficiencies are exactly what they sound like— the body is lacking something it needs. A lack of vitamins or minerals will typically cause certain systems not to function properly. For example, if we have a lack of iron or vitamin B12, we may become anemic. Our lifestyle choices, circumstances, and situations have caused our current health status. That is why evaluating the chemical side of the Health Triangle by examining diagnostic blood work is essential to the restoration of our overall health.

Complete blood count (CBC). The CBC is used to evaluate symptoms such as weakness, fatigue, or bruising, and to diagnose conditions such as anemia, infection, and many other disorders. It is also used to check the efficiency of your red blood cells, white blood cells, and platelets, and is concerned with how much oxygen your body is carrying and using. The CBC evaluates how strong your immune system is and will show how resistant your body is to disease. The CBC is often used to look for signs of cancer. Cancer is considered an anaerobic (without oxygen) disease. If your oxygen level is low, then you are opening the door for cancer.

CBC is also commonly used when a patient is suspected of being anemic.

Anemia means "lack of oxygen" and it often diminishes the physical capabilities of affected individuals and can impair immune function. The carriers of oxygen in the body are red blood cells (RBC) and hemoglobin. If any of these are low, you know your oxygen is low as well and you may be anemic.

Lipid profile. The word lipid means *fat.* The lipid profile deals primarily with how well your liver and gallbladder are functioning, and how your body handles fat. High cholesterol is the traditional indicator of potential heart disease, but new research shows that homocysteine is more of a risk than cholesterol. Cholesterol is manufactured in the liver. HDL (or high-density lipoprotein) is the good cholesterol, and LDL (or low-density lipoprotein) is the bad cholesterol. An overall cholesterol number of 170 to 200 is considered normal. When cholesterol drops too low, this negatively affects the hormone levels in both men and women. High cholesterol in the range of 250 and up usually means there is an imbalance in pancreatic function, which can impair the assimilation and use of fat. It also means that the liver could be congested.

Another component to cholesterol is called triglycerides. As a rule of thumb, these should always be half of the total cholesterol number. Triglycerides reflect the body's ability to normalize blood sugar and fatty acid levels. Extremely low triglyceride (or fatty acid) levels may suggest a dietary fat deficiency, and a deficiency of fat-soluble vitamins (vitamins A, D, K, and E) can result from this condition.

Elevated cholesterol levels may indicate the presence of excessive, rancid fats in the body due to overeating, extremely high fat diets, or poor hormone regulation. A decrease in HDL will not ultimately decrease the chance of coronary heart disease unless combined with low LDL levels. High LDL levels provide a big health risk and should prompt a complete study of dietary habits as well as a look at how your body is metabolizing sugars and fats. A great way to help keep cholesterol levels under control is to consume more whole organic vegetables and fiber.

Lipid Profile (Panel)

	Reference Range
Triglycerides	<150 mg/dL
Cholesterol, Total	125-200 mg/dL
HDL Cholesterol	> OR = 40 mg/dL
LDL Cholesterol	<130 mg/dL (calc)

Comprehensive metabolic profile (CMP). The CMP evaluates a large portion of the body's functions. You could call it the "multivitamin" of blood tests. It provides a tiny picture of everything. The CMP is used as a broad screening tool to evaluate organ function and check for conditions such as diabetes, liver disease, and kidney disease. The CMP may also be used to monitor known conditions, such as hypertension, and to monitor patients taking specific medications for any kidney- or liver-related side effects.

(CMP) Comprehensive Metabolic Profile

	Reference Range
Glucose	65-99 mg/dL
Urea Nitrogen (Bun)	7-25 mg/dL
Creatinine	0.5-1.2 mg/dL
GFR Estimated	> OR = 60 mL/min/1.73m2
Bun/Creatinine Ratio	6-22 (calc)
Sodium	135-146 mmol/L
Potassium	3.5-5.3 mmol/L
Chloride	98-110 mmol/L
Carbon Dioxide	21-33 mmol/L
Calcium	8.6-10.2 mg/dL
Protein, Total	6.2-8.3 g/dL
Albumin	3.6-5.1 g/dL
Globulin	2.2-3.9 g/dL (calc)
Albumin/Globulin Ratio	1.0 –2.1 (calc)
Bilirubin, Total	.2 – 1.2 mg/dL
Alkaline Phosphatase	33-130 U/L
AST	10-35 U/L
ALT	6-40 U/L
Creatine Kinase, Total	< OR = 165 U/L
Westergren	< OR = 30 mm/h

THE CANCER CONNECTION—FOLIC ACID AND B12

Blood testing is widely used to detect deficiencies in folic acid and B12. The overuse of trans fats in our diets has caused a widespread lack of omega-3 fatty acids in the body. Along with pesticides and toxic chemicals, trans fats have virtually eliminated the gene that converts folic acid in the body, a gene that needs omega-3 fats for the conversion. And because less folic acid is being produced, this in turn harms our DNA. Folic acid is used to convert enzymes that are essential to DNA formation and function. That is why pregnant women need folic acid to avoid birth defects in newborns. Folic acid deficiency is also one of the reasons cancer is so prevalent today. Folic acid helps increase our oxygen capacity in the body. Without the proper amounts of folic acid, our bodies are not producing enough oxygen, and as I stated previously, without oxygen, you are opening the door for cancer.

Folic acid deficiency is noticed in blood work when neutrophils (the most abundant white blood cells in the body) are low and lymphocytes are high. If a deficiency occurs, you will need a form of activated B12 specific to your genetic type, either adenosylcobalamin or methylcobalamin, and an activated form of folic acid called folinic acid. Your physician can perform tests to determine which version of folic acid and B12 you need. Most folic acid brands available in the stores will not absorb in the body. Each person is biologically different and needs a certain activated version of folic acid and B12 in one of two different coenzyme forms. Ask your doctor which supplement is right for you.

HOMOCYSTEINE AND YOUR HEART

Diagnostic blood work is the most accurate way to detect the levels of homocysteine found in the body. Homocysteine is now considered a more important marker for cardiac risk than cholesterol, and high levels are associated with a two- to four-fold increased risk of an acute heart attack. In contrast to the commonly held belief that cardiac disease primarily results from an abnormality in fat metabolism, homocysteine is actually a protein amino acid, and not a fat. High homocysteine levels indicate an increased risk for cardiovascular disease. Elevated homocysteine levels have also been linked to the narrowing of the blood vessels.

Elevated homocysteine levels are also considered to be an indicator of vitamin B6, vitamin B12, and folate deficiencies. Vitamins B6 and B12 both serve to keep homocysteine levels under control by converting it into less harmful substances. When either of these vitamins is deficient, homocysteine levels will increase in both blood serum and urine. Vitamin B12 deficiency not only prevents homocysteine levels from being regulated, but can also cause megaloblastic anemia to develop—this is a specific type of anemia characterized by enlarged and dysfunctional red blood cells (megaloblasts) in the bone marrow.

Folate deficiency can result from inadequate intake or improper absorption of this important water-soluble B vitamin. Individuals with nutritional folate deficiency may also develop homocysteine elevations. In addition, some experts feel that anemia caused by a B12 deficiency is really due to a folate deficiency in the tissue.

As you can see, having your blood tested is one of the most comprehensive ways to detect the source of problems and where deficiencies exist. By having your blood examined and then taking the correct measures to eliminate deficiencies found in your blood work, you can take an active role in empowering your health.

BLOOD WORK TO THE RESCUE

Samuel heard me on the radio and came in my office with sinus issues. He had been dealing with chronic sinus and allergy complications for over two years. No matter what he did, he was constantly congested and suffered from hay fever. He tried all of the traditional methods such as antihistamines and corticosteroids, but nothing gave him the relief that he needed. "I'm sick and tired of being sick and tired," he said. "Why is my body functioning this way?"

I had a hunch, but I never act on hunches. If I did, then I might head down the wrong treatment path. I treat every patient the same. I listen to them, and then pretend I don't know anything in regard to their specific condition. It keeps my mind open and unbiased. Like a puzzle, I put all the pieces together, and the root or cause of the health challenge will invariably reveal itself.

Samuel had alarmingly low numbers on his CBC tests for his red and white blood cell counts. That means he had low oxygen levels and low immune function. Samuel's sinus challenges were his body's way of saying that its immune system was low and not enough oxygen was flowing in his body. And as you now know, low oxygen levels in the body produce a breeding ground for cancer.

His low CBC numbers also indicated a breakdown in the folic acid gene system, which causes a nutritional deficiency of B12 and folic acid. Going to the grocery store and buying synthetic vitamins would not restore his health;

he needed the activated versions of those vitamins to get his health back. I placed him on an activated form of B12 and an activated form of folic acid. Because each person's needs are different, it is important to have your doctor find which forms of B12 and folinic acid are right for you.

In just one week, Samuel's sinus congestion cleared up for the first time in two years. In three months, we ran his blood work again. His blood work values had radically changed and were within the optimal ranges. Not only did correcting his nutritional deficiency clear up his sinus congestion (which was the symptom of the root cause of the underlying issue), but also helped his body increase its oxygen production, which lessened his predisposition for cancer. He was thrilled at how he felt, but even more excited about his body getting as far away from the edge of the cancer cliff as possible.

You should have your blood checked at least once a year. After the age of forty-five, I recommend having it checked every six months. There is power in prevention. Knowledge is power, and knowing where your body is, and where it is headed is extremely important for the extraordinary health you deserve.

Always remember, there's power in the blood.

Blood Work Quick Reference Guide

Components		Possible Causes or Conditions
Glucose	Low	Hypoglycemia
	High	Diabetes
Hemoglobin A1C	Low	Hypoglycemia
	High	Diabetes
Uric Acid	Low	Low protein/poor protein metabolism, edema
	High	Gout
BUN (Blood, Uria, Nitrogen)	Low	Low protein, low liver function, edema
	High	Poor kidney function
Creatinine	Low	Low protein, inactivity or low muscle exertion
	High	Poor kidney function
BUN/Creatinine	Low	Low protein
	High	Infection of urinary system
Sodium	Low	Chronic disease, possible Addison's disease (Hypoadrenal)
	High	Dehydration, possible Cushing's syndrome (Hyperadrenal)
Potassium	Low	Malnutrition, diuretics, Cushing's syndrome
	High	Dehydration, poor kidney function, Addison's disease
Chloride	Low	Poor digestion, poor kidney function, over hydration
	High	Dehydration
Magnesium	Low	Poor digestion/malabsorption
	High	Low thyroid function, poor kidney function
Calcium	Low	Poor digestion/malnutrition
	High	Dehydration, poor kidney function, low thyroid function
Phosphorus	Low	Low vitamin D, high carb diet
	High	Dehydration, excessive exercise, poor kidney and liver function
Calcium/Albumin	Low	Low calcium
	High	Protein deficiency, malnutrition, poor digestion
Total Protein	Low	Protein deficiency, poor digestion
	High	Dehydration, liver infection
Albumin	Low	Malnutrition, malabsorption, higher mortality risk
	High	Dehydration
Globulin	Low	Frequent/chronic infection/disease, protein loss, anemia
	High	Liver infection, CFS and similar, neoplasms
A/G Ratio	Low	Deficient protein, inflammatory diseases
	High	Excessive protein diet
Total Biliruibin	Low	Anemia, pharmaceutical toxemia
	High	Liver disease, gall bladder, pharmaceutical toxemia
Alkaline Phosphatase	Low	Mineral deficiency, anemia, malnutrition, pharmaceutical toxemia
	High	Degenerative joint disease, bone growth, CFS, liver disease, pharmaceutical toxemia
LDH	Low	none, possible inherited
	High	Destruction of cells, location unknown
SGOT (AST)	Low	B6 deficiency, severe liver infection, kidney infection
	High	Inflamed liver/pancreas/gallbladder, pharmaceutical toxemia

Blood Work Quick Reference Guide

Components		Possible Causes or Conditions
SGPT (ALT)	Low	Malnutrition, excessive alcohol intake, cancer
	High	Inflamed liver/pancreas/gallbladder, pharmaceutical toxemia
GGT	Low	Chronic pancreatitis, low thyroid function
	High	Excessive alcohol intake, inflamed pancreas/gallbladder/liver, pharmaceutical toxemia
Serum Iron	Low	Iron deficiency, blood loss, infection
	High	Excess iron, hepatitis, dialysis
Ferritin	Low	Iron deficiency
	High	Hemochromatosis, inflammation, liver disease
Cholesterol	Low	Malabsorption, malnutrition, infection/inflammation
	High	Unhealthy diet, low thyroid function
Triglycerides	Low	Malnutrition, excessive exercise
	High	Diabetes, liver or pancreas damage, kidney infection
HDL Cholesterol	Low	Sedentary lifestyle, low thyroid function
	High	Vigorous exercise, good diet, family trait
LDL Cholesterol	Low	Immunodeficiency
	High	High fat diet, diabetes, hypothyroidism
VLDL Cholesterol	Low	Immunodeficiency
	High	High fat diet, diabetes, hypothyroid
Chol/HDL ratio	Low	Low risk for coronary involvement
	High	Elevated risk for coronary
T4	Low	Low thyroid function
	High	High thyroid function
T3 Uptake	Low	Low thyroid function
	High	High thyroid function
T7	Low	Low thyroid function
	High	High thyroid function
TSH	Low	Normal thyroid function, low pituitary function
	High	Low thyroid function
White Blood Count	Low	Chronic infection, immunodeficiency
	High	Acute infection
Red Blood Count	Low	Anemia
	High	Dehydration
Hemoglobin	Low	Anemia
	High	Dehydration
Hematocrit	Low	Anemia
	High	Dehydration
MCV	Low	Microcytic anemia
	High	Macrocytic anemia
MCH	Low	Iron deficiency anemia
	High	Pernicious anemia (B12/folic acid deficiency)
MCHC	Low	Iron deficiency anemia
	High	Pernicious anemia (B12/folic acid deficiency)

Blood Work Quick Reference Guide

Components		Possible Causes or Conditions
Platelets	Low	Thrombocytopenia
	High	Infection, inflammation
Neutrophils	Low	Chronic infection, viral, bacterial
	High	Acute infection, most bacterial infection
Lymphocytes	Low	Immunodeficiency, viral infections
	High	Acute viral infection, food allergies, colitis
Monocytes	Low	Corticosteroids
	High	Bacterial infection, food allergies, colitis
Eosinophils	Low	None
	High	Allergies (environmental)
Basophils	Low	None
	High	Chronic sinusitis, lead poisoning, anemia
ESR	Low	None
	High	Inflammation
CRP	Low	None
	High	Tissue injury, inflammation, infections
Creatine Kinase	Low	Low muscle activity, low muscle mass
	High	Muscle breakdown, excessive exercise, increase cardiac risk

PART IV

STRUCTURAL HEALTH

NATURAL MEDICINE®
HEALTH TRIANGLE

15

OUR FRAMEWORK
The Structure of the Body

"Life is not merely to be alive, but to be well."
—MARCUS VALERIUS MARTIAL

In a scene in the 2006 James Bond movie, *Casino Royale*, the characters were in a building that rested on the beautiful inland waters of Italy, battling for a briefcase containing millions of dollars. One of the men shot an air-filled pontoon that was supporting the ten-story floating building. The building immediately began to shake and move until it finally crumbled into the water.

All it took for that enormous structure to come tumbling down was one shot to its foundational system. The support was solid, but one wrong move, and the entire structure collapsed. The construction of the building itself is important, but the foundation it's built on is of the utmost importance.

Structural balance in the body is often thought of as simply correct or poor posture, but that's only part of the picture. The structural side of the Health Triangle is the final side for discussion, but that does not mean it is of less importance. In fact, the structural side of health is literally the framework upon which all aspects of our body depend. In part II on mental health, we learned about the power of the mind, brain chemicals, and how you must make a conscious decision to be well. In part III, we turned our focus to the chemical side of the triangle and learned how to detect deficiencies and restore your systems to health. Part IV, the structural side, ties together both the mental and chemical side, as it encompasses all major systems and processes.

191

OUR TEN MAJOR SYSTEMS

Structural health includes every part of us—our cells, tissues, nerves, organs, glands, tissues, and the bodily systems to which each of these elements belong. The body has ten major systems:

Nervous system. The nervous system, the focus of part II on mental health, is the major controlling, regulatory, and communicating system in the body. It is the center of all mental activity including thought, learning, and memory. Together with the endocrine system, the nervous system is responsible for regulating and maintaining homeostasis (stable conditions in the body that are conducive to good health). The nervous system keeps us in touch with our environment, both external and internal.

Digestive system. The digestive system includes the digestive tract and its accessory organs, which process food into molecules that can be absorbed and used by the cells of the body. Food is broken down until the molecules are small enough to be absorbed and the waste products are eliminated. The digestive tract consists of a long continuous tube that extends from the mouth to the anus. It includes the mouth, pharynx, esophagus, stomach, small intestine, and large intestine. The tongue and teeth are accessory structures of the system. The salivary glands, liver, gallbladder, and pancreas are major accessory organs that have a role in digestion. These organs secrete fluids into the digestive tract. Part III examined the role of digestion and how the body processes your food choices.

Endocrine system. The endocrine system was covered in part III on chemical health, as it relates to hormones. Along with the nervous system, it functions in the regulation of body activities. The nervous system acts through electrical impulses and neurotransmitters to cause muscle contraction and glandular secretion. The effect is of short duration, measured in seconds, and localized, confined to a specific area. The endocrine system acts through chemical messengers (our hormones) that influence growth, development, and metabolic activities.

Respiratory system. When the respiratory system is mentioned, we generally think of breathing, but breathing is only one of the activities of the respiratory system. Body cells need a continuous supply of oxygen for the metabolic processes that are necessary to maintain life. The respiratory system works with the circulatory system to provide this oxygen and to remove the waste products of metabolism. It also helps to regulate pH of the blood, which we discussed in part III.

Muscular system. The muscular system is composed of cells called muscle fibers. Their predominant function is contractibility. When you turn this page, the muscles in your hand and wrist will contract. Muscles, where attached to bones or internal organs and blood vessels, are responsible for this movement. Nearly all movement in the body is the result of muscle contraction. (This is covered in chapter 17.)

Skeletal system. We rely on a sturdy internal frame that is centered on a prominent spine. The human skeletal system consists of bones, cartilage, ligaments, and tendons and accounts for about 20 percent of the body's weight. (This is covered in chapter 18.)

Lymphatic system. The lymphatic system has three primary functions. First, it returns excess bodily fluid to the blood. Of the fluid that leaves the capillary, about 90 percent is returned. The 10 percent that does not return becomes part of the interstitial fluid (or tissue fluid) that surrounds the tissue cells. Small protein molecules may leak through the capillary wall and increase the pressure of the fluid flowing through your lymph and blood veins. This further inhibits the return of fluid into the capillaries, and fluid tends to accumulate in the tissue spaces. If this continues, blood volume and blood pressure decrease significantly and the volume of tissue fluid increases, which results in edema (swelling). Lymph capillaries pick up the excess fluid and proteins and return them to the blood in the veins. After the fluid enters the lymph capillaries, it is called lymph. (This is covered in chapter 19.)

Cardiovascular system. The cardiovascular system (or circulatory system) consists of the heart, which is a muscular pumping device, and a closed system of vessels called arteries, veins, and capillaries. Blood contained in the circulatory system is pumped by the heart around a closed circle or circuit of vessels as it passes again and again through the various circulations of the body. In chapter 20, we will learn more about this system as it relates to one of the most common and deadly diseases we face today—heart disease.

Urinary system. The principal function of the urinary system is to maintain the volume and composition of body fluids within normal limits. It rids the body of waste products that accumulate as a result of cellular metabolism, and because of this, it is sometimes referred to as the excretory system. It is a vital system in eliminating inflammation from the body (which was covered in chapter 13). Be aware that the fluids you drink have a significant impact on how well this system works. Avoid sugary beverages when you can, and instead drink one half of your body weight in ounces of purified or filtered water each day.

Reproductive system. The major function of the reproductive system is to ensure survival of the human race. Other systems in the body, such as the endocrine and urinary systems, work continuously to maintain homeostasis (stable conditions and balance). You may live a long, healthy, and happy life without producing offspring, but if we are to continue existing on this earth, at least some people must reproduce! When you focus on making the right lifestyle choices and correct food selections, you will bring health to all your systems, including the reproductive system. The reason is simple—each system in the body affects the others. When one part of your body doesn't work right, every other part suffers as well. You must work towards total health for everything to work right.

Each system has its different roles and functions, and yet they all work together. The structural side of the Health Triangle is an often neglected but critical aspect of our overall health. Remember that no one side of the triangle is more important that the other two.

PAIN—THE BODY'S RED FLAG

Numerous patients come into my clinic with structural discomfort, saying, "Dr. Asa, my shoulder hurts, my side hurts, my back hurts." They use the word that resonates with all of us—pain. Pain is the body's indicator that something is wrong inside us, and it usually means something has been wrong for a while.

Cathy came into my office with recurring foot pain. She was twenty-eight and extremely active in biking and running, and her foot pain was affecting her active lifestyle. During the exam, I noticed that her hips were shifted. After examining the X-rays, I discovered a slight rotation in her lumbar spine (lower back) that was causing her entire hip placement to be out of balance. When this happens, it changes the biomechanics of the way a person walks. The twisting and rotational nature of Cathy's spine and hips was causing undue pain in her foot.

Cathy had suffered this challenge for several months and had taken large amounts of cortisone shots to numb the pain. It took us several months to balance her structure by placing her spine back into alignment and retraining her body's walking patterns, allowing them to return to normal. We also discovered that in addition to her foot not working properly, the misaligned area in the back was near the L5 vertebrate, which caused the front shin muscle (called the tibialis anterior) to malfunction. After correcting the misaligned area and reducing inflammation to the nerve root (the electric cord), her foot began functioning properly again.

When the structure of the body is misaligned, everything else begins to malfunction as well. A great house is built on a great foundation. If the foundation is crooked or shifted, the house will start to crumble. As the foundation shifts, the walls of the house distort, the plaster cracks, the doors don't fit, and the windows won't open. An accomplished carpenter can patch the cracks in the walls and trim the doors and windows to fit so that everything looks good and functions well—at least temporarily. But if the foundation itself is not corrected, it won't be long before the walls again crack, the doors won't fit, and the windows won't open. We have to take care of our foundational structure so our house will stand strong and be able to weather any storm that life brings our way.

The structure of the body is an essential part of the Health Triangle. It is of equal importance to the mental and chemical side in the overall picture of our health. Examination and evaluation is routinely done in Natural Medicine by using extensive orthopedic and neurological exams including extensive diagnostic testing. Let's look into the world of our structural environment and discover how you can firm up your foundation.

16

IS YOUR POWER ON?
The Nervous System

*"The nervous system controls and coordinates all organs
and structures of the human body."*
—*GRAY'S ANATOMY OF THE HUMAN BODY,*
29TH EDITION

My TV remote recently fell behind the sofa at my house. I climbed around the end table, trying not to knock anything over (I've been known to embody the term, "a bull in a china shop"), and accidentally yanked the lamp cord out of the wall with my leg. I plugged it back in and soon noticed that the lamp didn't have the same power that it had before. I looked down at the power cord and noticed that it had been partially severed. There was enough cord still attached to provide sufficient electrical current to keep the lamp lit; however, it did not have the full power it did before I ripped the cord from the wall. That lamp was only as good as the electric cord that gave it power. When the electric cord was damaged, the effectiveness of the lamp to produce light was greatly diminished. When I repaired the most important component of the lamp—the power cord—the power was fully restored.

This principle applies to our bodies. The nervous system is the part of the body that controls all major functions. It is our electric cord that keeps us running at full power. The body has millions of nerves and each one attaches to muscles, organs, tissues, or glands, and has a primary function. Nerves are what cause your heart to beat, your eyes to blink, your ears to hear, your skin to feel, and your muscles to move. More importantly, they keep the "power" on in the body.

Nerves originate in the spine and extend to their respective places within the body, functioning as the body's electrical power plants. They play a critical role in the structural side of the Health Triangle and are as important as our chemical and mental health to overall well being. If our nerves get irritated by inflammation or restricted when segments of the spine are out of alignment, then a loss of electrical power to their correlating organs, glands, muscles, or specific tissues occurs, just like when I partially severed the lamp cord.

BASIC FUNCTIONS OF THE NERVOUS SYSTEM

Like other systems in the body, the nervous system is composed of organs, specifically the brain, spinal cord, nerves, and ganglia (a mass of nerve tissue containing nerve cells outside the brain or spinal cord). These parts consist of various tissues, including nerve, blood, and connective tissue. Together these carry out the complex and essential activities of the nervous system.

The various activities of the nervous system can be grouped together as three general, overlapping functions:

- Sensory

- Integrative

- Motor

Sensory. Millions of sensory receptors detect changes (called stimuli), which occur inside and outside the body. They monitor such things as temperature, light, and sound from the external environment. Inside the body, the internal environment, receptors detect variations in pressure, pH, carbon dioxide concentration, and the levels of various electrolytes (material that dissolves to produce a solution that conducts an electric current.). All of this gathered information is called sensory input.[1]

Integration. Sensory input is converted into electrical signals called nerve impulses that are transmitted to the brain. There the signals are brought together to create sensations, to produce thoughts, or to add to memory. Decisions are made each moment based on the sensory input. This is the process of integration.

Motor. The term *motor* refers to any of the various power units that develop energy or impart motion. Based on the sensory input and integration, the nervous system responds by sending signals to muscles, causing them to contract, or to our glands, causing them to produce secretions. Muscles and glands are called effectors because they cause an effect in response to directions from the nervous system. This is the motor output or motor function.

Natural Medicine calls for evaluating the structure of the body to see how the nervous system is working. By evaluating specific diagnostic tests and extensive neurological exams, any neural imbalances that need to be addressed can be determined. If the spine is out of place to any degree, or there is any sign of degenerative joint disease, most likely the electrical current that travels through the nerves is restricted.

PLUG IN YOUR CORD

Sandra came to see me after hearing me on the radio, wanting to learn more about the widespread decrease in thyroid function that I often discuss. She suffered from an under active thyroid and was taking a drug in an attempt to lessen the symptoms. She came to me in desperation and said, "Dr. Asa, my hair is falling out, I'm overweight, I have no energy, and I have four kids and a husband to care for. Can you help me?"

In examining Sandra, I found that her sixth and seventh cervical verte-brae (the neck bones) had significant rotation. In addition, the discs between the bones had degenerated, causing an irritation and restriction of the nerves coming out of the area. She also displayed a muscular weakness in the triceps and finger muscles on the left side. The electric cords, or nerves, that come out of this area travel directly to the thyroid gland, and the thyroid gland is directly responsible for metabolism, mental clarity, and overall functionality. In essence, Sandra's power cord that operates the thyroid gland was restricted. Her blood work revealed that the numbers relating to her thyroid were com-pletely out of control. Sandra's thyroid was barely surviving.

Her underarm temperature—a clinical test for thyroid function—was 95.8 degrees, which was extremely low. Iodine is a highly deficient mineral in the thyroid, as we discussed in earlier chapters. In treating Sandra, I sought to restore joint function in the affected spinal area and reduce any restriction of those nerves that power the thyroid gland.

After two months of replacing the iodine and other nutritional deficien-cies in her system, Sandra's thyroid began functioning normally. Her new blood tests and the thyroid values were normal, and her endocrinologist determined that she did not need the medication anymore. She had more energy than she had in ten years, her hair stopped falling out, her skin tone evened, and her mental clarity increased. Her husband stopped by my clinic recently; I went to shake his hand, but he hugged me instead. He said he wanted to thank me for giving him back his wife. All I did was to provide the essential elements her body needed, and her body did the rest. Remember, the nervous system is the electric plant of the body. We must keep the electrical cords free of any irritation or restriction to achieve extraordinary health.

Misalignments of spinal vertebrae (the back and neck bones) and discs may cause irritation and restriction to the nervous system and negatively affect the structures, organs, glands, muscles, and tissues and their related functions. Here are the nerves and where they connect throughout the body:

Spinal Bone/Nerve to Body Relationships
Spinal nerve irritation may cause reduced function in associated areas of the body

Spinal nerve connection areas	Spinal Bone/ Nerve Area	Symptoms associated with an irritated spinal bone/ nerve area
Pituitary gland	C1	Headaches, nervousness, insomnia, head colds, high blood pressure, migraine headaches, chronic fatigue, dizziness
Inner/middle ear	C1	
Eyes, ears, optic, auditory nerve	C2	Sinus trouble, allergies, eye trouble, ear trouble, fainting spells
Tongue, sinuses, tongue	C2	
Teeth	C3	Neuralgia, neuritis, acne, eczema, skin trouble
Outer ear, cheeks, face bones	C3	
Eustacian tube	C4	Hay fever, ringing in ears, tonsils
Mouth, nose, lips	C4	
Pharynx, larynx, vocal cords	C5	Laryngitis, hoarseness, throat trouble
Tonsils	C6	Stiff neck, tonsillitis, whooping cough, croup
Neck	C6	
Shoulders	C6	
Thyroid gland	C7	Thyroid trouble, shoulder bursitis, common colds
Esophagus and trachea , throat	T1	Asthma, cough, shortness of breath
Heart, heart valves, and coronary arteries	T2	Functional heart conditions, chest pain
Breasts	T3	Bronchitis, pleurisy, congestion
Lungs	T3	
Gall bladder	T4	Gall bladder conditions, shingles
Liver	T5	Liver conditions, anemia, arthritis, low blood pressure
Stomach	T6	Stomach troubles, indigestion, heartburn
Pancreas	T7	Ulcers, gastitis, irritable bowel syndrome
Duodenum	T7	

Spinal Bone/Nerve to Body Relationships
Spinal nerve irritation may cause reduced function in associated areas of the body

Spinal nerve connection areas	Spinal Bone/ Nerve Area	Symptoms associated with an irritated spinal bone/ nerve area
Spleen	T8	Lowered immune function
Diaphragm	T8	
Adrenal glands	T9	Allergies, chronic fatigue
Kidneys	T10	Kidney troubles, hardening of the arteries, chronic tiredness
Skin	T11	Acne, eczema, psoriasis, boils, skin conditions
Small intestines	T12	Rheumatism, gas pains, sterility
Large intestines	L1	Constipation, colitis, diarrhea, hernias
Appendix and cecum	L2	Cramps, varicose veins, acidosis, difficulty breathing
Upper leg, abdomen	L2	
Genitalia, uterus, bladder	L3	Bladder troubles, menstrual trouble, impotency
Prostate	L4	Urination troubles, sciatic pain
Sciatic nerve	L4	
Lower leg	L5	Poor circulation in the legs, swollen ankles, weak ankles and arches, leg cramps
Ankles, feet, toes	L5	
Rectum and anus	Coccyx	Hemorrhoids, rectal itching, pain upon sitting
Hips and buttocks	Sacrum	Hip pain

Look at all these nerves! They travel throughout the entire body. It is crucial that you eliminate any restrictions in your electric cords. I told Sandra, just as I tell all my patients, *I can get you 50 percent better, and then we'll let God do the rest!* The next time you feel like someone ripped out your electric cord, you might want to have it checked out so you can get properly reconnected to the power source.

17

MORE THAN LOOKING FIT
The Muscular System

"A man too busy to take care of his health is like a mechanic too busy to take care of his tools."
—SPANISH PROVERB

Many young people are fascinated with characters such as Superman, The Incredible Hulk, Spiderman, Captain America, Rambo, Terminator, and Rocky. Because of such idols and the popularity of bodybuilding, most men believe big muscles are "cool," and women consider being fit as "sexy." Whether you are built like Arnold Schwarzenegger or lean like Amanda Beard, when we think of muscles, we often think about how we look on the exterior rather than the body's functionality and ideal build for optimal health.

We have close to 650 muscles in the body that control various functions and movements, and nerves that originate in the spine control every muscle. For example, if you try to perform a bicep curl and it's weaker than normal, this might be related to a dysfunction in your C5–C6 nerve (also called the musculocutaneous nerve). Our muscular system is involved in all the motion and movement in our lives, but healthy muscles are more than a big set of biceps—much more.

ANCIENT ENERGY PATHWAYS

For several thousands of years, civilizations in the Orient have used a system of treatment that involves studying the energy patterns of the body. The system was developed around 2600 BC by a Chinese emperor. The system, known as Meridian Therapy, was developed through the centuries correlating energy and health within the body. The goal of this medicine is to keep the energy patterns balanced to maintain normal health. Acupuncture is the most familiar name given to this healing system. However, with all the new methods and treatments today, needles are not the only way of performing treatment to get the maximum benefit.

The energy that is referred to in Chinese acupuncture is called "chi" (pronounced CHEE). This force travels through the body on predetermined pathways called meridians. There are twelve meridians that are based on a muscle-organ relationship. Acupuncture and meridian therapy both work to correct imbalances in the meridian system that have resulted in too much or too little energy, causing imbalances in the body. *The Standard Medical Textbook for Acupuncture, Chinese Acupuncture, and Moxibustion* explains the muscle-organ relationship. If one area has too much energy—take the heart, for instance—then muscles such as the subscapularis (a shoulder muscle) will be weak, and the heart will also begin to weaken. Such imbalances can arise from diet, trauma, environmental factors, seasonal changes, or stressful situations.

Imbalances are corrected by focusing on the acupuncture points and meridian pathways to balance energy, and by examining and adjusting the spinal-muscle-nerve-organ relationship, thus restoring balance to the body. The energy is electromagnetic in nature and can be "shorted out" by environmental factors, making organs and muscles weak. Methods to restore function include needles, digital pressure, and vibration called moxibustion. Stimulation of specific acupuncture meridian points immediately restores balance in the meridians, and the muscles and organs will return to their normal functioning states. In short, this ancient form of medicine recognizes that everything in the body is connected and must achieve balance for the body to function properly.

Do you remember elementary school science class? Our teachers taught us about atoms—small particles that make up all energy of both living and non-living things. They have three components: protons (positively charged particles), electrons (negatively charged particles), and neutrons (neutral particles). This was our first introduction to how everything from a plastic bottle to a chair to our bodies are made of material that contains these atoms, or particles. Each part of the atom contains energy, and these energy particles are always in motion. This is our basis for energy.

Despite preconceived notions that these ideas are "new age," Chinese medicine, acupuncture, meridian therapy, and chi are not new in any way. These treatments have been around for nearly five thousand years, long before our medical system. It is medicine that has stood the test of time and takes into consideration the body's structural-chemical-mental relationship and its role in Natural Medicine's Health Triangle. I consistently see this interconnection in my office, and I'm still amazed to see how it works every time. The following chart shows the correlation with the meridians and their respective muscles and how they affect the function of the body.

Body Meridians: The Muscle - Organ Relationship
Imbalanced muscle function can affect proper organ function

Organ	Muscle Relationship
Lung	(Shoulders) Deltoids, Serratus Anterior, Coracobrachialis
Large Intestine	(Legs) Tensor Fascia Lata, Hamstrings, Quadraus Lumborum
Spleen	(Back, Arms and Shoulders) Latissimus Dorsi, Triceps, Mid and Lower Trapezius
Pancreas	(Back) Latissimus Dorsi, Triceps, Mid and Lower Trapezius
Stomach	(Chest, Arms and Neck) Pectoralis Clavicular, Neck Flexors and Extensors, Sternocleidomastoid, Biceps, Brachioradialis, Supinator, Pronator Teres, Masseter, Temporalis, Internal and External Pterygoid
Triple Warmer (Thyroid)	(Shoulders, Rotator cuff) Teres Minor, Infraspinatus
Circulation/Sex	(Buttocks, Inner Thighs) Sartorius, Gracilis, Gluteus Maximus, Gluteus Medius, Adductors, Piriformis
Small Intestine	(Legs and Abdominals) Quadriceps, Abdominals
Heart	(Shoulder; Rotator Cuff) Subscapularis
Gall Bladder	(Behind the Knee) Popliteus
Liver	(Middle Chest and Upper Back) Pectoralis Sternal, Rhomboid
Bladder	(Shins, Lower Leg, and Lower Back) Tibialis Anterior, Peroneus Longus & Brevis, Sacrospinalis
Kidney	(Shoulders and Hip Flexors) Psoas, Iliacus, Upper Trapezius

This chart may look intricate and intimidating, but the concept is an easy one. If your shoulder hurts, it could indicate that you have a health issue in your lung. If you have problems with your quadriceps (thigh muscles), then you could be dealing with issues in your small intestines. Stomach issues? That could be a problem with your bicep muscles. Remember, these are all *energy meridians*—the nerves that travel from the spine to the organs also have alternate pathways through muscles. If the muscles are not working well, the respective glands or organs might not be working well either.

Ben was a new patient. He had been suffering from severe stomach pains that increased when he ate, especially if he ate a lot of fat. His doctors treated him for ulcers, colitis, irritable bowel syndrome, reflux, and a host of other conditions, but he had never gotten any relief from these treatments.

He also told me he was upset because he had been an avid runner for years, but his knees had been bothering him lately and he had been forced to decrease his running considerably. Doctors told him it was "runner's knee," and he was probably showing the early stages of arthritis. They put him on pain-relieving steroids, which further decreased his joint function.

A major element in Natural Medicine, is the specific relationships between the body organs and the muscles. With this in mind, I performed tests on the rotation of the tibia bone at the knee joint, which is controlled by the popliteus muscle, a tiny muscle located behind the knee and considered to be connected to the gallbladder. This muscle prevents over-rotation, and when weakened, it can cause severe internal knee pain.

As I examined Ben's knees, I found that they were weak and unable to show any strength as I gave resistance. Ben was amazed that he couldn't withstand the light pressure that I applied. I asked him to touch the meridian point on his body that was correlated to the gallbladder. When he touched that point, it caused a reconnection in the chi, or energy flow, and the strength in Ben's muscle immediately returned. I asked him if anyone ever said anything to him about his gallbladder. He nodded and replied, "The doctors want me to have it taken out. I am scheduled for surgery in two weeks."

I strongly suggested that he wait before going through with the surgery. Ben helped reset his body by doing a liver and gallbladder cleanse, which eliminated numerous stones and toxins from the organs. Ben also restored nutritional deficiencies that were discovered in his blood work, and his gallbladder began working normally again.

Surgery is necessary at times, and advances in modern medicine are amazing. However, before you ever go cutting out body parts, have *everything* checked out. You never know, it just might be one of those meridians in need of a little balance.

18

KEEPING THE STRUCTURE STRONG
The Skeletal System

*"Age does not depend upon years, but upon tempera-
ment and health. Some men are born old, and some
never grow so."*

—TRYON EDWARDS

I remember walking into seventh grade science class the first day and seeing a tall structure that I had never seen before—his name was Tyrone. Tyrone was about six feet tall and weighed five pounds. He exemplified everything a person wants to be; he was strong, firm, and well put together. Tyrone was our class skeleton, and all 206 of his bones were put together in the masterpiece that is the human skeletal frame.

Our skeleton is the framework onto which everything else is built. Our joints and bones connect the body, and without our skeletons, we would be nothing but a pile of skin, organs, and glands. But when all these body parts are hanging so exquisitely on the skeleton, you have the art of the human body.

Along with bones, we also have joints and cartilage. Cartilage is the substance in joint areas such as our knees, shoulders, hips, and spine to help create a padded area so the bones can't rub together. Over time, our bones can deteriorate through osteoporosis, which is seen more often in women, and degenerative joint disease or osteoarthritis, which is equally seen in both males and females.

It's essential to keep the skeletal system strong, but a myriad of factors contribute to skeletal deterioration and dysfunction. Our sedentary lifestyle is one of them. The body is designed to move, and sitting around each day watching TV or sitting for hours in an office chair is not going to get our framework where it needs to be. The simple pounding action of walking is a great way to naturally build our bones and offset the effects of a sedentary lifestyle. Weight-bearing movement creates a natural response in the body to increase and maintain what is called bone density, or the thickness of our bones. The older we get the more brittle we become, accelerated by improper nutrition, limited sunlight, and little or no exercise.

Our skeleton is vital in our health, as it provides the home for our muscles, organs, glands, and systems. For example, when our spine begins to deteriorate, such as with degenerative joint disease, our nerves become inflamed and reduced in function. If we can eliminate spinal degeneration, we can eliminate decreased bodily function, arthritis, and other inflammatory joint diseases. Proper exercise and nutrition are great protocols for increasing bone health. Let's look at how we can best increase this important part of our health.

TAKE CARE OF YOUR BONES

Neal was a truck driver who had been listening to my radio show regularly for a while. He called in and told me he had recently been feeling, as he put it, "down in his back." He drove five days a week, for twelve to fifteen hours per day, and had done so for the last thirty years. He led a life of extreme wear and tear on his body, and now excruciating pain throbbed down his left leg into his foot. That indicated that there might be something wrong in his lower back with possible nerve damage, so I asked him to come into the clinic.

Neal came in hunched over, unable to straighten and stand erect. His pain was so intense that he assumed a wheelchair would be his next means of transportation. We ran several tests, including X-rays and an MRI, to find out with what we were dealing. Neal had a deteriorating disc and joint in his lower back around the fourth and fifth lumbar. He had degenerative joint disease that had decreased the width of the disc between the spinal bones to the point where it was causing irritation to his nerves—thus the pain traveling down the leg.

His orthopedic doctor wanted him to have surgery, but had first referred him to my office. The spine is an amazing piece of the human anatomy, and it has the ability to regenerate, just like every other part. I began using spinal decompression, a way of restoring an intervetebral disc back to its normal state. Through a series of spinal decompression treatments, his normal function began to return.

In accordance with the Health Triangle, I also examined his mental and chemical functions. His blood work revealed that he had high phosphorus levels and low levels of calcium. His excessive phosphorus content was causing his bones to become weak and brittle, and was breaking down the bone enamel. This causes the bones in the spine to degenerate faster than normal. We increased absorbable calcium in his body and lowered his phosphorus intake, and the degeneration ceased. After only two months of therapy, his back began to improve drastically, and now he is driving his normal routes, having successfully avoided surgery altogether.

Our skeleton plays such an important role in our overall health. If the structure is out of balance, we are out of balance.

OSTEOPOROSIS AND BONE DENSITY

Osteoporosis has become a twenty-first century epidemic. It results in more deaths among women than ovarian and breast cancer combined. With osteoporosis, men and women as young as forty can suffer intense bone pain, muscle weakness, and difficulty walking. Conventional medical approaches to treating osteoporosis have traditionally been with calcium and estrogen replacement therapies. But taking estrogen to treat osteoporosis is the equivalent to burning down a barn to get rid of the mice.

Heavy exposure to estrogen over a woman's lifetime increases the risk of cancer—particularly breast cancer. This fact has been largely overshadowed by the fact that estrogen increases the body's absorption capacity, which in turn increases bone mass. Estrogen levels are so closely linked to bone mass that researchers now tell us that they can predict a woman's cumulative lifetime exposure to estrogen simply by measuring her bone mass. The higher the bone mass, the more exposure a woman has had to estrogen; the greater the estrogen exposure, the greater the risk of developing breast cancer.

Calcium bone levels are being depleted because calcium levels in American diets are not sufficient to reverse the onset of osteoporosis, and phosphorus levels in food are increasing. Currently, only children under the age of eleven are getting sufficient calcium in their diets to replace what is lost during bone remodeling (the lifelong process in which old bone is removed from the skeleton and new bone is added). At adolescence and early adulthood, more calcium loss occurs than can be replaced from diet alone—and this becomes worse with age. Calcium becomes more difficult to assimilate due to the lack of sufficient digestive acids. Limited exposure to the sun results in lower body levels of vitamin D, a vitamin that is essential for strong bones and proper calcium assimilation.

Interestingly, the reason that many people crave sodas is because their bodies are deficient in phosphoric acid, which is a key ingredient in all soda drinks. If you find yourself craving soft drinks, take organic phosphorus in a liquid form, which you will find at your local health food store, to replenish the levels and support proper bone health. You can easily take in adequate amounts of phosphorus by adding a milliliter to each gallon of water you drink.

GOAT'S MILK—NATURE'S REMEDY

Most people think cow's milk is a great source of calcium and a healthy drink. While cow's milk does contain calcium, it is a common misconception that cow's milk is always good for us. We undoubtedly need calcium, especially as we age. Women in their thirties and forties and those on estrogen replacement therapy should get at least 1,000 milligrams of calcium daily. I recommend that postmenopausal women not on estrogen get approximately 1,500 milligrams daily, and most men should get approximately 1,000 to 1,200 milligrams daily. I also recommend you obtain vitamin D from a whole food organic source rather than take a calcium supplement or drink more cow's milk, and this is available in one product alone—goat's milk yogurt. By eating one eight-ounce serving of plain goat's milk yogurt a day (with no added sugar), your body can assimilate all the calcium it needs.

Like cow's milk, goat's milk is low in essential fatty acids (EFAs), because goats and cows have EFA-destroying bacteria in their stomachs. But goat's milk is reported to contain more of the essential linoleic fatty acids (omega-3 and -6), in addition to a higher proportion of short-chain and medium-chain fatty acids, which are easier for intestinal enzymes to digest. Goat's milk does not contain agglutinin (a protein found only in cow's milk). Consequently, the fat globules in goat's milk do not cluster together as they do in cow's milk, which also makes them easier to digest.[1]

210

Goat milk protein forms a softer curd (the protein clumps that are formed by the action of your stomach acid on the protein), which makes the protein more easily and rapidly digestible. Goat's milk may also have advantages when it comes to allergies. It contains only trace amounts of an allergenic casein protein, alpha-S1, found in cow's milk. Goat's milk casein is more similar to human milk, yet cow's milk and goat's milk contain similar levels of the other allergenic protein, beta lactoglobulin. Goat's milk also contains slightly lower levels of lactose (4.1 percent versus 4.7 percent in cow's milk), which may be a small advantage for people who are lactose-intolerant.

In children under two years of age, goat's milk has often been called the "orphan formula." When a woman cannot breast-feed, goat's milk is one of the best forms of milk or dairy product you can give a child because it contains highly absorbable calcium.[2] Goat's milk has the highest assimilated forms of calcium over any other kind of dairy product, and it provides profound nutritional benefits. Goat's milk and goat milk products are available at most health food stores and some larger conventional grocers.

In addition to consuming more goat's milk products, here are some great ways to keep a strong skeletal system:

- Exercise with weights five to six days per week.
- Get plenty of sunshine to help your body form vitamin D.
- Have your blood checked twice per year for calcium, magnesium, and phosphorus levels.

By incorporating a few of these simple changes into your lifestyle, you can avoid the onset of osteoporosis and keep your structure strong. Start by making little changes—enjoy a cup of goat's milk yogurt during the day and go outside to soak up some sunlight during your lunch break. Over time, these small steps can equal big improvements in your health!

19

THE BODY'S FIRST LINE OF DEFENSE
The Lymphatic System

"Be careful about reading health books. You may die of a misprint."

—MARK TWAIN

The body has its own system for eliminating toxins and foreign substances, called the lymphatic system. Every single day, the air we breathe, the water we bathe in and drink, the environment in which we live, and the activities we choose determine the levels of toxins that enter our bodies. Our lymphatic system is like a toxin pump, flushing poisons out. God designed the lymphatic system to rid the body of these toxins.

Jill is a wife, a mother of three, and a grandmother of ten. She had been diagnosed with high blood pressure years ago, and came into my office after developing a new pain under her arm near her breast. Nodules and large knots were present that concerned me. I sent her to be tested for cancer, and thankfully, the results showed the lumps to be benign. The tests revealed that the lumps were inflamed and swollen lymph nodes. The doctors wanted to put her on prednisone and other drugs to reduce the inflammation.

She was not feeling comfortable with their diagnosis, and returned to my office to give me the report. She didn't understand why these lumps were there in the first place. Jill's immune system was suppressed and her white blood cell count was high, while her platelets were extremely low. She was still dealing with the high blood pressure that had previously been diagnosed. She had begun implementing some lifestyle changes, and told me she would try to exercise more. Then she revealed another issue. "Oh, by the way, I smoke," she said.

That explained a lot. She smoked heavily, up to two packs per day, didn't exercise, and sat at a desk in front of a computer all day. No movement on the outside and no movement on the inside made Jill a toxic woman.

I told her that her high blood pressure and swollen lymph nodes were all interrelated. Her body was filled with toxins and getting no air and no movement, and if she didn't change something soon, cancer was the inevitable conclusion. Jill started walking five days a week, and I also recommended that she go outside and take full, deep breaths for five minutes, two times per day. Then I told her about a great tool for stimulating the lymph systems—the mini trampoline. I suggested that Jill jump each day for five minutes and work up to twenty minutes. This is one of the greatest tools to help lower blood pressure and clean out the lymphatic system. We then corrected her structural issues, balanced her neurotransmitters, and replaced the nutritional deficiencies that we found in her blood work.

But Jill had to do this work on her own. She had to become selfless and think outside herself, focusing on people who needed her, such as her husband, children, and grandchildren. I told Jill, "Think about your family when you are tired and don't feel like walking, jumping, taking your supplements, or eating well. You must be 'others' focused." And that is truly what she became.

By following the regimen, her body began to rid itself of toxins and restore its function. In about eight weeks, I reexamined her and was amazed. Her lymph node inflammation was gone, she had lost forty pounds, and even more amazing, her blood pressure was normal, and she no longer needed high blood pressure medication. She also had quit smoking. I was simultaneously shocked and proud of such an accomplishment. "Why did you quit smoking?" I asked her.

She smiled and said, "When I look at my grandkids and see the excitement and joy in their eyes, I want them to be as healthy as they can possibly be as they continue to grow. I realized that I am their example, and what kind of example was I being?"

Not only did Jill get her health back, she got herself back, and her family got an incredible role model.

FIRST LINE OF DEFENSE

The makeup of the lymphatic system is much like the circulatory system—a system of thin tubes called lymph vessels branch through us like the arteries and veins that traverse the body. Instead of blood, however, the lymphatic system carries a liquid called "lymph." Lymph is a clear fluid that circulates to the body tissues.

The lymphatic system defends the body from foreign invasion by disease-causing toxins such as viruses, bacteria, and fungi. Lymphatic vessels also prevent the dangerous backup of lymph fluid so that the fluid can continue to flow and carry those deadly toxins with it. The vessels have specialized organs called lymph nodes, which filter out destroyed microorganisms that would harm the body if left in circulation.

Let's look at the lymphatic system from the microscopic level. White blood cells seek to remove dangerous toxins and foreign substances that are harmful to the body. If a white blood cell senses unwanted bacteria in the blood, it will find these bacteria and encase them. After a type of white blood cell known as a T-cell has the bacteria trapped, it releases a deadly toxin that destroys the bacteria. In other words, your body is constantly battling and eliminating harmful substances, and the lymph system manages this complex and essential process.[1]

You have lymph nodes in your neck, under your arms, and in the groin area. When you get sick, your throat often becomes "lumpy." Those lumps are your lymph nodes in full battle mode. They are filled with the toxins that are making you feel ill and are attempting to rid the body of them. You also have lymph nodes that you can't feel located in your abdomen region, pelvis, and chest cavity.

Most people know we have these organs, but are often unaware that they are all related and connected. Besides the lymph nodes, the lymphatic system includes the spleen, thymus, tonsils, and adenoids.

As children, the first surgery many of us ever undergo is a removal of the tonsils. They are removed at the first sign of dysfunction, despite the fact that they are a part of the very system that helps prevent future problems. I'd recommend keeping your tonsils as long as possible.

The lymphatic system is one of the first lines of defense against cancer. If cancer cells break away from a tumor, which is how cancer becomes systemic (attacking the entire body), they often become stuck in the nearest lymph nodes. The nodes trap the cells in an attempt to keep the deadly disease from affecting more systems. This is why doctors check the lymph nodes first when they are trying to determine how far a cancer has spread.

The lymph system performs countless essential bodily processes such as draining excess fluid into the bloodstream. As the blood circulates, fluid leaks out into the body tissues. The lymph vessels transport fluid away from the tissue and return it to the blood stream.

Remember that all the body's systems are connected, including the lymph system. In fact, lymph contains a high number of white blood cells. Plasma leaks out of the capillaries to surround the body tissues, and then drains into the lymph vessels. It all works together to make you work![2]

WARNING SIGNS

Several conditions let doctors know to check your lymph system for poor drainage. The first and best indication is any kind of infection. The most common infections that indicate a lymph drainage problem are ear, nose, and throat infections, common colds, and upper and lower respiratory infections. Often, structural problems such as tennis elbow and sore knees also indicate issues in the lymph system. If you often feel run down, have cold hands and feet, swelling in the ankles, or numbness in the extremities, these are strong indications to evaluate the lymph system. This is critical because excessive fluid concentration is not clinically observable until the level is far above normal. Consequently, there may be no outward sign of poor lymphatic drainage until the condition becomes significantly worse.

BREATHE YOUR WAY TO LYMPH HEALTH

Like the cardiovascular system, the lymphatic system is made up of channels and valves. Unlike the cardiovascular system, however, the lymphatic system lacks any central organ (like the heart) to pump lymph throughout the lymph vessels. Instead, the lymphatic system depends on muscular movement, gravity, and breathing to move lymph fluid throughout the body. The lymph drains into the blood through two ducts at the base of the neck, and breathing is the fuel that drives this action. When you take in a deep breath and fully exhale, this massages the ducts so that the fluid flows more freely.

Proper breathing is critical for correct lymphatic function. But there is a wrong way and a right way to breathe. We typically breathe from the chest in a rapid and shallow manner. However, deep breathing is best, especially when it comes to the lymph system. I recommend taking a few minutes each day to practice deep breathing.

Here is a breathing exercise designed to promote proper lymph drainage. It is called the Bellows Breathing Technique (or the Stimulating Breath):

- Sit in an upright position with your spine straight.

- With your mouth closed, breathe in and out of your nose as rapidly as possible. Think of using a bicycle pump to pump up a tire. Both the inhalation and exhalation are equal in length.

- The rate of breathing is rapid with as many as two to three cycles of inspiration and expiration per second.

- While performing the exercise, you should feel effort at the base of the neck, chest, and abdomen. The muscles in these areas will increase in strength the more you practice this technique.

- Do this for no longer than fifteen seconds at first. Over time, increase the length of the exercise by five seconds each time. Do it as long as you are comfortably able, not exceeding one full minute.

- There is a risk for hyperventilation that can result in loss of consciousness if this exercise is overutilized in the beginning. For this reason, it should be practiced in a safe place such as a bed or chair and should be practiced with sense and moderation.

"BOUNCING" THE LYMPH SYSTEM

Anything that can stimulate the movement of lymph fluid inside the lymph vessels is beneficial, and one of the most efficient ways to stimulate the flow of lymph fluid is by jumping on a mini trampoline. Bouncing up and down on a trampoline may not sound like a strenuous aerobic exercise, but that is a misconception. Rebounding, as it is often called, is a safe, low-impact exercise that actually burns more calories than jogging.

The lymph fluid travels through channels (similar to blood vessels) that are filled with one-way valves to ensure that the lymph fluid also flows in the same direction to prevent a backup of fluid. The main groups of lymph vessels run up the legs, arms, and torso. That is why the vertical bouncing movement of rebounding is so effective to maintain the proper flow of fluid. The up and down motion causes the lymph valves to open and close simultaneously, increasing lymph flow dramatically.

Start rebounding, even if you can only jump for a few minutes at a time. You will start to feel immediate calming of the digestive system as well as the knowledge that you are greatly aiding your lymph system's proper function.

DETOXIFY THE LYMPH SYSTEM THROUGH SWEAT

The skin is our body's largest organ, with an intricate system exquisitely created to eliminate toxins from the body. It's known as perspiration! Many people simply don't sweat enough. Antiperspirants, artificial environments, smog, synthetic clothing, and a physically idle lifestyle all serve to clog skin pores and inhibit the healthy flow of perspiration.

For thousands of years, people of all cultures have indulged in the soothing warmth of sweat baths. The Romans are known for their elaborate baths. The legendary Turkish bath has been popular in Asia and Europe for centuries. Hippocrates, the founder of Western medicine, said more than two thousand years ago, "Give me the power to create a fever, and I shall cure any disease." The artificial fever created by steam bathing works as an immune system stimulant by increasing the number of white blood cells in the body. In addition, the raised temperature reduces the growth rate of most bacteria and viruses, giving the immune system time to mobilize its own forces.[3]

Sweat therapy is one of the most effective and painless detoxifying treatments available. As the pores open up and the millions of sweat glands start to excrete, the body rids itself of metabolic and other waste products. Heat speeds up the chemical processes in the body, making steam and sauna bathing one of the simplest and most comfortable ways to rid the body of accumulated toxins. It's time to bring this fundamental cleansing and healing therapy into our modern lives. If you don't have access to a sauna or steam bath, a hot shower is a great substitute, provided you use a shower filter to eliminate the chlorine and toxins. Sweating naturally during activity is also beneficial, but be sure to drink plenty of fluids to replace the water that is lost. Do not wear excessive clothing or garbage bags in order to sweat more. It is simply unwise to cause your body to sweat more than it would on its own because this can quickly lead to dehydration. Just let your body perspire naturally.

THE BODY'S FIRST LINE OF DEFENSE—The Lymphatic System

We were given this system to flush poisons out of our bodies. The lymphatic system is truly our first line of defense against sickness and disease. Make the effort to build up your defenses by helping your lymphatic system do its job and flush toxins from the body. Take more deep breaths during the day, jump on a mini trampoline, and don't be afraid to do a little sweating!

PART V

ASA PRESCRIPTIONS

20

AVOIDING THE TOP DISEASES
Beating the Odds

"The deviation of man from the state in which he was origially placed by nature seems to have proved to him a prolific source of disease."

—EDWARD JENNER

Now you know about all three sides to the Health Triangle: how the mental and chemical sides can affect each other and that the structural side ties all the system together. In the following chapters, we will uncover the secret to exercise and weight loss—and that is that there are no secrets. It requires genuine effort and a desire to feel better, but it is attainable, and we will discover how. We will also briefly discuss weight management (but the best weight management tools are given throughout this book, and not confined to a single chapter). Every food choice, supplementation, and lifestyle choice we make affects the entire body, including your weight. We will also address the concept of rest and discuss how to prevent the onset of the most prevalent diseases we face today.

No cure, natural or otherwise, can guarantee a lifetime free of sickness or disease. However, we have been given the knowledge of positive steps we can take that lessen our exposure to chemicals, pollutants, and toxins, and through the advances of modern medicine (such as diagnostic blood work), we can now determine where we have deficiencies. Then we can correct them! It is truly an amazing gift—the ability to choose a healthy lifestyle.

LIFESTYLES THAT BREED DISEASE

I walked into my patient exam room and saw Samantha. She wore a brave smile and a look of anticipation. Cancer had run rampant in her family for generations. Her great-grandmother had colon cancer; her great-grandfather had cancer of the prostate; her grandmother suffered from leukemia; her grandfather had skin cancer; her mother had breast cancer; and now Samantha, in her early 40s, had a lump in her breast. She went to an oncologist to remove the lump. Thankfully, the tumor was benign, and doctors believed they were able to remove all of it. She had also been diagnosed with type 2 diabetes and was taking insulin to help regulate the condition.

I assured her that just because her other family members suffered with cancer didn't mean she had to. Most diseases are lifestyle and diet related. We usually aren't born with these conditions, but through poor dietary and lifestyle choices, our bodies produce harmful cells that create cancer, heart disease, diabetes, and others.

Remember the good news—if we can *lifestyle* our way in, then we can *lifestyle* our way out. Although Samantha faced an early breast cancer scare, and the doctors believed they successfully removed all the tumor, in actuality, her lifestyle choices, influenced by her genetic predispositions, had caused the lump to develop in the first place; and if she didn't make certain lifestyle changes, the lump would most likely come back and next time may not be benign. Benjamin Franklin once said, "Insanity is doing the same thing over and over and expecting a different result." And he was right. Samantha had to make radical changes to achieve radical new results in her health.

I assured her that we could get her body working normally again if she was willing to do some work. Before she left that day, I told her, "Samantha, regardless of your fears or how you're feeling right now, I want you to know something—you can get well."

With a tear rolling down her cheek, Samantha said, "I've been to doctors all my life, and I've never had anyone tell me that. Thank you, Dr. Asa. I'm ready to do whatever it takes to get well." Samantha's attitude is the necessary one to overcome your afflictions and to become well again.

Diseases are frightening, intimidating, and overwhelming. However, getting educated on your body processes, focusing on what you can and cannot control, and deciding that you want to get well are some great places

224

to start. In the next few pages, we will discuss the top four diseases that plague our nation and discover some of the ways that Natural Medicine can help you avoid these common afflictions. All you have to do is adjust your mind, get ready to learn, and implement some changes—everything else will follow.

CANCER

Cancer is formed when the body cannot make healthy cells, and instead makes abnormal cells, or cancer cells. Some tumors are benign, which means the cells do not invade surrounding tissues and do not spread to other parts of the body; other tumors are cancerous or malignant, in which the cells invade and destroy nearby tissues.

If you are diagnosed with cancer, your oncologist will most likely design a personal cancer protocol for you. But you can also fight the disease by following a three-week liver detoxification protocol followed by a four- to six-month antivirus/antiparasite protocol, followed by another eighteen-month standard anticancer protocol. These protocols involve eating raw foods and whole food extracts that will enhance detoxification and the removal of parasites and viruses. Not all of your raw food intake will be eaten; some of it should be taken in the form of supplement capsules. In addition, see chapter 9 in the headache protocols for the liver cleanse I recommend.

While working with your oncologist and receiving traditional treatments, including radiation and chemotherapy, strengthen your body's own immune system by implementing Natural Medicine strategies such as proper food intake, plenty of antioxidants, and regular exercise. By doing so, you will give yourself the best chance for survival and recovery.

Natural Medicine seeks to provide natural ways to fight cancer, such as proper food for healthy cell growth and powerful antioxidants to fight oxidation and further damage to cells. When surgery and radiation are needed, then we must do it all. If you

Cancer Prevention Super Foods

Pineapple	Kiwi
Corn	Aloe vera
Yellow peppers	Broccoli
Mustard	Spinach
Tumeric	Green peppers
Green peas	Green olives
Lettuce	Horseradish
Courgettes	Avocados
Green Grapes	

are faced with that decision, then make it your goal to get all three sides of the Health Triangle in balance. Give your body the means to protect its good, healthy cells, and then use the conventional cancer therapies to eliminate the cancer cells. It's not an either/or situation. Physicians of all specialties work together as a team with the goal of restoring you to extraordinary health.

CHEMOTHERAPY AND PHYTONUTRIENTS

Chemotherapy is used to shrink tumors and keep the cells from migrating in the body. Unfortunately, poisoning the cells with chemo does not always seem to work. Even a more recent treatment, target chemotherapy, which targets specific cells, does not have a consistently effective medical track record.

One of the nation's most respected cancer experts, Guy Faguet, explained the battle over chemotherapy and its effect on cancer: "Three decades later, the process of anticancer drug development remains mostly anchored on this century-old, conceptually antiquated, technically inefficient, labor-intensive, costly, and low-yield 'hit and miss' screening approach engineered and sponsored by the National Cancer Institute."[1]

But there is more hope for survival through phytonutrients, compounds found in plant-derived foods. Because each cancer is different and each patient is unique, a phytonutrient protocol should be specifically designed for your body's needs. Regardless of whether or not you choose radiation or surgery, the best course for success is achieved when you incorporate a phytonutrient protocol in addition to any other treatments. For a complete list of phytonutrient-rich food sources, see chapter 9. Here are my recommendations for making phytonutrients part of your health protocol:

- Drink "green drinks" three times daily. Green drinks contain grasses, sprouted grains, and green vegetables, which infuse your body with easily absorbable vitamins, minerals, and amino acids. They usually come in a powder form and mix easily with water or juice. Many varieties of green drinks are available at most health food stores, and a number of conventional grocery stores now carry them as well.

- Take buffered vitamin C (as many milligrams to bowel tolerance) daily.

- Take 800 IU of vitamin E daily.

- Take one to three tablespoons omega-3 oil (including cod liver oil) daily.

THE FEMALE PLIGHT—BREAST CANCER

If you are a woman, you are probably aware of the critical risk factors for breast cancer (but be aware that men, too, can get breast cancer). Some of the classic factors include age, early onset of menstruation, delayed childbirth or inability to conceive, a family member who has had breast cancer, lumps in the breast tissue, and any diagnosis of atypical hyperplasia (increase in cell numbers causing organs or tissues to grow to abnormal sizes).

These risks are considered so important doctors urge women to get annual mammograms and learn how to administer breast self-examinations, and many women are prescribed anti-breast cancer drugs. Many women who had several high-risk situations have resorted to having single or double mastectomies.

Several cancer experts have claimed that Tamoxifen, an anticancer prevention drug, has been a wonder drug in preventing breast cancer. The drug Herceptin is believed to cut the risk of breast cancer recurrence in half. However, the drugs were found to be cardiotoxic, causing heart disease and death in a small number of women. If you must use these drugs, give your body everything possible to fight the disease naturally. These drugs offer some dangers, but it may be even more dangerous to do absolutely nothing. Consult with your physician to find out what you can actively do to decrease your risk of cancer or speed recovery.

Here are some steps to help lower your risk of developing or experiencing the recurrence of breast cancer and other forms of cancer:

- Stay away from synthetic hormone supplementation.

- Quit smoking and begin exercising. You can cut your odds of getting breast cancer by exercising regularly.

- Eat more fruits and vegetables, especially anticancer foods such as kale, beets, collard greens, brussels sprouts, and broccoli.

- Use a filtration system to remove the chlorine from your bathing, showering, and drinking water.

- Go outside and get some sunlight. High levels of vitamin D from sunlight exposure are powerful anticancer agents.

THE MALE PLIGHT—PROSTATE CANCER

If you have been diagnosed with prostate cancer, as with any cancer, treatment and surgery will more than likely be recommended. However, if you do not treat the disease systematically—cleansing your entire body of toxins and diseases—you decrease your chances of survival. Removal of the prostate and radiation therapy may neglect the possibility of microscopic seeds of cancer spreading throughout the body and planting themselves in tissue and bone.

Most men with prostate cancer do have systemic prostate cancer, the type of cancer that is not localized in one area of the body. Those who survive typically have enhanced immunity or a response system that destroys the cancer cells and seeds, no matter where they end up in the body. Unfortunately, there is no medical procedure that can improve the body's natural defense mechanisms. The only thing that can help is to have a strong immune system, and the body's defensive mechanisms will help keep you alive, even after a cancer diagnosis.

A study at the University of California at Los Angeles found a correlation between pomegranates and prostate cancer. After patients underwent surgeries and radiation treatments, doctors monitored their PSA (prostate specific antigen) levels, which helps determine if there are cancer cells in the prostate. If the PSA levels were out of an acceptable range, that indicated the presence of cancer. Once the PSA levels began increasing, more conventional treatments were pursued.

The California study involved forty-six patients, and ones whose PSA levels were detectable following treatment drank eight ounces of pomegranate juice a day. PSA levels in the men who drank the pomegranate juice took twice as long to double. Researchers concluded that pomegranate juice may slow the progression of prostate cancer; however, the evidence remains inconclusive. Nevertheless, there is no reason that pomegranate juice should not be added to an anticancer prostate protocol. Here are my recommendations for restoring or maintaining a healthy prostate, some of which are the same as the protocols for breast cancer:

- Eat more fruits and vegetables, especially anticancer foods such as kale, beets, collard greens, brussels sprouts, and broccoli.

- Use a filtration system to remove the chlorine from your bathing, showering, and drinking water.

- Go outside and get some sunlight. High levels of vitamin D from sunlight exposure are powerful anticancer agents.

- Take 50 to 100 milligrams of zinc daily.

- Take 8 to 10 grams of pumpkin seed oil daily.

- Take 1,500 milligrams of saw palmetto daily.

- Make sure that one-third of your daily caloric intake consists of healthy fats such as cod liver oil, fish, coconut oil, nuts, and avocados.

SYSTEMIC PROTOCOLS FOR CANCER

Here are some points to remember about cancer. Those with genetic predispositions to cancer (other family members faced cancer) should:

1. Avoid foods that contain mercury, gallium, and thallium such as farm-raised fish. Consume only fish caught in the wild, and even then limit your intake. Fish oils such as cod liver oil—one of my foundational four supplements—are a great way to get the essential oils found in fish while avoiding toxic effects.

2. Have all silver, amalgam-mercury fillings removed from your mouth to avoid mercury toxicity.

3. Take a liquid B12 supplement (the scientific name is adenosylcobalamin).

4. Increase immune function by taking magnesium and potassium chloride.

5. Eat plenty of vegetables, including broccoli (a natural methyl conversion food).

6. Avoid all dairy products except goat's milk. The lactose in cow's milk will increase risk for the disease.

7. Eat super foods (see the following graph for list of super foods).

HEART AND VASCULAR DISEASE

Heart disease has been a personal issue for me throughout the years because my greatest hero dealt with it in his mid-thirties. His name was Ben Ellingson, but I will always call my grandfather "Pap." He was the epitome of a man's man—an avid farmer, bull rider, and rodeo champion. He was my champion, too. Pap was highly active, had a strong work ethic, and was an exemplary husband, father, and friend. It was 1950, and he and his family (including my mother) lived in Palm Springs, California, where Pap worked as a horse breeder and trainer. You may recall an old TV show called *The Lone Ranger*. My grandfather was the one who bred and raised most of the horses used to play "Silver" on the program over the years. *Hi, ho, Silver away,* indeed!

Because of the amount of time he spent breeding horses, he had not been able to work on the farm and compete in rodeos as he once did, and he was getting no daily exercise. After several years, he decided to move his breeding and farming operation to Tennessee. He drove out ahead of the family to make the necessary preparations for the move. As he was driving back to California to pick up the family, he stopped in Arizona for the night. Sitting in a hotel room and exhausted from the long drive, he began to feel a pain in his chest that slowly crept down his left arm. The next thing he knew, he was lying in a hospital bed having suffered from a major heart attack. At only thirty-six years old, *how could this be?*

He was moved to St. Thomas Hospital in Nashville, Tennessee, to be put under the supervision of Dr. Thomas Frist Sr., a world-renowned heart specialist. After careful monitoring in the hospital

Heart/Vascular Disease Prevention Super Foods

Broccoli	Beetroot
Watercress	Watermelon
Red Grapes	Red Peppers
Blueberries	Tomatoes
Blue plums	Huckleberries
Blackcurrant	Lingonberries
Blackberries	Rowanberries
Bilberries	Hibiscus
Black grapes	Ginger
Black olives	

for a month, Dr. Frist released him, but strictly warned him to not do anything strenuous. He was to stay indoors, never exert himself, and be on a restrictive diet for the rest of his life! These orders were not unusual, but rather were the standard way of thinking at the time in regard to heart attack survivors.

He returned to his new home in Loretto, Tennessee, a five-hundred-acre farm complete with cattle, horses, peacocks, and chickens. Stay indoors and in bed? That just wasn't Pap's style. The next morning at five o'clock, he began milking the cows, rounding up cattle, and feeding the chickens. This was his routine every day, and his strength slowly returned to him a little more each morning. He also had the benefit an all-organic diet because everything the family ate was raised or grown on the farm (of course, my granny's world-famous cooking didn't hurt, either). Once a month, he went to see Dr. Frist for a checkup. Just one year after his heart attack, the doctors were amazed at the state of his overall health. His heart had reduced in size and was no longer swollen, his arteries were clean, and his blood pressure was within the ideal range.

My grandfather's story of extraordinary recovery became a landmark study and sparked research on heart health and the power of an organic diet and exercise. My Pap lifestyled his way out of his health challenge. He could have listened to the doctors and sat idly by as his life slipped away. But he chose to overcome. He set the standard for the importance that the medical field places on exercise, lifestyle, and diet choices for heart health today.

It's next to impossible to find anyone who has not lost a friend or loved one to heart disease—it is the second leading killer in the United States. Carefully monitoring risk factors, knowing your genetic tendencies, and keeping the heart healthy with proper diet and exercise are absolutely critical.

THE TRUTH ABOUT YOUR HEART

There are several real risk factors for heart disease to consider. In the 1970s, an amino acid called homocysteine was discovered, which is thought to be one of the culprits behind heart disease. Homocysteine is a by-product of methionine, an amino acid found in luncheon meats and high-fat pork products such as bacon, bologna, sausage, ham, and hot dogs. Studies found that high levels of homocysteine produced high levels of arterial plaque formation.

Elevated blood levels of homocysteine have been linked to increased risk of premature coronary artery disease, stroke, and thromboembolism (venous blood clots), even among people who have normal cholesterol levels. Abnormal homocysteine levels appear to contribute to heart disease in at least three ways: a direct toxic effect that damages the cells lining the inside of the arteries, interference with clotting factors, and oxidation of low-density lipoproteins (LDL), or good cholesterol.

As mentioned earlier, it is believed that high levels of homocysteine produce high levels of arterial plaque formation. But it is quite simple to naturally correct high levels of arterial plaque formation. Two ways to achieve this are through food choices—whole eggs are a good option—and supplements such as vitamin B6, vitamin B12, lecithin, and folic acid. Vitamins B6, and B12, and folic acid convert homocysteine back to methionine and help eliminate it from the body. Whole eggs contain coline, which removes plaque off the walls of the arteries. Lecithin liquefies fat and removes it from the body.

CHOLESTEROL—KEEPING IT UNDER CONTROL

Heart attacks have also long been associated with high cholesterol levels. The theory is that if you eat foods high in cholesterol, you will have high blood cholesterol levels, and this will cause you to have a heart attack. However, this theory is not necessarily true. Cholesterol is a modified fat called sterol, which mimics a wax more than it does a fat or oil. Your liver naturally produces cholesterol, and as mentioned earlier, if you tried to eliminate it from your diet, your body would simply produce it on its own. Researchers and doctors cite high cholesterol as the main cause for heart disease, but eating cholesterol *does not* necessarily cause high levels of cholesterol.

There are plenty of natural ways to lower your cholesterol level to a healthy range, which is generally around 200. One of the chief ways to keep your cholesterol at this level is to avoid hydrogenated oils. Canola oil is a prime example—when canola oil is heated and a hydrogen atom is added (a catalyst called nickel commonly found in cookware), the product becomes solid. It is important to note that *nothing in nature* eats hydrogenated fat except humans. It is extremely toxic and is labeled on food items as trans fats; that's why it is important to read all food labels.

In 2006 the FDA required food companies to list the presence or absence of trans fats in their products, and the amount of trans fat present. A word of caution: The phrase "zero trans fats" does not ensure that the product is totally free of trans fats. If there is any mention of hydrogenated oils or partially hydrogenated oils, that product does contain some form of trans fat. Even in small amounts, hydrogenated oils are not recommended. As a matter of fact, just 1.5 milligrams of hydrogenated oil is enough to change our bodies' cellular structure and DNA.[2]

Protocol for lowering cholesterol:

- Red yeast rice—200 milligrams daily

- Vitamin B-3 (niacin)—1,000 milligrams daily

- Co-Q-10—1 milligram per pound of body weight

- Vitamin C—1,000 to 3,000 milligrams daily

- Selenium—100 micrograms daily

HIGH BLOOD PRESSURE—THE RED FLAG

Experts in the field of health and the majority of Americans now recognize that high blood pressure is almost always a precursor to both strokes and heart attacks. In fact, hypertension (high blood pressure) is the number one reason patients visit their physicians, and the treatment of hypertension is responsible for the single highest use of prescription drugs.

It seems that patient awareness of hypertension is on the rise; 85 percent of the adult population in the United States has their blood pressure taken regularly.[3] Blood pressure is the force your arteries use to push blood through the arteries and venous system. This process is analogous to a water hose—if the hose is larger than the amount of water flowing through it, water does not back up. However, if the hose is smaller than the force of water attempting to go through it, the water cannot move through freely, and begins to build back up. In the human heart, when vascular resistance increases, the heart must work harder to overcome this resistance. As a result, the blood backs up much like the water in the narrow hose, and this causes hypertension.

Over the years, medical experts have argued over exactly what level of high blood pressure is too high. After years of research to discover at what blood pressure the body begins to exhibit adverse effects, a 1988 report of the

Joint National Committee on Detection, Evaluation, and Treatment of High Blood Pressure reported that blood pressure above or equal to 140/90 is considered to be high.[4] This does not mean, however, that if your blood pressure is 139/89, you are not at risk.

When going to the doctor to have your blood pressure checked, you are typically given numbers that represent how well your heart is functioning, such as 140/90, which is a higher than average blood pressure range. To understand the meaning of these numbers, you need to understand the beating cycle of the heart. The heart has two basic phases—systole and diastole. In the diastole phase, the heart relaxes and fills with blood. This corresponds to the number on the bottom, or 90 in this example. In the systole phase, the heart squeezes and pumps the blood into the arteries. This corresponds to the number on top, or 140. As blood is forced through the venous system, the measurement is 140. Between beats, or in the resting phase, the pressure is 90.

When a person is diagnosed with high blood pressure, health insurance rates soar. That means this problem not only affects you—it also affects your wallet. High blood pressure, high cholesterol, and high triglycerides cause insurance rates to increase because insurance companies do not want to offer coverage to unhealthy people. Insurance companies see such individuals as "walking time bombs."

Insurance companies have a valid reason to hike rates after a high blood pressure diagnosis—blood pressure is statistically linked to life expectancy. The following statistics show just how critical the correlation is between blood pressure and the length of your life:

At age thirty-five: If your blood pressure is 120/80, you are expected to live forty-one more years. If your blood pressure is 150/100, you are expected to live twenty-five more years.

At age forty-five: If your blood is 120/80, you are expected to live about thirty-two more years. If your blood pressure is 150/100, you are expected to live another twenty-three years.

At age fifty-five: If your blood pressure is 150/100, you are expected to live only seventeen more years.[5]

Statistics like these scare countless people into doctors' offices for pills to fix their problems, but there is good news—you do not have to take prescription drugs to lower your blood pressure. The greatest medicine you can ever use is food. Food is powerful; it can completely change the biochemistry in your body. Instead of turning to a pill to fix your problems, turn to your lifestyle choices. Change the way you view things; change the way you do things; change your habits to include exercise; begin to *do things* that will affect your health positively.

HIGH BLOOD PRESSURE RISK FACTORS

Numerous risk factors have been linked to the development of hypertension. The list of contributing factors includes gender, race, obesity, tobacco use, diabetes, family history of hypertension, physical inactivity, stress, type A personality, caffeine abuse, dangerous amounts of fatty molecules in the blood, excessive alcohol intake, less than 30 grams of fiber in the diet, and over-consumption of animal fat and vegetable oil.

Some commonly used products have been pegged as contributing risk factors of hypertension and should be eliminated from the diet. These include caffeine, margarine or hydrogenated oils, pork products, shellfish, luncheon meat, alcohol, monosodium glutamate (MSG) found in many commercial oriental foods, and mainstream non-organic dairy products that are homogenized and pasteurized. To help fight hypertension, use only organic milk products and goat's milk yogurt, which is available at most health food stores. In addition, avoid traditional mayonnaise made with soybean oil and switch to a canola-oil based mayonnaise. Avoid traditional cooking oils and use organic butter or coconut oil instead. Other oils such as canola and olive oils break down under heat and become trans-fatty acids.

NutraSweet, or aspartame, interferes with the blood sugar regulation in the body, so avoid consuming products that contain this artificial sweetener.[6] Aspartame is also extremely toxic to the body because it is a neurotoxin (poisonous to the nervous system). It is even argued that the use of aspartame can actually cause people to gain weight because it disrupts the blood sugar levels in the body. That is not exactly what the makers of diet sodas would like us to believe.

SODIUM VS. POTASSIUM

Another significant factor that contributes to high blood pressure is the ratio of sodium to potassium in the diet. In many respects, potassium and sodium are chemically similar, although organisms in general—and animal cells in particular—treat them quite differently. Potassium is a soft silvery-white alkali metal that occurs naturally bound to other elements in seawater and many minerals, and unlike sodium, potassium is never found free in nature. Eating a variety of foods that contain potassium is the best way to get an adequate amount. Healthy individuals who eat a balanced diet rarely need potassium supplements. Foods with high sources of potassium include potatoes, bananas, avocados, apricots, pomegranates, kiwi, and turnips, although many other fruits, vegetables, and meats contain potassium.

Sodium plays a major role in maintaining healthy cell liquid levels. Pressure inside the cell maintains the liquid levels both inside and outside the cell to preserve a state of equilibrium. This pressure is maintained by sodium inside the cell and potassium outside the cell. Excess consumption of sodium produces an influx of water into the cells in the body and causes swelling. This produces an increase in pressure around the blood vessels, which leads to higher blood pressure in individuals who are susceptible.

Potassium works outside the cell to offset the effects of sodium. Most of us do not consume sufficient potassium, and this is compounded by the fact that the body does not conserve potassium as it does sodium. Therefore, the body is in a constant state of crisis as it tries to hold on to sodium, and that is what creates the imbalance. Although the body excretes potassium, it maintains more sodium than potassium because the levels of sodium in the typical diet are excessively high.

A question often asked is, "If I just cut down on my sodium intake, will that help reduce my blood pressure?" Unfortunately, simply eliminating sodium-rich food is not the answer. It's not the sodium content that's the problem—it's the ratio of sodium to potassium. When sodium levels far exceed those of potassium, susceptible individuals may become hypertensive. Sodium restriction alone may not reduce blood pressure, but can if accompanied by potassium supplementation.

Three separate studies confirm the benefits of increasing potassium in the diet. In one study, 10,000 adults monitored their dietary intake of seventeen nutrients. The results demonstrated an inverse relationship between the amount of potassium consumed and the average systolic blood pressure. The *American Journal of Clinical Nutrition* reported a comparison of ninety-eight vegetarians to a group of non-vegetarians. The average blood pressure for the vegetarian group was 126/77, and for the non-vegetarians, the average was 147/88. Both groups had similar sodium intake and excretion; however, the vegetarian group had significantly higher levels of potassium. In 1982, a medical journal called *The Lancet* reported that among patients with high blood pressure, those who received potassium supplementation had significantly lower blood pressure than those who received a placebo.

Be aware that many of the diuretics used to combat high blood pressure rapidly deplete the body's store of potassium. If you must take a diuretic, keep your electrolytes high and eat plenty of organic fruits and green leafy vegetables. Despite the possible ill effects of blood pressure medications, however, it is critical that you *do not* stop taking your high blood pressure medication without first discussing the issue with your physician. Take notes from this book, share them with your doctor, and get his or her professional opinion.

FIBER AND YOUR HEART

Fiber is an excellent weapon against high blood pressure. The U.S. recommended daily allowance of fiber is thirty grams per day, but most of us do not take in even half of the recommended amount. Monitor how much fiber you actually consume and you will be shocked—the Western diet is dangerously deficient in fiber.

Studies show that people who increase their dietary fiber experience a decrease in blood pressure. One study took 300 health food store customers—shoppers who were already health conscious—and increased their dietary fiber by 100 grams per week. The results showed a 3 to 4 mm difference in both systolic and diastolic pressures.[7]

People suffering from diabetes often have hypertension. In a research program, twelve diabetic men were placed on a special diet for two weeks. They consumed raw fruits, raw vegetables, and three times their normal dietary intake of fiber. After only two weeks, the men showed a 50 percent increase in potassium levels.

Researchers also changed the diet of thirty-two subjects so that 62 percent of their caloric intake came from raw foods. In less than seven months, the average diastolic blood pressure of the group dropped by 17.8 mm.[8] That is a significant decrease, which should give hope to all sufferers of high blood pressure.

If you begin to make dietary changes today—regardless of your blood pressure level—it won't be necessary to continue taking pills for the rest of your life, as you've likely been told. Dietary fiber should be increased to the recommended level of forty grams per day. This can be accomplished by eating whole grain, high-fiber cereals or through using natural fiber supplements. Remember, you have eaten your way into the condition you are now in, and *you can eat your way out.*

NUTS AND YOUR HEART

Nuts stand out as a powerhouse of nutrition and are an effective way to maintain good heart health. Studies have shown that eating 20 percent of your daily caloric intake in pistachio nuts can dramatically increase your levels of HDL cholesterol (the good cholesterol), and lower triglyceride levels by a remarkable 26 percent. The amazing part is that this drop was accomplished in just three weeks.[9] It's worthwhile to include nuts as a part of a healthy heart regimen such as almonds, walnuts, hazelnuts, brazil nuts, cashews, and macadamia nuts. However, avoid peanuts due to a highly allergenic mold found in most of them.

BEATING HYPERTENSION

Hypertensive patients typically possess low intake levels of vitamins A, C, and potassium. Alterations in calcium metabolism have also been implicated as a primary factor in the development of hypertension. Hypertensive patients also tend to excrete more calcium in their urine, thus increasing their dietary needs. So it is essential that people with hypertension add supplements to counteract the depletion of calcium.

Supplements not only treat the effects of hypertension on the body, but can also serve as a way to overcome the condition. One study concluded that the use of the following supplements significantly lowered blood pressure: Vitamin B complex (consisting of 50 milligrams of thiamine, 40 milligrams of riboflavin, 200 milligrams of pantothenate, and 200 milligrams of nicotinic acid), and 50 milligrams of lipoic acid. These supplements lowered blood levels of saturated fatty acids, while increasing polyunsaturated fatty acids, in as little as ten days.[10]

Magnesium helps regulate the function of smooth muscles such as those surrounding arteries at the cellular levels. It is a potent vasodilator, (a substance that reduces blood pressure by relaxing blood vessel walls), and hypertension is a symptom of its deficiency. If you look at profiles of most hypertensive people, most have a serious magnesium deficiency. The *British Medical Journal* reported that when twenty hypertensive patients were given magnesium supplementation for six months, the average blood pressure in the group dropped 12/8 mm—that's a significant decrease!

Coenzyme Q-10 (Co-Q-10) is a well-known nutrient that helps with hypertension. Co-Q-10 is an essential component of the organelles that are responsible for producing cellular energy. (An organelle is to the cell what an organ is to the body; think of them as tiny "cell compartments" that help cells manufacture energy.) Co-Q-10 can be synthesized in the body, but deficiencies related to hypertension have been reported.[11] When a cardiovascular disorder develops in the body, organelles and body tissue require increased levels of Co-Q-10 to help fight the disease and maintain energy levels.

Here are my recommended supplement protocols to reduce your risk of developing hypertension:

- Calcium citrate—1,000 to 1,200 milligrams per day.

- Magnesium—500 milligrams per day before bed.

- Coenzyme Q-10—30 milligrams twice per day.

- Vitamin C (in ascorbic form)—1 to 3 grams per day.

- Zinc—15 to 30 milligrams per day (males take 50 to 100 milligrams).

- Omega-3 oil—1 tablespoon per day.

- Evening primrose oil—four capsules per day.

- Vitamin E—400 IU per day.

- Follow the Anti-Inflammatory Diet.

- Rebound on a mini trampoline each day, working up to twenty minutes a day.

- Take vitamin B12 (determine what form you need from blood work).

- Exercise five to six days per week, thirty minutes a day.

- Adjust your lifestyle to reduce stress.

- Rest one full day per week.

If you are currently being treated for hypertension or have high blood pressure, remember to discuss any changes you wish to make with your physician as you begin the journey toward controlling your blood pressure naturally. If your physician does not wish to discuss natural health alternatives, I recommend finding a more open-minded physician who is experienced in alternative medicine.

OBESITY

You may have noticed how many people are overweight or obese today. In fact, the number of obese people appears to be growing at an alarming pace.[12] While it's true that many people need to exercise more and eat less fattening foods, there must be some reason our generation has eaten or lifestyled its way into obesity. Many children already experience adult onset diabetes, a price we are paying for the foods we eat.

Even with all the overweight people, it seems as if everybody is on a diet—with most of those diets filled with high levels of harmful fat and toxins. It is a diet of convenience, which emphasizes meats and refined foods, rather than raw vegetables that are nutrient rich. With fast food at every street corner, Americans are constantly tempted. Our nation has no health model and is blindly following the S.A.D.

THE OBESITY-HYPERTENSION CONNECTION

We discussed vascular disorders in great detail in the previous section. The majority of patients who suffer from heart issues have one thing in common—excessive weight. This can be attributed to the Western diet, which is high in rich foods and low in fresh fruits and vegetables. Exacerbating matters further is America's love affair with a sedentary lifestyle. Not all people with high blood pressure are overweight, but in my experience, the majority of patients with hypertension are clinically obese.

A group of scientists at Harvard University has been studying the effects of hypertension for more than thirty years. Called the Framingham Study, these experiments clearly demonstrate a direct link between obesity and blood pressure. In subsequent studies of the children of those participants in the original study—aptly named the Framingham Offspring Study—up to 78 percent of hypertension in men and 64 percent of hypertension in women was directly connected to obesity.

The distribution of body fat is an important variable because blood pressure and triglyceride (blood fat) as well as plasma glucose (blood sugar levels) are highest in patients with "trunk" obesity. Obesity in the midsection, or trunk, of the body is common in men as they are prone to carry excess weight around their stomachs. This type of obesity leads to the highest levels of hypertension.

Alarmingly, studies show that adults who were obese as children are at particular risk to the ravages of heart diseases. This is of special concern because of the dramatic rise in childhood obesity today. If you ever wonder if American children eat too much, just visit your local mall and look around. It is clear that we are setting up our children for a lifetime of health problems.

In school, one of my professors said that if his patients with cardiovascular issues would maintain a realistic goal of staying no more than 20 percent over their ideal body weights, 70 percent of them could eliminate their dependencies on medications. According to the 1983 Metropolitan Height and Weight Table, this means that a medium-framed 5-foot 10-inch male, whose ideal body weight is 151 to 163 pounds, could weigh from 181 to 196 pounds and still only have minimal increase blood pressure due to his excessive weight. The average 5-foot 6-inch woman, whose ideal body weight is 130 to 144 pounds, could weigh from 156 to 173 pounds. In reality, most Americans' weight problems don't stop at a mere 120 percent of their ideal body weights. Many keep going . . . and going . . . and going.

The first line of defense in the war against disease is weight reduction and a fitness program designed to meet your individual needs. The importance of exercise cannot be overstressed. I jumped on the exercise bandwagon at sixteen years old when I began bodybuilding. My passion for exercise helped me excel in competitive sports, and now it helps me maintain a great level of fitness, and a faithful and consistent effort to stay physically fit will carry me into my later years with vitality.

THE 5 BASIC PRESCRIPTIONS FOR EMPOWERING YOUR HEALTH

1. Decide you want to get well.

2. Drink half your body weight in number of ounces in pure, non-chlorinated water daily.

3. Eat three balanced meals per day, fasting one day per week.

4. Take the foundational four supplements, and get your blood checked twice per year.

5. Exercise five to six days a week for twenty to thirty minutes a day doing something you enjoy.

SUGAR AND OBESITY

Sugar is an addictive substance, and Americans ingest more than fifty-four pounds of it a year. It is not refined sugar or carbohydrates that are the real problems—it's high fructose corn syrup, also called the anti-diet drug. This is lethal over time and in the doses that the average American ingests regularly, its effects are extreme. This poison is manufactured from cornstarch, and raises your levels of hormones, causing you to gain weight. You will find it in all types of foods, from a loaf of whole wheat bread to a bottle of catsup.

Alarmingly, no matter how much you ingest, it does not suppress hunger when you are full, allowing you to keep eating more. This is why we often overeat foods with empty calories. Since high fructose corn syrup became prevalent in our foods, diabetes and obesity have been at an all-time high. Between 1970 and 1990, our intake of this substance increased by 1,000 percent. There has never been another food additive that the intake and demand increased so quickly.

The food industry introduced it because it was cheaper to use, and not until later did researchers learn that it made you uncontrollably hungry. Food industries will deny this, as it is an ingredient that helps them sell billions of dollars of food a year. However, removing this substance from your diet may cause you to lose weight, feel fuller when you eat, and regain energy as your body will be able to use what you are putting into it.

XYLITOL—A BETTER SWEETENER

I know what you're thinking right now . . . *But Dr. Asa, I can't give up all sweets!* Well, you don't have to. Studies conducted in Finland have been studying a sweetener substitute called xylitol for several years. It is a sweet compound naturally found in certain vegetables, strawberries, raspberries, plums, and jute, as well as various hardwood trees, such as birch. Ingesting xylitol may aid in curing sinus infections, bronchitis, pneumonia, and middle ear infections.

When xylitol is used in chewing gums, it serves as a powerful dental tool in fighting tooth decay. Researchers have also discovered that when xylitol was used instead of sugar, bacteria levels dropped in the mouths of those chewing the gum. Researchers found that rather than killing the bacteria, the xylitol simply does not allow the it to adhere. Trident brand gums are now sweetened with xylitol and are an excellent substitute to gums sweetened with artificial sweeteners like aspartame. Xylitol is available at most health food stores, and many traditional grocery stores now carry it as well. Look for xylitol under such names as Xlear and the Ultimate Sweetener.

CONJUGATED LINOLEIC ACID—THE "MAGIC" PILL

The latest nutritional research indicates that a dramatic decrease in the consumption of conjugated linoleic acid (CLA) is linked to the rise of obesity rates and other health problems.[13] CLA is one of the good omega-6 fatty acids, and if you are looking for a "magic pill" for weight loss, you may have found it. CLA is found in health food stores, nutritional stores like GNC, and even some mainstream drug stores.

CLA is found in range-fed beef, lamb, turkey, and milk products. When cows eat prepared feed rather than grass, the CLA content of the animals' milk drops to less than half its normal amount. Even if we increase our intake of dairy and beef, we are not likely to get the CLA we need. However, it is available in a pill form.

In 1998 the *American Journal of Physiology* reported that researchers in Louisiana discovered a 43 to 88 percent reduction in body fat in just six weeks when they added CLA to the diets of mice.[14] The area that appeared most responsive to CLA supplementation was the fat in the abdomen region—the trouble zone for most men. CLA triggers the loss of body fat by increasing the metabolic rate, decreasing the appetite, and causing a greater percentage of body fat cells to be used for energy production. Follow-up studies by the same group of researchers revealed that CLA's ability to lower body fat worked in both high- and low-fat diets. In addition to body fat reduction, the substance also increased muscle mass.

Even if weight loss is not an issue, there are other compelling reasons to include CLA in your daily diet. CLA has a significant impact on the immune system, bone and joint health, cancer and diabetes rates, and cardiovascular disease because it converts into hormone-like substances called prostaglandins—lipid compounds with a variety of positive physiological effects. CLA can reduce tumor growth and slow the development of prostate and breast cancer by inhibiting tissue inflammation. It also helps move glucose into cells, reducing the need for insulin, and prevents clogged arteries by stabilizing LDL cholesterol (the bad cholesterol). When lowered, LDL becomes less harmful to the body and allows the heart to function better. I recommend 6,000 milligrams of CLA, taken in two doses throughout the day.

OBESITY AND CHOCOLATE

There is some good news if you are a "chocaholic." You can still eat chocolate. Dark chocolate—not milk or white chocolate—lowers high blood pressure, according to an article published in *The Journal of the American Medical Association.* Of course, this does not mean that you can consume unlimited amounts. It is still a calorie dense food, but eating moderate amounts of dark chocolate may help lower your blood pressure. Dark chocolate (at least 70 percent cocao) is the best form because it contains the highest amounts of cocoa phenols. These naturally occurring chemical compounds found in cocoa are proven to help regulate blood pressure.[15] Remember, this does not give you license to eat large amounts of dark chocolate; rather, you must balance the extra calories by eating less of other foods on the days you consume chocolate.

FIBER—THE NATURAL ENEMY OF OBESITY

Fiber is the indigestible part of the plant that forms its structure. Increasing the amount of fiber in your diet can be one of the least expensive and successful tools in reducing harmful fat and combating obesity. Higher fiber food products take longer to break down and digest more slowly. If you are hungry all the time, it is likely due to eating a low-fiber, high-carbohydrate diet that keeps your hunger spiking and dipping, causing similar fluctuation in your blood sugar levels. Fiber causes the food to move out of the stomach much slower, causing you to feel full longer.

Due to the lack of whole, natural, high-fiber foods in most diets today, Americans are greatly lacking in fiber consumption. Considering that increased fiber intake is one of the most effective ways to lose weight, it is illogical that some of the most popular diets only suggest an average of fifteen grams of fiber per day. Your intake should be around twenty-five grams of fiber per day, at a minimum. Here is a short list of quality fiber sources and the fiber they contain:

- 1 cup of berries (blackberries, strawberries)—5 to 6 grams

- Handful of nuts (almonds, hazelnuts, pecans)—6 to 9 grams

- 1 cup of beans and legumes, cooked (chickpeas, lentils)—12 to 14 grams

- Handful of dried fruits (apricots, prunes, raisins)—4 to 6 grams

- Whole fruits (apple or pear with skin, kiwi, orange)—3 to 5 grams

- 1 cup raw vegetables (broccoli, carrots)—8 to 10 grams

- 1 cup cooked vegetables (beets, cabbage, peas)—8 to 12 grams

DIABETES

Because of the refined, prepackaged low-fiber foods we consume regularly, a constant "yo-yo effect" occurs in the body as insulin levels continually rise and fall. Blood sugar repeatedly reaches peak levels, which in turn, require high amounts of insulin excretion to stabilize them. After years of struggling to maintain healthy blood sugar levels, eventually the pancreas has had enough; it doesn't have any insulin left to give, or at least not enough to maintain your body, particularly if you are overweight. When this occurs, the result is *diabetes*—arguably the leading health crisis in America today. If we do not change our consumption patterns, by 2010, one out of every three children under the age of eleven will probably develop diabetes.[16] Health experts warn of the dangers of inactivity and of consuming increased sugar and refined carbohydrates, but have gained little ground in convincing the public that these habits often lead to diabetes.

There are two types of diabetes—type 1 and type 2. Type 1 diabetes was once referred to as *juvenile diabetes* because it typically occurs early in life. It is also sometimes referred to as insulin-dependent diabetes because insulin injections are required to provide the body with adequate levels of the hormone. Type 1 diabetes involves the complete failure of the body to produce insulin, and cannot be prevented by dietary or lifestyle changes. This type of diabetes accounts for only 5 to 10 percent of all diabetic cases.

Type 2 diabetes used to be called adult-onset diabetes, or sometimes non-insulin dependant diabetes. However, because it is now not uncommon in children, and because some type 2 diabetics do require insulin, type 2 is the preferred term. This form of diabetes develops over a longer period of time and is generally diagnosed in adulthood. It is the most common form of diabetes, affecting 90 to 95 percent of all sufferers.

Type 2 diabetes begins with insulin resistance as the body begins to need ever-increasing amounts of insulin for cells to open and allow blood sugar to enter. This resistance continues undetected for years because the pancreas is usually able to compensate by producing large quantities of insulin. Over time, the quality of the insulin produced lessens and the pancreatic cells begin to lose their ability to produce insulin altogether. When insulin production drops to the point that blood sugar levels can no longer be brought to normal levels, an individual has type 2 diabetes—although it may not be diagnosed until much later.

People with type 2 diabetes weren't born with a pancreatic condition or a lack of insulin; they created the problem through their own poor eating, exercise, and lifestyle habits.

But the FDA states the only problems related to sugar are dental cavities.[17] Influential members of the U.S. sugar industry founded a group called the Sugar Association "to promote the consumption of sugar as part of a healthy diet and lifestyle through the use of sound science and research." With the support of the American Dietetic Association, the Sugar Association holds firm to the assertion that sugar is a healthy, low-calorie sweetener that is no different from any other carbohydrate. While it's less harmful than high fructose corn syrup, the fact is that eating too much sugar can contribute to diabetes—and many of us do eat far too much of it.

It is possible, however, to develop type 2 diabetes simply by eating too many processed carbohydrates, drinking too much fruit juice, and not exercising. Simple carbohydrates such as flour and potato chips break down in the body to form sugar, and fruit juices are full of sugar (however natural), and except in small or dilute proportions, are not part of a healthy diet.

BLOOD SUGAR AND INSULIN

The first step to managing weight and fat loss is to maintain healthy levels of a hormone called insulin. The carbohydrates we eat are converted into simple sugars in the body called glucose, or blood sugar. After food is converted into glucose, it enters the bloodstream to be transported throughout the body. Blood sugar is the primary energy source used by all the major systems in the body such as the muscular and nervous systems. To be used, blood sugar must travel from the bloodstream into the nerve and muscle cells—this is where insulin comes into the process.

Insulin is the pancreatic hormone that opens up cell walls so blood sugar can enter, and it is the key to the body's energy processes. Insulin is secreted in two phases: The first surge of insulin releases immediately following a meal or when sugar is detected in the mouth or digestive system; a second round of insulin releases shortly after a meal and continues to release gradually for several hours.

For insulin to work properly, it must be present in sufficient quantities, and the cells in your body must be sensitive to its effects and willing to let it in. When cells don't react to the effects of insulin and block the sugar from entering through the cell wells, a condition develops called *insulin resistance*. Insulin resistance isn't fully understood; however, we do know that insulin resistance is often directly related to obesity. This is especially true for people who carry excess fat in the abdominal area. Excess waistline fat and fat deposits around the liver increase the amount of circulating fatty acids in the blood; as these fatty acids break down, they cause toxicity in the body. Increased toxicity inhibits the production of insulin and makes muscle tissue cells less sensitive to the insulin that is available.

Muscle tissue is a critical part of balancing blood sugar levels. Under normal circumstances, muscle cells use at least 80 percent of the blood sugar released directly following a meal. Studies prove that obese people can often overcome insulin resistance simply by losing weight and gaining muscle, without making any changes in blood sugar levels. With less fat, existing insulin in the body becomes more effective in lowering blood sugar levels on its own. Once you get insulin levels under control, not only will you reduce inflammation in the body, but you will also increase the production of a hormone called glucagon, a beneficial fat-burning hormone secreted by the pancreas. When blood sugar levels are low, glucagon has the ability to take over and use fat in the body for energy.

Here are my recommendations for people with predispositions to heart and vascular disease and diabetes:

1. Avoid foods and products that could contain metals such as aluminum, fluoride, indium, and palladium, like cow's pasteurized cheese, tap water, deodorant, soaps, and other personal care products.

2. Take liquid B12 (methylcobalamin), according to the prescribed dosage.

3. Increase immune function by taking magnesium and potassium iodide. You can easily intake adequate amounts of magnesium iodide (available at most health food stores) by adding one milliliter of the liquid form to a gallon of water. For potassium iodide (also available at most health food stores in liquid form) simply add one drop per gallon of water per week.

4. Eat plenty of organic hormone-free meat.

5. Avoid and/or limit intake of most grains, especially anything containing wheat.

6. Eat plenty of mustard and horseradish.

7. Eat your super foods (see the lists on pages 225 and 230).

Being diagnosed with any of the diseases covered in this chapter can be incredibly frightening, and it can make you feel helpless. But you aren't! Your doctor wants to beat the disease, and now that you have learned some positive steps you can personally take to prevent the onset of a major illness, you can go forward with increased confidence that you know how to help your body defend itself against sickness.

21

DESIGNED TO MOVE
Exercise

"It is amazing how much crisper the general experience of life becomes when your body is given a chance to develop a little strength."

—FRANK DUFF

It's two in the morning and you can't sleep because your blood sugar has dropped (the reason most people wake up during the night), and your body finds itself in a pre-diabetic state. You grab a bag of chips or a bowl of ice cream because that's what you're craving. You turn on the TV and begin to flip through the channels. A man on channel 58 is assuring you that you can have personal power and get his edge if you buy his audio series. The next channel has a modern version of Richard Simmons, updated with a ponytail, using a stairstepper screaming *You can do it!* And what's the favorite mantra? *Money-back guarantee!* You glance at your belly, your bag of potato chips, and your slouched position, and think, *It's time to make a change!* You order it all; after all, there's always the money-back guarantee. We all have bought on impulse at some point, and these products do work when properly applied. Statistics show that 95 percent of people who buy exercise machines never use them;[1] but the equipment makes great units to hang your clothes on. Sound familiar? It's so true, and it's so America.

Exercise has gotten increasingly large amounts of attention over the last fifteen years. Scores of people joined gyms, purchased ab-rollers, and ordered cardio equipment advertised in infomercials—machines guaranteed to "change your life forever." Despite the buzz surrounding the fitness craze, most people still *detest* exercise. When I tell patients to get moving and *do something*, most of them get frustrated with me. They plead: "I will eat right; I will fast; I will drink purified water; I will get my rest; but *please* don't tell me to exercise—don't tell me to *get moving.*" They try to find any way other than exercise.

Excuses are nothing more than creative avoidance—and yes, it's easier not to exercise. However, empowering your health and regaining control of your life is not about what's easy. Despite all the reasons you may come up with that you don't need to or don't have time to exercise, one fact remains—the body was created to move. Before the invention of the automobile and public transportation, everyone walked, and past generations didn't have the heart conditions and health problems that exist today, because they were so much more active in their everyday lives. No matter what you do, what you drive, or what your reasons are for not exercising, you must *get moving* if you are going to get healthy.

The bottom line is it's time to make a change. You can have the physique you had when you were twenty years old, the energy, the vitality, the excitement in life—but only you can make that decision.

The hardest thing for most people to do is exercise. I can get people to change their eating habits, stop smoking, stop addictive behaviors, stop negative thought patterns, and drink more water. However, it's so difficult to get people moving. The easiest way to get yourself healthier and in shape is to begin exercising. If you walk five minutes today, it is more than you did yesterday. If you walk back and forth to your mailbox, then you are on your way! It doesn't matter what activity you choose; just choose to do something.

Charlene came into my office with a look of fear, sadness, and anxiety. She was nervous and didn't know how to explain her situation. She was unhappy with where she was in life. She was a single mom with three kids, and working two jobs. She had gained more weight in the past year since her divorce than she ever had. I asked her what she wanted to do, and it was a resounding, *I want to get my health back!* Charlene was about thirty pounds overweight, and after testing, I found several things wrong with her overall health, including some arthritis in her hips.

She quickly jumped on the bandwagon. She ate perfectly, detoxed her body, and started drinking more water. However, I noticed that she was not losing the weight that she should have been. So I asked, "Charlene, how is the exercise routine going?"

She paused in silence. "Dr. Asa, that's one area that I just haven't gotten to yet." She began to tell me all the reasons why she couldn't exercise. *The kids have day care. I have to get up early and make breakfast. I work two jobs. It was raining. I had to get my hair done.* It went on and on.

I said, "Charlene, you don't have time not to exercise. You are overweight, you have three kids, you are reaching the forty-year mark, and cancer is your predisposition genetically. You don't have time not to exercise. Your body needs the increase of oxygen from aerobic activity for extraordinary health. Come on, Charlene!"

Finally, she was motivated! She began exercising five to six days per week, walking at first. She found that she really liked biking. She purchased a road bike and began riding every morning. She made time for her health. It's a discipline, just like anything else. The motive for her discipline, however, became different. She became selfless, thinking how her kids needed her to be around, rather than maintaining a selfish attitude that said, "I don't feel like exercising today." Her motivation to regain her health went outside herself.

Our bodies were designed to move. We weren't designed to sit in front of a desk all day and look at a computer. We weren't designed to sit on the sofa at home, get in our cars, and find the absolute closest parking spot to the building. No wonder we are sick as a nation and our obesity rate is the highest in the world. It really shouldn't be this hard. If you just took twenty to thirty minutes a day doing something active you enjoy, you can cut your risk of disease in half. Exercise is so important to our overall health, and not just for how we look and feel, but for the health of our cells.

GET A TRAINER

Your best option to get started is to use a personal trainer. It costs money, but isn't your body worth it? Thoroughbred horses are some of the most expensive animals in the world. Trainers spend countless hours with them, feeding them the finest foods, ensuring they get proper rest, and providing them with world-class training facilities. We can spend thousands of dollars on animals, yet we struggle to spend hundreds of dollars on our health.

Working with a certified personal trainer will benefit you in several ways. Because there is money involved, you are more likely to actually show up. You will learn how to exercise properly and reduce the chance of injury.

A trainer provides accountability, and you will increase your chances of success by exercising with someone. Once you have worked with a trainer for while, you will able to do it on your own. A good trainer teaches you how to take responsibility for your fitness and how to exercise properly. Most gyms, such as the YMCA, have trainers on staff, and four, six, or eight weeks with a trainer should be enough to get you started. The cost of training varies depending on what is available to you, but in general, the price is between thirty to fifty dollars a session—a bargain to pay for good health and fitness levels!

I know that some health books have pictures of someone doing exercises—stretches, lunges, floor exercises, and movements on inflatable balls. Many times those workouts are fantastic, but most people aren't going to learn correct form from a picture, especially if you are new to exercise. Radical action achieves radical results, and radical action is not looking at a black and white photo of someone doing lunges. You must reach for a higher level of fitness, and the best way to achieve this is by using an educated personal trainer. Whether it's yoga or circuit training with weights, just get out and do it. I will explain a few types of exercise and what they are. I will also give you my personal workout routines for beginner, intermediate, and advanced trainees.

AEROBIC AND ANAEROBIC EXERCISE

Aerobics was a buzzword in the seventies and eighties. Dr. Kenneth Cooper of the Cooper Clinic in Dallas was the father of the aerobic movement. People started going nuts on treadmills and stationary bikes, and with jogging and walking. Aerobic training was in high gear. The word "aerobic" means "with oxygen," and this style of exercise increases our bodies' oxygen levels. Increasing oxygen means increasing health. Our bodies thrive on oxygen, and cancer cannot survive in an oxygen-rich environment. It's an excellent way to help our bodies create new, healthy cells. That's why I tell patients who are unaccustomed to exercise to start with walking. Move at a brisk pace for a period of time, even just five minutes, and this will produce an aerobic environment and yield positive benefits.

The opposite of aerobic exercise is anaerobic exercise. It means "without oxygen," and includes the short bursts of energy during resistance training (weight lifting) or sprints while running. A good rule of thumb is mixing anaerobic and aerobic exercise.

In the eighties and nineties, an exercise guideline became overly popularized—we were told at least one hour of constant aerobic exercise was the best thing for overall fitness. This theory was based on old studies regarding high cholesterol and clogged arteries and their relationships to constant motion. This "cardio-crazed" mentality resulted in worn-out cartilage, hurt knees, damaged shoulders, injured hips, and increased lower back pain. Long periods of intense aerobic activity cause the immune system to weaken, which increases the chances for the body to contract illnesses.[2]

This is why I recommend exercise sessions of thirty-five to forty minutes. Some activities, of course, take longer (a long bike ride, a canoe outing, playing golf)—this is fine, as long as you rest regularly. If you participate in marathons, triathlons, or other high-endurance sports, simply allow your body to periodically rest by scheduling less intense workouts during the off-season.

NON-FUNCTIONAL AND FUNCTIONAL EXERCISE

In the late eighties and early nineties, I was heavily involved in weight training and bodybuilding. Like many young men, I emulated Arnold Schwarzenegger; I read every article about him because I wanted to look just like Arnold. I worked out two hours a day for six days a week. It consumed my life, but I know now that excessive weight lifting was counterproductive to my health. I am in far better shape now after I adopted a different approach.

Most traditional weight training is termed "nonfunctional." Our bodies are designed for full, natural movements, not to sit in a Nautilus machine and be restricted in our motions. The majority of the exercise you choose should mirror real life motions. This does not mean that weight training harms your body. In fact, it is an important part of most workout regimens, but you must be careful to balance the use of weights with daily stretching and movements that utilize the entire body.

One of the best forms of full body exercise is called functional exercise. Better results and health are attained when you use your entire body combined with moderate weight training. Some examples of functional aerobic exercises are swimming, tai chi, yoga, Pilates, and even ballroom dancing. The key to these fun exercises is that they are low impact, and require smooth, controlled movements while strengthening the body's core. Just be sure not to exceed thirty to forty minutes of aerobic exercise.

In the nineties, the world was introduced to a new superstar in the fitness world, Billy Blanks. You might recall his infomercials in which Billy took the country by storm with his Tae Bo routines, classes, and videos. He made fitness fun again. I like his program because it is low to medium impact, involves the entire body doing functional movements, and can be done with others. It's filled with great functional movements to provide increased functional fitness.

The mini trampoline is a great form of exercise. Jumping benefits your reflexes, your digestion, and your lymphatic system, in addition to the obvious benefits of toning and cardiovascular activity. It's ideal to jump twenty to thirty minutes a day. Wear good arch-supported shoes, and if you struggle with balance, have a chair nearby to hold onto for stability. Start slowly—you may not be able to jump that long in the beginning. You can jump on both feet at first, and as your comfort level increases, you can try different variations (on one foot, jumping jacks, etc). Start with one minute a day and increase the amount of time daily. The key is to *just get started!* Try walking up and down your driveway, or even out to your mailbox. Take baby steps toward reaching a healthier you. Before long, you will notice how much more vitality and energy you have in every area of life!

EFFECTIVE FREQUENCY AND DURATION

How long should I exercise? The primary reason people don't ever get started is because they think that exercising involves spending two hours every day in the gym. Actually, that couldn't be further from the truth. Have you ever heard the old adage, *less is more*? It's applicable to every area of life, and especially to fitness. Exercise and its benefits are not difficult. Rather, they are easy if you are doing something you enjoy and you do it consistently. Here are some recommended tips for frequency and duration of exercising:

1. Exercise at least five days per week, twenty to thirty minutes per day.

2. Do something you enjoy.

3. If you struggle with motivation, exercise with a partner, as you will be less likely to skip.

4. As a general rule, don't exceed forty-five minutes of non-stop aerobic activity. Production of cortisol, a muscle-wasting and fat-storing hormone, increases after this point.[3] Of course, if you are participating in a sport such as biking or distance running, you will go beyond that time limit. Just use common sense and do not push yourself every day; take intermittent breaks to allow your body to rest.

5. Be consistent and you will attain consistent results.

FIND YOUR TARGET HEART RATE

You have likely heard about the importance of proper pace during exercise, especially for those who are not accustomed to physical activity. A monitoring method called target heart rate (or exercising heart rate) is helpful to determine the correct pace. You can measure your pulse throughout your workout and stay within 50 to 85 percent of your maximum heart rate, which is called your target heart rate.

Here is a simple way to determine your target heart rate (the correct heart rate for you while exercising):

1. Subtract your age from 220.

2. Multiply this number by how hard you want to work based on the scale (use .70 for 70% up to .85 for 85%). See the table below for the list of ranges. The resulting number is your target heart rate.

You can use a lightweight heart rate monitor from a sporting goods store, or you can manually take your heart rate:

1. Take your pulse with your first two fingers on your wrist on the thumb side for 15 seconds.

2. Multiply that number by 4 to get your heart rate.

The suggested target heart rates in the table below allow you to measure your initial fitness level and monitor your progress as you continue a regular exercise regimen.

For those who can't or don't wish to take their pulses while working out, use this simple guideline: If you can talk during your activity, you are not overexerting yourself. If you try to speak, but are short of breath, slow your pace until you can speak clearly again.

Heart Rate Chart

Age	Light 55%	Fairly Light 60%	Fairly Hard 70%	Hard 80%	Very Hard 85%
15	19	21	24	27	29
20	18	20	23	27	28
25	18	20	23	26	28
30	17	19	22	25	27
35	17	19	22	25	26
40	17	18	21	24	26
45	16	18	20	23	25
50	16	17	20	23	24
55	15	17	19	22	23
60	15	16	19	21	23
65	14	16	18	21	22
70	14	15	18	20	21
75	13	15	17	19	21
80	13	14	16	19	20
85	12	14	16	18	19
90	12	13	15	17	18
Max Rate	55%	60%	70%	80%	85%

GETTING STARTED OR TAKING IT TO THE NEXT LEVEL

Here are some workouts and fitness routines to help you get started. If you use a personal trainer to help you, make sure he or she is certified by a reputable organization such as the American Council on Exercise (ACE) or the Aerobics and Fitness Association of America (AFAA). Conversely, if you are already working out and simply want to take your fitness to the next level, there is also a fitness chart for you.

Asa's Total Body Workouts
Please consult with a certified personal trainer before starting.

	Beginner Workout	Intermediate Workout	Advanced Workout
Monday	Resistance training: Chest, back, biceps, calves; 3 sets, 12-15 reps, 60-second rest periods. Cardio: 5-minute warmup, 12 minutes at high intensity 65-70% MHR, 5-minute cooldown...	Resistance training: Chest, back, biceps, calves; 4 sets, 12-15 reps, 30-second rest periods. Cardio: 5-minute warmup, 12 minutes at high-intensity 70-75% MHR, 5-minute cooldown...	Resistance training: Chest, back, biceps, calves; 5 sets, 15-20 reps, 30-second rest periods. Cardio: 5-minute warmup, 12 minutes at high-intensity 75-85% MHR, 5-minute cooldown...
Tuesday	Do some type of activity that you enjoy for 30 minutes. (Run, walk, bike, swim, yoga, tennis, etc.)	Resistance training: Quads, hamstrings, shoulders, triceps; 4 sets, 12-15 reps, 30-second rest periods. Cardio: 5-minute warmup, 12 minutes at high-intensity 70-75% MHR, 5-minute cooldown...	Resistance training: Quads, hamstrings, shoulders, triceps; 5 sets, 15-20 reps, 30-second rest periods. Cardio: 5-minute warmup, 12 minutes at high-intensity 75-85%, MHR, 5-minute cooldown...
Wednesday	Resistance training: Quads, hamstrings, shoulders, triceps; 5 sets, 12-15 reps, 60-second rest periods. Cardio: 5-minute warmup, 12 minutes at high-intensity 65-70% MHR, 5-minute cooldown...	Do some type of activity that you enjoy for 30 minutes. (Run, walk, bike, swim, yoga, tennis, etc.)	Resistance training: Chest, back, biceps, calves; 5 sets, 12-15 reps, 45-second rest periods. Cardio: 5-minute warmup, 12 minutes at high-intensity 75-85% MHR, 5-minute cooldown...
Thursday	Do some type of activity that you enjoy for 30 minutes. (Run, walk, bike, swim, yoga, tennis, etc.)	Resistance training: Chest, back, biceps, calves; 4 sets, 8-12 reps, 45-second rest periods. Cardio: 5-minute warmup, 12 minutes at high-intensity 70-75 % MHR, 5-minute cooldown...	Resistance training: Quads, hamstrings, shoulders, triceps; 5 sets, 12-15 reps, 45-second rest periods. Cardio: 5-minute warmup, 12 minutes at high-intensity 75-85 % MHR, 5-minute cooldown...
Friday	Resistance training: Chest, back, biceps, calves; 3 sets, 12-15 reps, 60-second rest periods. Cardio: 5-minute warmup, 12 minutes at high-intensity 65-70% MHR, 5-minute cooldown...	Resistance training: Quads, hamstrings, shoulders, triceps; 4 sets, 8-12 reps, 45-second rest periods. Cardio: 5-minute warmup, 12 minutes at high-intensity 70-75% MHR, 5-minute cooldown...	Resistance training: Chest, back, biceps, calves; 5 sets, 8-12 reps, 60-second rest periods. Cardio: 5-minute warmup, 12 minutes at high-intensity 75-85% MHR, 5-minute cooldown...
Saturday	Do some type of activity that you enjoy for 30 minutes. (Run, walk, bike, swim, yoga, tennis, etc.)	Do some type of activity that you enjoy for 30 minutes. (Run, walk, bike, swim, yoga, tennis, etc.)	Resistance training: Quads, hamstrings, shoulders, triceps; 5 sets, 8-12 reps, 60-second rest periods. Cardio: 5-minute warmup, 12 minutes at high-intensity 75-85% MHR, 5-minute cooldown...
Sunday	Rest.	Rest.	Rest.

257

An optimal fitness regimen must be functional—a combination of both aerobic and anaerobic—and be of short duration. Thirty minutes of activity is plenty; this will keep your hormone levels in balance and avoid overtraining. A good guideline for exercise is to work out until you reach a level just outside your comfort zone. Let your activities stretch you a little, but don't let them wipe you out. In doing this, exercise will remain enjoyable rather than something you dread doing every day. My personal journey of fitness has been one of trial and error. I have tried almost every fad workout and fad diet, and through these experiences, I discovered that in the long run, shorter duration and variety in both anaerobic and aerobic activity work most effectively.

ASA'S LIFETIME FITNESS PROGRAM
(I strongly suggest you wear a heart rate monitor)

1. **First 30 days**
   Fast walking at a speed that elevates your heart rate up to 70% of your maximum heart rate for 30 minutes a day, three days per week.

2. **Days 31-60**
   Exercise at a pace that elevates your heart rate to 75% of your maximum heart rate for 30 minutes a day, three days per week.

3. **Days 61 and beyond**
   Exercise (doing whatever activity you enjoy) at a pace that elevates your heart rate to 75-85% of your maximum heart rate for 30 minutes a day, three days per week.

   Day 1 exercise at 75%
   Day 2 exercise at 80%
   Day 3 exercise at 85%

Functional fitness activities that follow the natural motion of the body are ideal. Examples include walking, deep breathing, and rebounding on a mini trampoline. Weight training is encouraged in your exercise regimen, but not mandatory. If you include weight training, work out in a functional manner—in other words, use natural motions such as full-bodied movements with free weights rather than being bound to a stationary machine. Nautilus and stationary machines are not harmful to your health and can, in fact, help you build and tone your muscles. However, the pulley systems of these machines do not allow for free movement and as a result, your muscles become trained to pull up or down in one line of movement. The most effective form of weight training allows for freer motion, and when combined with stretching before and after your workout, develops muscles with more movement and flexibility; this in turn helps to prevent other sports injuries brought on by stiff muscles.

Find an activity you enjoy and *do it*. By doing an activity you enjoy, you are more likely to repeat that activity rather than dread the daily trip to the gym. It is also important to incorporate variety in your exercise regimen. Try doing something fun but challenging five to six days a week, for twenty to thirty minutes at a time. Make exercise a part of your regular routine; you are not only designed for it, your life and state of health depend on it.

You were created to do something great with your life—to live, work, play, overcome obstacles, and experience great victories. *If you don't use it, you'll lose it.* That applies to everything in your life, and is especially applicable to your body and your overall state of health. Bodies are made to move; the heart is made to pump blood; the joints are made to allow motion in the body. When you increase your heart rate, blood pumps more effectively to body tissue, which increases oxygen levels, making tissues healthy and able to create new healthy cells. There are so many benefits to be gained from exercise! By continuing to exist in a sedentary, lethargic state, we help our bodies to decrease in function and eventually to die. The body is designed to move; so get moving!

22

LOSING WEIGHT THE HEALTHY WAY
The Prescription for Weight Management

*"When it comes to eating right and exercising, there is no
'I'll start tomorrow.' Tomorrow is disease."*

—V.L. ALLINEARE

Weight management is on everyone's mind; it is next to impossible to turn on the TV and not hear stories about the growing obesity rate or the latest Hollywood diet. You've seen the infomercials, and you may own one or more of the widely marketed ab rollers, butt tuckers, tummy suckers, and electronic fat removers. You've probably also tried an assortment of firming creams and fat burning pills. People are on a relentless search for the answers to weight loss and physical fitness.

IN SEARCH OF THE MIRACLE DRUG

Everyone is looking for that magic pill. Wouldn't that be nice? Take a pill and all your stubborn fat and cellulite will vanish. But reducing your waistline is more than doing abdominal crunches on a special device. The models you see on TV did more than crunches; they have quite a bit of discipline to get where they are.

Claims of the miraculous effects of fad weight-loss products may have enticed you enough to purchase them, but how much difference did they make in your own physique or health? Exercise and weight management require hard work and dedication. There is no guaranteed weight-loss gimmick, so don't waste your money. There is simply no such thing as a "quick fix." Searching for the remedy on late-night infomercials is not the solution.

If these companies actually sold you the answers, they would bankrupt their multi-billion dollar industry.

When I refer to weight loss, I am not talking about the specific number on the scale. You must lose targeted body fat—and more specifically, abdomen fat. This is especially true for men because they typically carry body fat around their waistlines. When you carry excess abdominal fat, statistics show that you have a higher risk of both heart disease and heart attack. People with large waistlines almost always have high blood pressure—that's because there is a clear correlation between abdominal fat and heart health. Proper diet and exercise can reduce body fat, but the choice is up to you. It's time to stop looking for the quick fix and discover how to bring about permanent and lasting change.

Effective weight management is something that medical science has known about for years; after all, the chemistry of our bodies hasn't changed. Society and our lifestyles have changed, but our bodies, the way they function, and how to achieve extraordinary health certainly haven't. You can reach the weight that you desire—but you need to do it for health reasons and not for vanity alone. Just because a Hollywood star you saw in the newsstand magazine is skinny doesn't mean she's healthy. The outside does not always reflect what's on the inside. Health is determined solely by the quality of our cells, which means that losing weight does not necessarily equal extraordinary health. The secret to health lies in balancing all three sides of the Health Triangle. We must be balanced mentally, chemically, and structurally to achieve the health we desire.

HORMONES—THE SECRET WEAPON

What weight management plans and pills tend to promote are the "secret ingredients" that make their formulas unique. Allow me to dispel a myth: There are no such things as secret ingredients. Keeping the body balanced is the ultimate goal. The endocrine system controls hormones within the body. Each of our bodies contains some basic hormones: estrogen, progesterone, testosterone, human growth hormone, and other important regulatory hormones for thyroid and fluid balance. By keeping our hormones in balance, we will reverse the negative hormone pathways in our bodies; our bodies will do most of the work to burn unwanted body fat, and we will lose the weight we desire. How do we do it? Let's go to back to science class for a moment.

The most underestimated gland in the body for weight management is the thyroid gland. The thyroid is responsible for controlling our body's internal furnace. It helps the body convert our food into energy. If your thyroid is over- or under-functioning, then all the processes in the body will be slower than normal, and the body will convert much more of the food you eat into fat stores than is necessary. A large contributor to an underactive thyroid is lack of organic iodine, covered in more detail in chapter 11. I strongly recommend the underarm temperature test found in that chapter to determine the state of your thyroid. If your temperature consistently runs below 97.6 degrees, then you have a sluggish thyroid and need organic iodine (but do not start on iodine without being under the supervision of a physician).[1]

Each of our bodies has an inherent ideal weight called the *set point*. This is what our bodies desire to weigh. When we go outside this set point, our bodies are in a constant fight to return to it. However, without changes in our lifestyle choices (which made us overweight to begin with) we usually continue to fight with our own set point, and that is when something in the body finally breaks down and disease sets in. It's time to stop the vicious cycle.

You must accept the fact that there is no magic pill that will flush away the unwanted pounds. Eating right and exercising are difficult; it is much easier to sit on the couch than it is to exercise, but the fact remains that we live a too-sedentary lifestyle. We are used to sitting around watching TV, so the first step is to get moving, and make a commitment every single day to *do something*.

YOUR OWN FOUNTAIN OF YOUTH

Throughout the ages, people have searched for the fountain of youth, but it's been inside our bodies all along. We just have to tap into it. This youth hormone is called human growth hormone (HGH). All the anti-aging clinics today focus on this wonder hormone, which regulates all the other hormones in the body. Around age twenty-five, we slowly begin to lose this hormone that is largely responsible for how we look. When HGH levels are high, we have tighter skin, less body fat, better memory, more muscle tone, shinier hair, and that radiant glow that people notice.[2] Time and our dietary choices tend to lower our HGH levels. Highly refined diets with sugar and carbohydrates and not enough protein and healthy fats, and too little exercise, are some of the culprits—along with nasty environmental toxins, heavy metals, and electromagnetic radiation. All these factors serve to lower the powerful HGH level.

Once we restore the hormone function naturally through proper diet and exercise, body fat and cellulite melt away, and your other hormones, such as testosterone, progesterone, estrogen, and even thyroid hormones, will begin to rebalance themselves. Then you will be well on your way to maintaining your body's ideal weight.

THE PRESCRIPTION—PUTTING IT ALL TOGETHER

This prescription is designed to keep your body healthy and to jump-start a stubborn metabolism at the same time. Consult with your physician before beginning any diet or exercise regimen, but once you do begin, follow it precisely and you will see incredible results. It is simply a matter of helping your body to function in the way it was originally designed. For those who do not need to lose weight, the great thing about this prescription is that it will help reposition your body. That means that although you may not lose weight on the scale, you body composition will change because you will increase lean muscle tissue and decrease body fat that is harmful to your overall health.

Be sure to exercise for forty-five minutes a day during this time. You must do some form of exercise each day. If you don't like to exercise and it is new to you, just get out and walk. Also drink half your body weight in number of ounces of pure, non-chlorinated water daily away from meals (a 150-pound woman would drink 75 ounces of water daily).

Get ready for you and those around you to be shocked at the transformation in your body.

NOTE FOR DIABETICS: If you are diabetic please tell your physician that you are starting this plan and do so under his supervision. Drink chicken or beef broth on your partial fasting days to take the edge off. *Do not* use anything with sugar.

This is a modified version of the Anti-Inflammatory Diet (discussed in chapter 13), but the fundamental goal remains the same: to reset the body's chemistry by reducing inflammation in the digestive system. Weight loss must never equal health loss. Don't sacrifice your health in the quest to lose weight. You can lose weight effectively and permanently if you do it correctly by keeping overall health your top priority. Forget the diet pills and starvation. Focus on what will give you maximum health, and you will lose the weight your body wants to lose.

Don't forget that we all have our own set point. You can fluctuate above or below this point, but in doing so, you are fighting your body's attempt to find balance. Don't be discouraged if someone who is the same height as you is 105 pounds and your weight is 155. If you are healthy, your tests are within normal ranges, and your yearly checkup is positive, then you are most likely where you need to be, regardless of what the scale says. Learn to accept and love yourself the way God designed you.

These weight management techniques are useful for those of you who have gone past your set point, and need help to get rid of the extra weight. Follow the principles outlined in the chapter and watch your body transform into the new body you desire. Once you have reached that point, then be happy with the new you! Stop looking for perfection and look for peace in who you are.

23

NO REST FOR THE WEARY
The Rest Principle

"Early to bed, early to rise makes a man healthy, wealthy, and wise."

—BENJAMIN FRANKLIN

Burnout is all around us, in our careers, in our families, in various areas of our everyday lives. We use stimulants such as coffee and sugar to "get our fix" in the morning, and take drugs such as Ambien and Lunesta to allow us to unravel from the stress of the day so we can sleep—only to wake up and start the vicious cycle all over again. We race home from our jobs and then it's off to the kids' soccer games and piano lessons. We just don't have enough time; we are overworked, overstressed, and under-rested.

We need a solution—we need something that will slow us down so that we can regain our health. The busy American lifestyle is a contributing factor to most of the poor health conditions today: heart disease, type 2 diabetes, stroke, and cancer—all diet- or lifestyle-related. We must change the way we are doing things if we are going to achieve the optimal health that our Creator designed for us.

If our responsibilities can't be lessened, or at least slowed, there is one time-proven principle that will restore our health. This is *rest*. You may think you "rest" because you sleep every night—but is that really rest? You may lie on the couch and do nothing one evening—but that is not true rest. That is only a few hours in the day, and the rest of that day was likely spent working, running errands, or stuck in traffic. True rest is achieved when you take one day out of your busy schedule to allow for complete mental, physical, emotional, and spiritual rest—a time to experience relaxation and rejuvenation. True rest involves a complete break from the normal routine. It is not only necessary; it is vital to overall productivity and health.

TWO TYPES OF REST

There are two types of rest—the first is called active rest. Active rest occurs on the typical Saturday afternoon on the couch watching TV or on the golf course. Active rest occurs when you break from your daily activities and responsibilities and do something you enjoy. The second type is passive rest. When you experience passive rest, you are not doing chores, cleaning, working in the garden, exercising, or engaging in recreational activities. Passive rest occurs when you do *absolutely nothing*. This is the type of rest on which you want to focus.

Every working creature needs rest—this includes people, animals, and even soil. People and animals need rest every seven days, and the soil prospers when rested at least every seven years. Wise farmers use field or crop rotation so the soil can replenish for one growing season every seven years. In a study of two similar farming soils, one was farmed continuously for eight years, while the other was allowed to stand fallow, or unfarmed, during the seventh year. The rested soil was two times more nutrient-dense than the soil that had no rest.

In France after the bloody French Revolution, the monarchy decided to change the nation's schedule from a seven-day workweek to a ten-day cycle. Before long, the country's horses and mules became diseased and died at alarming rates. After scientists investigated, they discovered that a return to the "seventh day principle" was necessary to maintain physical welfare, health, and long life.

Rest is crucial to the health of the body and soul, and sleep is an absolute and undeniable necessity of life. Lengthy regular periods of rest are equally important over time. Europeans are far ahead of Americans in this arena. In fact, it's normal for European families to take extended vacations each year for four to ten weeks; most Americans struggle just to take a two-week vacation every few years—and many take no vacations at all.

TAKE A DAY OFF

Nighttime is designed for regular sleep, but we are also programmed to perform best when we experience complete rest every seventh day. Even the

Creator rested on the seventh day, and I believe He was setting an example for us. The Bible is replete with suggestions for achieving better health; however, there is only one health *commandment*. This fourth of the Ten Commandments must be abided by or there will be major consequences. The Bible commands us simply to rest.

Years ago, a businessman named S. Truett Cathy decided to build a business on the rest principles in the Bible. Today, his franchise, Chick-fil-A is among the top ten fast food chains in America.[1] Chick-fil-A gained this success despite the fact that its restaurants are open fifty-two fewer days per year than the other fast food chains. Cathy does this because he believes in applying the rest principle to the work week. This principle also applies to the human body. The way to achieve optimal health and avoid burnout and exhaustion is to practice the seventh-day rest principle.

Important biological functions occur when we rest, the kind of rest that involves stepping out of the stresses of everyday life and taking a day off from your usual busy tasks: Cortisol, the muscle-wasting hormone in the body decreases; creativity returns; hormones balance; body toxins reduce; the aging process slows; and our immune system rejuvenates, which decreases our chances for cancer. We give our bodies the chance to restore themselves during complete or *passive* rest—the type of rest that requires you to take one day each week to totally disengage from your usual responsibilities.

SWEET DREAMS

Sleep is another key component of rest, and yet it is something that many Americans struggle with night after night. People constantly complain of sleep problems—they feel they are just not getting enough. Tranquilizers and sleeping pills are some of the most prescribed medications on the market.[2]

The pharmaceutical companies have found a gold mine in the making and marketing of tranquilizers and sleeping pills. TV advertisements suggest that there is not an individual on earth who wouldn't benefit from one of these drugs. In these commercials, the actors smile as they drift off to sleep. But if you take these drugs, your body won't be smiling on the inside.

A far cry from simple medications to relieve anxiety and sleeping problems, these drugs can cause dizziness, memory loss, decreased mental function, confusion, and loss of coordination. To make matters worse, these drugs are also highly addictive. Elderly patients are the most susceptible to these problems, and not surprisingly, they receive the majority of these drugs. As we get older, our bodies have more difficulty clearing drugs from our systems, and this increases our sensitivity to them. If a doctor isn't monitoring the situation carefully, memory dysfunction and coordination problems are written off as aging problems, perpetuating the symptoms and making them worse.

For elderly patients in hospitals or institutions, the problem is even more widespread. A large number of these institutionalized individuals receive some form of tranquilizer or sleeping pill. If you have a friend or loved one under care, list all the medications they are taking, and have a doctor review the list. Eliminating these sleeping pills and tranquilizers can improve their quality of life dramatically. I wouldn't recommend a "cold turkey" approach to eliminate medication because this can cause problems due to the addictive natures of these prescriptions; but drug use can be reduced slowly to wean patients away from unnecessary medications, under the watchful eye of a physician.

WHY DO WE SLEEP?

Thirty-three percent of our lives are spent asleep. Sleep gives the body time to repair itself, but sleep patterns have changed dramatically since the invention of electricity. Sleep once was a bodily function that relied heavily on the daily cycle of the sun. Before the advent of electricity, civilizations arose when the sun came up and went to sleep when the sun went down. There were no twenty-four hour grocery stores or nightclubs. When it was dark, people slept.

Sleeping gives our brain the time it needs for processing and filing new information collected during the day. Studies in the 1920s revealed that electrical conductivity within brain cells decreased the longer people stayed awake.[3] Based on this early research, the activity of the brain was compared to a battery that must constantly give off an electrical charge to maintain consciousness. Only during unconsciousness did the battery (the brain) have the opportunity to recharge; this is unlike the heart, which rests between beats, and other organs that function periodically. The only time the brain can rest and recharge is during sleep.

A basic understanding of sleep phases and how to influence them will help you deal with insomnia and other sleep disorders more effectively. The practice of sleeping and waking are processes that your body uses to synchronize many functions, such as body temperature, hormone levels, and respiration. Increased levels of serotonin, a neurotransmitter in the brain, help initiate the sleep process, and as certain nerve impulses are blocked, several events begin to unfold.

First, your heart rate slows, and you begin to slip into the lightest level of sleep, Stage One. As your brain activity slows even more, you gradually reach Stage Two sleep. After about forty minutes, you pass through Stage Three and into Stage Four, the deepest level of sleep. In Stage Four, your brain shuts itself off from the outside world. Many of us have been awakened from a Stage Four sleep to discover that we have drooled all over the pillow, can't move a muscle as if our arms have fallen asleep, or can't shake ourselves from a deep, zombie-like state. Stage Four sleep is closely related with the restoration and repairing of the physical body, while the other stages of sleep are closely linked to memory, learning, and the ability to adapt to changes in the environment.

THE SCIENCE OF SLEEP PATTERNS

It is difficult to determine exactly how much sleep we actually need. We do know that as we grow older, we appear to require less sleep, while babies may sleep as much as sixteen hours a day. Moreover, Stage Four sleep periods begin to decline as we age. This deepest of sleep stages almost disappears for many people over the age of fifty. After studying the sleeping habits of teenagers, researchers concluded that teens feel best after ten to eleven hours of sleep each night; college students perform well when they receive about eight hours of sleep; and those between the ages of forty-five and sixty get sufficient rest with seven hours of sleep.[4]

While some individuals claim to need only a few hours of sleep each night, no one can function totally without sleep. There are variations in the exact amount needed, depending on factors such as proper diet and a resilient immune system. The former prime minister of Great Britain, Margaret Thatcher, reportedly slept only four hours a night.

Numerous studies show that insomniacs have a difficult time judging exactly how long they remain awake each night. Time appears to pass much more slowly when you lie awake worried about trying to fall asleep; so without a proper sleep study, it is often impossible to determine exactly how much sleep insomniacs lose.

Patients repeatedly ask me how to improve their sleep patterns. First, I suggest going to sleep earlier at night. If you go to bed around nine or ten o'clock, you will be much better off than if you go to bed after midnight. Each minute of sleep that you get before midnight is worth four minutes after midnight. Our ancestors didn't have computers, late-night talk shows, the Internet, or the nightly news to keep them up late at night, and they didn't encounter the levels of stress and responsibility that we experience today. They went to bed at dark and rose with the sun—this may be one reason why they suffered from fewer diseases as a whole and had sufficient energy throughout the day.

Another key to regulating sleep patterns is regular, vigorous exercise. If you exercise six days a week for twenty to thirty minutes at a time doing something you enjoy, this helps maintain the *circadian rhythm* in your body—this rhythm is a twenty-four hour cycle that occurs in the physiological processes of all living beings. It reduces the stress of the day and increases your blood flow and oxygen levels. Thanks to the balance it maintains, when it is time to sleep, your body will be ready for a good night's rest. Exercise is critical to preserve this natural body rhythm that flows in each of us.

NATURAL SLEEP AIDS

Guava. If you suffer from insomnia, several natural remedies may help relieve sleepless nights. A fruit called guava helps many people overcome addictions to sleeping pills and anxiety medications. It is also available in a supplement form. Generally, the best results are achieved with 200 milligrams of guava four times daily.

Melatonin. Melatonin is a hormone supplement and is a great aid for insomnia and jet lag, but it is still a hormone. Hormones are powerful forces in the human body, and their effects can be far reaching. For this reason, I don't recommend using melatonin on a continuing basis. Use it for a day or two to overcome jet lag, shift changes at work, or to reset your biological clock to correct insomnia, but it is not recommended for extended use.

Once your body's clock has been reset, you shouldn't need additional melatonin and other natural remedies unless your system gets out of its circadian rhythm again. You can increase your levels of melatonin naturally without resorting to supplementation through your diet, as certain foods are high in melatonin. These include bananas, barley, ginger, rice, and corn.

WHAT'S KEEPING YOU AWAKE?

A number of situations could be causing your sleeping problems. Here are a few possibilities:

Bad habits. If you suffer from insomnia, sleeping late in the morning, taking afternoon naps, and lying in bed all day are just a few habits that contribute to sleep disorders. Eating starchy carbohydrates such as bread right before you go to bed also perpetuates insomnia, and stimulating drinks such as coffee or tea prolong the time it takes for you to wind down and go to sleep.

Medications. The widespread use of medications is one of the biggest detriments to sleep—this includes both over-the-counter and prescription drugs. Monitor your body to determine if your inability to sleep coincides with the use of a new medication. Even seemingly harmless over-the-counter sinus and nasal congestion medications can be strong nervous system stimulants that interfere with sleep. Never accept a new prescription from your doctor until you have provided a complete list of drugs that includes any over-the-counter medications you are taking, and discuss how they may interact with each other. Any time you develop a new symptom after starting a new drug, consider the new drug to be the culprit until you can prove otherwise.

Blood sugar. Hypoglycemia, or low blood sugar can also contribute to insomnia. Your brain uses glucose as its main source of energy. If glucose or blood sugar levels fall below normal while you sleep, your adrenal glands automatically release hormones that stimulate glucose production—and this is often what wakes you up in the middle of the night. If you fall asleep easily, but frequently awaken and have difficulty returning to sleep, this could indicate falling blood sugar levels.

The only long-term solution is to correct the hypoglycemia through dietary choices and supplementation. However, on a temporary basis, consuming a small amount of unsweetened juice or a teaspoon of cottage cheese or peanut butter when you awaken in the middle of the night will help stabilize your blood sugar enough to allow you to return to sleep. Persistent insomnia problems may take a couple of months to normalize using these natural remedies, but unlike pharmaceuticals, once good patterns have been reestablished, these natural remedies can be slowly phased out without experiencing the addictive side effects of prescriptions.

Environmental factors. The cycle of sleeping and waking is intricately connected to thousands of bodily functions. The process is like a complex clock with millions of gears that intertwine to help control hormone levels, blood pressure, body temperature, the nervous system, and virtually every other phase of our lives. Our stressful environment can make this wonderful clock gain or lose time. Ordinarily, your body will automatically reset itself, but when it doesn't, you can use one or more of these natural methods such as guava or melatonin to reset your body clock in the right direction—going forward.

SLACKER'S SYNDROME

Are you sick and tired of being . . . well, sick and tired every day? Do you constantly crave sleep? Do you wake up exhausted each morning? Do you have extreme mood swings that often have little to do with external influences? If you answered "yes" to any of these questions, you may be suffering from a condition that afflicts countless Americans—chronic fatigue syndrome. Chronic fatigue syndrome, loosely termed a "disease" by doctors, impairs a human being's core vitality. This illness has many names, including myalgia, chronic mononucleosis, and chronic Epstein-Barr virus. Numerous insurance bureaucrats and health care professionals have demonstrated their lack of respect for chronic fatigue syndrome sufferers by labeling the disease "slacker's syndrome," and the media has portrayed chronic fatigue syndrome as the *yuppie flu*—as if the sufferers are malingerers or just plain lazy. This is simply not the case: Studies show that vitamin deficiencies and lifestyle can cause characteristic chronic fatigue symptoms.[5]

Everyone experiences fatigue—it is impossible to avoid at the pace in which we live. However, in a healthy person, fatigue should be a temporary problem associated with strenuous activity or emotional stress worsened by a sedentary lifestyle, poor diet, or lack of sleep. Health practitioners often call this *acute fatigue*. This type of fatigue is commonly thought to serve a protective function by alerting the body of a heightened need for rest or better nutrition. By definition, acute fatigue should not last more than a few days, and with rest and proper diet, symptoms should resolve themselves.

This does not adequately explain the daily feelings of fatigue that disrupt every area of life for many individuals. Sufferers of ongoing fatigue may find that rest lessens the symptoms, but the benefits are only temporary; even more perplexing, chronic symptoms of fatigue may or may not be indicative of chronic fatigue syndrome itself. Other diseases such as multiple sclerosis and rheumatoid arthritis include severe fatigue as a symptom. More than 500,000 people in the United States have symptoms related to post-polio syndrome, which often causes a sudden loss of energy and feelings of extreme exhaustion.[6] Cancer can also bring about extreme fatigue, and cancer treatments can leave a patient "wiped out," to say the least. Because of these diverse and potentially disastrous consequences, people who experience severe, unrelenting fatigue should seek qualified medical care immediately.

DEFINING CHRONIC FATIGUE

Chronic fatigue syndrome is a debilitating disorder characterized by profound feelings of exhaustion or lethargy. Patients suffering from this illness become completely exhausted following even the lightest form of physical exertion; as a result, they are forced to substantially lower their activity levels as the illness progresses. Mundane tasks such as going to the grocery store become increasingly taxing until the patient no longer has the stamina to accomplish even the simplest of daily responsibilities. Meal preparation often requires more energy than the chronic fatigue syndrome patient has available, which only compounds the problem as malnutrition or poor eating habits drain the person even further. Victims of chronic fatigue syndrome also report symptoms such as sore throat, low-grade fever, muscle and joint pain, headaches, and the loss of the ability to concentrate. Patients may also notice small bumps on their neck and throat indicative of swollen lymph nodes.

DETERMINING THE CAUSE

The precise causes of chronic fatigue syndrome are yet unknown; however, some theories provide plausible explanations. One explanation is that the disease is brought on by an infection called the *Epstein-Barr virus*. The Epstein-Barr virus is in the same family of viruses that causes herpes, chickenpox, and shingles. These viruses all have one thing in common—the ability to establish themselves in the body and remain in dormant states for long periods of time after the initial infection.

Normally, these sub-acute infections are kept under control by the body's immune system. However, the immune system can become compromised when you get too tired, experience extremely high stress levels at work, deal with difficult family issues, or persistently make poor nutrition choices. When the immune system is weakened by these factors, those opportunistic viruses are likely to become active. These sudden "outbreaks" are commonly seen with herpes patients. Patients can live for years without an occurrence of this infection until major stress factors reduce the power of the immune system.

The Epstein-Barr virus is also responsible for mononucleosis, commonly known as the "kissing disease." Most of us can remember classmates who had mono. If you endured this illness in your teenage years, you likely remember feeling fatigued with a painful sore throat. Laboratory experiments have isolated antibodies to the Epstein-Barr virus in the blood of patients with mononucleosis and chronic fatigue syndrome. Some researchers contend that infection with Epstein-Barr is inevitable. According to some studies, by the time Americans reach the age of thirty, most of them will have the Epstein-Barr virus in their blood systems.

Another possible cause of chronic fatigue syndrome may be food allergies. Millions of people have allergies to common foods and do not even realize it. When someone is allergic to foods such as wheat and peanuts, dramatic symptoms can develop, or may cause milder symptoms such as red, burning eyes or exhaustion.

Your immune system is designed to recognize, seek, and destroy offending organisms such as cold germs. However, when you suffer from allergies, your body's immune system becomes confused, and reacts to substances such as pollen, cat hair, wheat, corn, or even broccoli. The body sees that harmless element as a threat, and is attacked by its own immune system. In food allergies, symptoms can vary tremendously. If you suspect you might be suffering from food allergies, start by eliminating all wheat and cow's milk dairy products from your diet for at least three weeks. If your symptoms do not improve, seek professional help from an allergist or natural health care practitioner to determine whether there are some or many foods that your body perceives as a threat.

FIGHTING BACK

I recommend several supplements to help battle chronic fatigue syndrome. These supplements help boost your body's defenses and promote a healthy immune system so your body can stave off chronic fatigue:

- Beta-carotene: Up to 10,000 IU per day

- Vitamin C (ascorbic form, buffered): 3,000 to 10,000 milligrams per day

- B complex supplement: 100 milligrams three times per day

- Coenzyme Q-10: 75 milligrams per day

- Probiotic: 4 to 8 capsules per day

- Vitamin E (a natural source): 400 to 800 IU per day

- Licorice root: 0.5 to 2 milliliters daily until symptoms begin to improve. (Note: when taking licorice root, increase your potassium-rich foods such as ripe bananas.)

- Vitamin B5 (pantothenic acid): 250 to 500 milligrams per day

Whether your exhaustion and illnesses are associated with your pace, work schedule, bad lifestyle habits, diet, or all of the above, the seventh-day rest principle discussed earlier is an essential process—a *standard* to which humans must adhere. Passive rest is both essential and critical to your over-all health. For those of you who live with chronic fatigue, insomnia, or other sleep disorder, I encourage you to wean yourself off anti-anxiety drugs, sleep medications, and tranquilizers. Talk with your physician about this before attempting to end any medication or treatment, as stopping a medication too quickly may cause problems.

WAYS TO SLEEP WELL

Here are my prescriptions for a good night's rest:

- Go to bed by 10 PM—every minute of sleep you get before midnight is worth four minutes after midnight.

- Start dimming the lights two hours before bedtime. This will signal the pineal gland (gland in the brain that produces a hormone that regulates wake and sleep patterns) to start producing melatonin (the sleep hormone).

- Use a fan or a white noise machine.

- Put an air purifier in the room. Cleaner air circulating in the room ensures that you breathe in fewer toxins and allergens from the air while asleep.

- Set the thermostat on 65 to 68 degrees. Your body naturally warms by several degrees at night, so keep the temperature a little lower than you would during the day to allow for this body temperature increase.

- Drink at least 10 ounces of pure, non-chlorinated water before bed for hydration. Often when the body is dehydrated, it will be unable to rest, and cause you to wake up in the middle of the night.

- Take any nutritional supplements needed, such as 5-HTP and probiotics.

- Drink a cup of chamomile tea. The soothing warm comfort of the tea is a great way to help calm you down and prepare you for a good night's rest.

Follow these simple prescriptions to experience the rest your body needs to become rejuvenated, and you will find you can face each subsequent day with increased energy and vitality. Seek natural methods and restore your body to a state in which your hormones reach balance and your body desires sleep on its own according to its natural rhythms. You must listen to your body! Sleep, combined with both active and passive rest, is one of the essential principles to living a healthy, long life.

24

GETTING WELL
Staying Well

"Look to your health; and if you have it, praise God and value it next to conscience; for health is the second blessing that we mortals are capable of—a blessing money can't buy."
—Izaak Walton

Health is really a lot of common sense combined with the desire to be well. All you have to understand are a few of the basic principles outlined in this book, not all the research and statistics. My advice to you is to take one healthy step at a time. Don't put this book down and try to do it all at once. If you do, you'll end up feeling overwhelmed. Pick one idea you can accomplish, embrace, and implement in your life today—not tomorrow. A common phrase is, "I'll get to that tomorrow," but with that outlook, you'll never get *anything* done. Have faith that you can begin today. If you will give at least a 50 percent effort, and put your trust in God to walk with you in the journey, you will acquire 100 percent of the most vibrant health you could ever imagine.

Take healthy steps, and take them one day at a time. Just pick one and get started. We've only just met, and I believe in you! And whether you believe in Him or not, God believes in you. It's time that *you* believe in you. Life is short, death is sure, our wrong choices are the cause, and our faith in God and ourselves is the cure.

THE 90/10 PRINCIPLE—NOBODY'S PERFECT

Natural Medicine is not all about cod liver oil, water filters, and mini trampolines. The 90/10 principle is the simple guideline that keeps us encouraged, and answers these questions: *Can I ever have a piece of cheesecake again? Will I ever be able to eat another pizza?* The answer is yes! This is where balance comes in. The human body is resilient. You can give it junk every now and then and it will withstand it with relative ease. It's when we feed it junk all the time that it breaks down. If you eat and practice a healthy lifestyle 90 percent of the time, then you can indulge yourself a little bit the other 10 percent.

The average person in America does the exact opposite. He or she eats one healthy meal per week and exercises one day per week. That's not going to get the job done. In your pursuit of health, understand that it's okay to be balanced. Don't feel like it's "all or nothing." You can still have fun and do what you want in life. If you are truly living well and following the principles outlined in this book, you will attain the extraordinary health that you have been looking for.

Here are some examples of applying the 90/10 principle. If you consume twenty-one meals in a week, during two meals a week, eat what you want. Have a dessert or an appetizer that you have been craving. I also recommend that you take a week off exercising every eight weeks. During this week, you can do exercises such as yoga or Pilates. However, more intense anaerobic activities and high impact aerobics should be avoided during the eighth week to give the body a chance to rest. Remember, it's all about balance.

YOUR BEST DAYS ARE STILL AHEAD

David walked into my office one day. I saw the desperation. I saw the despair. I saw the need for something bigger and greater than himself. He sank into a chair beside me and simply said, "Dr. Asa, I can't anymore."

"Can't what?" I asked.

"I can't live like this anymore," he replied. "I was told by another doctor that my heart is in really bad shape, and if I don't do something, I probably won't live much longer. I've already had two heart attacks, and I'm only forty-five."

David had finally reached it—the point at which he had had enough. There really isn't a word for it. It's a pain beyond description. I asked David, "Do you have a family?" He replied that he had a wife, a new baby, and two other children, and he wanted to be there to watch them grow. David's father had died at age fifty from heart disease, and he didn't want his story to end that way.

I asked him the pivotal question: *Do you want to get well?* David replied with a resounding "Yes!" By proclaiming that he wanted to be well, he had overcome the hardest challenge that we all face—ourselves. It's not the program, the diet, or the lifestyle changes. The greatest battle is not the one *around* us, but the one *within* us. David had overcome, and now he was on his way.

I found his heart was indeed in horrible shape. But I assured David that his body would regenerate. And it did. Today, David has lost eighty-five pounds, lives a thriving life with his family, has the heart of a twenty-year-old, and the life of a champion. He chose to look past himself and become selfless in the process. His health became more about others than about himself. He finally got it.

I'm your physician and health coach, and I'm here to coach you toward your health goals. Your health is determined by your choices. No one else can do it for you. The doctor can't do it for you, your husband can't do it for you, your wife can't do it for you, your kids can't do it for you, and your friends—they can't do it for you either. Only *you* can take responsibility for your health. The choices you make today will determine the health you will have tomorrow. Do I sound like a broken record? Good! Maybe then you'll remember what I am saying.

Thank you for reading this book. I hope and pray you signed the commitment card in the beginning. All I ask as you close this back cover is the most pivotal question you will ever be asked. Just as Jesus asked the man by the pool at Bethesda who had been sick for thirty-eight years . . .

Do you want to get well?

Do you?

Then get up and move into the extraordinary health that you deserve. That is what this book is for, and that is what I am here for—to show you how to take responsibility for your health right now. Wherever you are in the health process—beginning the journey, struggling to get your health back, absolutely thriving, or challenged in a hospital bed—you can get to that next level in your health transformation. Remember, your health is your greatest wealth. You can get it back, and it all depends on your first making the decision that you do indeed want to get well. Forget about the past—it's gone.

Focus on today because that's your gift, and realize, my friend, your best days are still ahead.

Talk with you soon.

Asa

"Dear friend, I pray that you may enjoy good health and that all may go well with you, even as your soul is getting along well."

3 John 1:2

25

ASA'S HOME REMEDIES
A Quick Reference Guide

Every patient carries her or his own doctor inside.
—ALBERT SCHWEITZER

Some things just work, even though we can't always explain them. Home remedies are often like that—we many not always have research articles, journals, or medical studies to back them up, but their track records speak for themselves. No doubt, your grandma had plenty of these remedies that were never published, yet they worked. The home remedies listed below are like that; these are helpful hints that I have used for years, simple things that you can do in your own home. So take these with the proverbial grain of salt and implement them as you feel necessary. Remember, give the body what it is lacking, and it will generally heal itself.

Home Remedies

Acid reflux	Vitamin A and omega 3 oils help thin bile; beet greens can cause the gallbladder to contract, flushing itself. Try taking a tablespoon of apple cider vinegar.
Acidosis	Acidosis is overactivity of the sympathetic nervous system. The person is usually breathless, sighs a lot, and feels as though there is a lump in his or her throat.
Adrenal fatigue	To relieve adrenal fatigue, add fresh celery juice and celtic sea salt to the diet until energy is restored.
Aerobic fitness	Aerobic fitness is improved with iron and omega 3 oils.
Alcohol	If you drink alcohol, make sure to supplement your diet with zinc, glutamine, and natural sodium to avoid any primary nutritional deficiencies.

Home Remedies

Allergies (seasonal)	Seasonal allergies usually indicate HCL (hydrochloric acid) insufficiency. Take 1-2 HCL tablets with each meal during peak allergy seasons. A lack of sodium can increase allergies.
Allergies (chronic)	For chronic allergies eliminate all wheat flour, flour, sugar, grains, and cow's milk dairy products for four weeks. Follow the adrenal building protocol on page 123 and monitor acid/alkaline balance.
Allergy to tomatoes	If you are allergic to tomatoes, you are deficient in niacin and pantothenic acid.
Alzheimers	Cooking utensils are made from stainless steel, iron, and glass. These items contain iron and chrome, which are needed by the body. Teflon products contain aluminum and should be avoided.
Anaerobic fitness	Anaerobic fitness is improved with panothenic acid.
Arthritis	Persons with too much alkalinity show signs of arthritis and can be helped by taking calcium.
Aspirin	Bromelain, found in pineapple, is a great alternative to aspirin.
Asthma	For asthma, eliminate all wheat flour, flour, sugar, grains, and cow's milk dairy products for four weeks.
Bags under eyes	Dark rings under the eyes are a result of a toxic liver and kidneys.
Bloating	Bloating is a symptom of vitamin B1 (thiamine) deficiency.
Blood clotting issues	To increase blood clotting, increase vitamin K. It is best found in chlorophyll.
Blood transfusion	If you are told you need a blood transfusion, try a mixture of 6 oz. of pure concord grape juice, 1 raw organic egg, and 50mg of liquid B12 (activated form) until energy is restored; this reduces the need for a transfusion.
Bone pain	People who experience frequent bone pain or perspire from the head need vitamin D.
Bone spurs	Bone spurs and calcium deposits may result if your system is too alkaline. Increase your intake of acidifying foods.
Burning in soles of feet	Burning in the soles of the feet is a symptom of vitamin B1 (thiamine) deficiency.
Calcium absorption	Calcium absorption is disrupted for four days with the ingestion of sugar.
Cardiovascular disease	Walnuts may help reduce cardiovascular disease.

Home Remedies

Cataracts	Cataracts are usually caused by defeciencies in vitamins B2, B6, B12, and D. Glutathione helps negate the cloudy effects caused by cataracts in your eyes.
Congestion	When your nose is congested, increase your intake of sodium and potassium. A congested right nostril indicates the need for potassium, and the left for sodium. Heavy localized congestion in the throat usually reveals a need for sulfur. Consider taking methionine, taurine, glutathione, bananas, eggs, garlic, and onions.
Constipation	For constipation, increase water intake to half your body weight in ounces (a person who weighs 150 pounds should drink 75 ounces of water per day) and increase your daily intake of natural fiber in foods to 40 grams. Eat peas such as black-eyed or green. Increase exercise, add omega-3 oils, and increase B vitamins. Always check your prescription drugs for constipation side effects.
Diarrhea	For chronic diarrhea, consider montmorillonite clay.
Digestion	Drink green or black tea with high fat meals to increase digestibilty of the meal.
Dizziness	If you experience dizziness when you sit up quickly, you may have adrenal fatigue and need B vitamins and vitamin C.
Drowsiness	Drowsiness after meals is a symptom of vitamin B1 (thiamine) deficiency.
Eye issues	Eye issues are usually associated with the liver and kidney. Look to an activated form of vitamin A and essential fatty acids such as omegas 3, 6, and 9.
Fat allergies	If you eat fats and have an allergic reaction, try taking sulfur.
Fatigue	If you are enduring ongoing fatigue, think anemia. You may need either vitamin B12, vitamin B1 (thiamine), or iron.
Fever in children	Calcium lactate or omega-3 oils, can be helpful in controlling fever in children who are sick or cutting teeth; they also lessen the severity of chicken pox.
Fluid retention	Fluid retention indicates a need for B vitamins.
Gallbladder	If your gallbladder has been removed, consider taking bile salts with your meals.
Gastroesophageal reflux	If you suffer from gastroesophageal reflux (GERD), consider taking digestive enzymes with your meals. Also check for a hiatal hernia.
Gastrointestinal bleeding	Licorice root, cayenne pepper, and rhubarb are great for preventing gastrointestinal bleeding.

Home Remedies

Head pressure	Tight bandedness around the head is a symptom of vitamin B1 (thiamine) deficiency.
Headaches	Headaches with pain in specific areas require certain nutrition. Pain in the right eye indicates the need for iron; pain in the left eye shows a need for zinc, and a pain in the back of the head may be alleviated by taking some choline.
Heart disease	If you deal with heart disease, add niacin, coenzyme Q10, vitamin C, lecithin, citris pectin 9 (found in grapefruit), and selenium to your daily routine.
Heart issues	If you have a heart condition, do not drink tea. It contains tannic acid, which will further deplete your already low potassium levels.
Heavy metals	Heavy metals can be eliminated from the body with methionine, cysteine, and superoxide dismutase (SOD).
Hemorrhoids	Hemorrhoids are usually due to venous congestion. Try collinsonia root and comfrey.
High blood pressure	To lower blood pressure, use a product with L-citrulline and L-arginine, such as Restore Balance (www.EmpowerRx.com).
High cholesterol	Persons with high cholesterol may need more essential fatty acids. Tumeric, green tea, rosemary, and quercetin can reduce bad cholesterol (LDL), protect against cancer, and provide strong antioxidants.
High triglycerides	If your triglycerides are high, consider taking 1 tablespoon of salmon oil per day.
Hot flashes	If you are experiencing hot flashes, take your underarm temperature as described on page 149. If it is below 97.6, consider organic iodine. If it is above 97.6 look into a possible estrogen-progesterone balancing formula.
Hypertension	Cadmium is a metal that should be avoided. It is found in enamel pots, cigarette smoke, car fumes, and urban pollution. It is a primary cause of hypertension.
Hyperthyroid	If you are hyperthyroid, vitamin A and thymus supplementation may help.
Immunodeficiency	When the immune system is low, consider supporting the thymus gland with alfalfa, spirulina, kelp, and bee propolis.
Impotence	Impotence can be helped by eliminating sugar from your diet and including herbs, such as ginseng, sarsaparilla, damiana, yohimba, and saw palmetto, and foods high in zinc, arginine, and selenium in your diet.

Home Remedies

Indigestion	Indigestion twenty minutes after a meal shows the need for HCL. Indigestion one to two hours after a meal shows the need for digestive enzymes. For chronic indigestion, consider L-glutamine.
Insomnia	Inability to fall asleep may be due to a calcium deficiency.
Leg cramps	Leg cramps usually show the need for calcium, magnesium, or vitamin E; they may also be caused by dehydration.
Ligament weakness	If you have loose ligaments and sprain joints easily, or you experience reccurring back pain, you are probably deficient in manganese.
Liver issues	If you have any condition associated with the liver, such as cirrhosis or jaundice, consider increasing your natural sodium intake by eating green vegetables.
Loose teeth	Loose teeth usually indicate a calcium deficiency.
Low body temperature	A low body temperature indicates a need for B vitamins.
Lung disorders	Most bronchitis, asthma, and lung disorders are due to a severe sodium deficiency. Consider increasing your "greens" by eating more celery, cabbage, cucumbers, spinach, lettuce, and green beans, and by using celtic sea salt.
Lupus	Most Lupus symptoms will disappear when sodium and potassium levels are regulated. Also consider checking the pituitary gland, and taking the amino acid L-ornithine and B6 (pyridoxal 5 phosphate).
Lyme disease	For Lyme disease consider the homeopathic remedy of teasel.
Memory	If your memory is not what it used to be, take an RNA supplement or lecithin. Poor memory also indicates a need for B vitamins.
Memory loss	Cooking utensils are made from stainless steel, iron, and glass. These items contain iron and chrome, which are needed by the body. Teflon products contain aluminum and should be avoided.
Migraines	Migraine headaches usually stem from one of two primary sources: aluminum in the diet or food allergies. Migraines on top of the head can be alleviated by taking wood betony.
Morning sickness	Vitamin K along with vitamin C are good for morning sickness.
Muscle soreness	Take vitamin B1 thiamine for excessive soreness after exercise.
Muscle tone	B vitamins provide muscular tone.
Mucous secretions	Try using some organic iodine.

Home Remedies

Nausea	A queasy, nauseated stomach needs organic phosphoric acid.
Nervousness	People who bite their fingernails, chew hair, and crave dirt (pica) may need organic trace minerals.
Neuritis	Persons with too much alkalinity show signs of neuritis and can be helped by taking calcium.
Night blindness	Vitamin A is a good remedy for night blindness.
Night sweats	A person who sweats a lot at night, has blood shot eyes, or jerks erratically while relaxing may need vitamins B2 and B3.
Nightmares (recurring)	A person who deals with reccurring nightmares will usually show a rise in blood pressure when going from standing to lying and needs the amino acid L-arginine.
Noise intolerance	Noise intolerance indicates a need for B vitamins.
Osteoarthritis	If you are suffering with osteoarthritis, consider eating 8 to 16 ounces per day of plain goat's milk yogurt.
Overweight	Fennel and chicory are great fat burners.
Parkinson's disease	Parkinson's disease may mean a malfunctioning parathyroid gland and calcium deficiency. Consider bone meal calcium and B complex vitamins. Sunshine is a great therapeutic addition, helping to increase calcium absorption through vitamin D.
Perspiration	People who perspire a lot from the head need vitamin D.
Plantar warts	Plantar warts may be helped by taking a trace mineral supplement.
Prostate	Prostate health is helped with 100 mg zinc, 2000 mg of saw palmetto, and 10 g of pumpkin seed oil daily.
Ringing in the ears	Constant ringing in the right ear is an indication of a wheat allergy. Stop eating all wheat products. If the left ear is ringing, try maganese.
Schizophrenia	When dealing with schizophrenic symptoms, niacin, cysteine, glutathione, and vitamin C may assist.
Sciatica	In sudden nerve pain such as sciatic pain, mega doses of B vitamins with 5-20 mg of calcium may be used for a brief time. Persons with too much alkalinity show signs of sciatic pain and can be helped by taking calcium.
Seizures	If you struggle with seizures, eliminate coffee from your diet. It disrupts choline, which is essential for proper brain function.
Sinus issues	Try using some organic iodine.

Home Remedies

Skin disorders	For skin disorders eliminate all wheat flour, flour, sugar, grains, and cow's milk dairy products for four weeks.
Sleep issues	Inability to stay asleep might indicate a vitamin B deficiency or low blood sugar.
Slow heart rate	Slow heart rate indicates a need for B vitamins.
Smoking habit	Smokers should use the amino acid Taurine to help negate side effects (but I strongly suggest you quit smoking altogether.) A great method to stop smoking is to take vitamin B3 in the form of niacinimide. Nicotinic acid is a version of "nicotine" and will replace and help eliminate the cravings.
Spider veins	Spider veins indicate a need for B vitamins.
Sun exposure	Apply safflower and olive oil to the skin after sun exposure. They contain vitamin F, which enhances skin regeneration.
Sun poisoning	Overcoming sun poisoning and skin rashes can be helped by calcium lactate and omega 3 oils.
Swelling	Persons with "wedding band sydrome" or swollen hands usually need P-5-P (pyridoxal 5 phosphate). If you are unable to flex your fingers to your palm and have swelling of the hands, consider adding vitamin B6 to your daily regimen.
Tooth decay	If you have "bad teeth," usually you are too acidic. Try eating more alkaline foods.
Ulcers	For relief of ulcers, drink 8 ounces of freshly juiced cabbage juice daily for 1–3 months.
Urination issues	Frequent night urinations is a symptom of vitamin B1 (thiamine) deficiency. If you have frequent urination but a small volume of fluid, you may need B vitamins.
Viral infection	If you have any type of virus, avoid foods or supplements containing arginine (chocolate and almonds) during the flare up. Take L-lysine and vitamin B5 (pantothenic acid) instead.
Voice pitch	If there is a sudden drop in your voice pitch, then you are probably deficient in sulfur.
Weak blood vessels	If you are prone to weak blood vessels, try taking rutin and absorbable calcium such as calcium lactate.
Yawning	If you yawn frequently, you may be too acidic on the pH scale and need alkalizing foods. Frequent yawning is a symptom of vitamin B1 (thiamine) deficiency.

APPENDIX A
Asa's Healthy Top 40 Countdown

Here are forty things you can incorporate into your life to regain proper body function. You probably won't ever do all of them in one day, but choose a few every week to highlight. Then watch your health consistently get better!

40. Wear a magnet. It protects you from the damaging effects of electromagnetic radiation that we encounter daily from cars, microwaves, lights, computers, etc. It will also restore your energy by 50 percent.

39. Spend 30 minutes in the sun each day without sunscreen. Sunlight is one of the best ways to stay healthy, promoting vitamin D production and absorption. Sunscreen is laden with chemicals and should be avoided when possible. For times when you will be exposed to longer periods of sunlight, use natural sunscreens available at most health foods stores. I also recommend wearing a hat and covering the more sensitive parts of your body that are prone to burn, including your shoulders and back, and not going out during peak hours.

38. Get one Thai massage each week—fully clothed and without lotions. It's great for toxin release and stimulation of the lymphatic system. It's also a great stress reducer and increases immune function.

37. Eat two tablespoons of extra-virgin coconut oil daily. It increases thyroid function, stimulates metabolism, and is an anti-fungal. An easy way to achieve this is to use coconut oil when you cook.

36. Eat organic grapefruits and chocolate. They contain powerful antioxidants and enzymes that burn body fat. Organic chocolate must be dark, such as bakers' chocolate, and include 70 percent cocoa. It's high in flavinoids, and antioxidants, which lower LDL bad cholesterol and reduce chances of heart attacks and strokes.

35. Drink green, yerba matte, chamomile, and eleotin tea daily. All will promote energy, reduce toxins, and provide antioxidant protection.

34. Do a heavy metal cleanse weekly. It helps remove toxic metals such as aluminum, arsenic, mercury, and cadmium. Use a liquid metal cleanse supplement that contains chlorella, which you can find in your local health food store. You can also use chelation for extreme cases, which are discussed in greater detail in chapter 10.

33. Eat organic eggs every day. Eggs are one of nature's complete foods, great for keeping cholesterol normalized because of choline and lecithin in the egg yolk. Eat the yolks!

32. Eat three regular meals and two snack meals per day. Regular meals promote healthy digestion and metabolism and provide the right nutrients for healthy cells to grow.

31. Don't eat later than 6:00 or 7:00 PM and stop eating at least three hours before your bedtime. This allows proper resting of the digestive system.

30. Use cinnamon and 40 grams of fiber daily. Both of these help maintain healthy digestion, elimination, and blood sugar levels.

29. Jump on a mini trampoline at least five to ten minutes per day. This is helpful for proper pumping and functioning of the anti toxin system, the lymphatics.

28. Seek out healthy salt. Forget all you know about sodium. Stay away from table salt; use Celtic sea salt and eat high sodium foods such as celery, beets, beet greens, carrots, kale, mustard greens, and spinach. Don't use this an excuse to load up on salty foods like ham! Use some common sense, and this will strengthen adrenal glands and help your body manage stress throughout the day.

27. Go to bed at 10:00 PM and wake up by 6:00 AM. Key hormones and body regeneration happens between 11:00 PM and 2:00 AM. Make sure to have your body clock asleep during these times of "body repair." This will replenish your energy to meet the next day.

26. Stop using non-organic personal care products. Read labels and look for the toxic chemicals mentioned in the personal care products section. What you put on your skin goes directly into your bloodstream.

25. Get a shower filter. Chlorine is one of the most toxic chemicals known. Use a shower filter to avoid chlorine toxicity. Whatever touches your skin goes in you.

24. Stop using fluorescent lights. Use full spectrum lights to lower fatigue levels and strengthen your adrenal (stress handling) glands. Full spectrum light is light that covers the entire spectrum from low infrared to ultraviolet and above. Sunlight is considered full spectrum, so choose select lights that are the closest you can get to real sunlight.

23. Breathe. Regular deep breathing is essential for adding oxygen to our cells; it also cleans out toxins and increases lung capacity.

22. Use music in the morning and evening. Music therapy has been used for years and has profound effects on our mental state. It can stimulate, activate, and inspire you in the morning and calm you in the evening.

21. Do a liver and gallbladder cleanse. These two organs tend to hold on to toxins and become congested. Do a liver and gallbladder cleanse regularly. See cleanses in chapter 9 under headache protocols.

20. Exercise with weights at least two days per week. Everyone needs to use some form of weightlifting or resistance type exercise to increase bone density and increase muscle mass for greater structural stability and to prevent osteoporosis.

19. Have houseplants. They are a great natural way to increase oxygen within the home.

18. Do not use an alarm clock. Waking the body with this shock-like mechanism will create stress and increase cortisol, a fat promoting, muscle-wasting hormone.

17. Check yearly for candida yeast and parasites. These are some of the greatest challenges in our digestive system that keep our bodies malfunctioning. Overgrowth can cause such things as gas bloating, headaches, nausea, allergies, asthma, fibromyalgia, arthritis, diabetes, acne, dandruff, bad breath, fatigue, and depression. The most common side effect is the inability to lose weight.

16. Take absorbable calcium before bed. Lack of calcium is the number one reason people wake up and can't sleep through the night. Try eating eight ounces of plain goat's milk yogurt about three hours before bedtime as an excellent source of calcium.

15. Walk as much as you can. We were meant to move. Stop trying to get the closest parking spot, and take the stairs rather than ride elevators to the second and third floors. Get off your duff and get moving.

14. Have mercury fillings removed. Mercury is extremely toxic and causes everything from cancer to Alzheimer's. If you have any silver amalgam fillings, have a dentist who is trained in the removal of such fillings replace them with porcelin fillings. Choose your dentist carefully; improper removal can lead to mercury sickness.

13. Eat an organic apple each day. It has tons of fiber and nutrients to help normalize blood sugar and is loaded with antioxidants.

12. Check your body pH saliva and urine once per week. Keeping your body pH balanced helps improve energy and increase overall health.

11. Change your home air filters monthly and use an air purifier. Air quality is critical to overall health. Keep all your rooms at the highest air quality they can be, and open your windows in your home frequently—

just thirty minutes a day of fresh outdoor air will drastically increase immune function, healthy cell growth, and increase energy levels.

10. Have your blood checked yearly for disease prevention and nutritional deficiencies. Diagnostic blood work is the foundation of all medicine. Get checked yearly to prevent disease and repair any nutritional deficiencies.

9. Fast one day per week. The digestive system needs time to repair and rest. Give it a break once per week and decrease your risk of cancer, heart disease, and inflammatory diseases.

8. Forgive others. Stop holding grudges. There is always something you don't know about a situation when you've been hurt. Get over it and get on with it.

7. Keep your hormones checked and balanced. Thyroid, estrogen, progesterone, and testosterone are very important for optimal balance; have them checked at least annually.

6. Supplement your diet with the foundational four. These include a whole food multi vitamin, digestive enzymes, omega-3 oils (cod liver oil), and probiotics. Don't leave home without them. You must supplement these things, as we don't get enough of them in our normal food supply anymore.

5. Drink half your body weight in ounces of pure, non-chlorinated water daily. Dehydration is an issue with poor health. Our bodies are over 70 percent water. Get hydrated with water; don't count all your teas and other beverages throughout the day. For example, a person who weighs 140 pounds should drink 70 ounces of water per day.

4. Rest and do nothing one full day per week. Our bodies need rest for mental, chemical, and structural reasons. Take one full day a week and do only what is absolutely necessary.

3. Exercise five to six times per week for thirty minutes per day. Regular exercise of any type will promote health.

2. Have your health checked monthly by a qualified physician. Have your Health Triangle checked monthly or at least every two months to remain aware of your current condition. Daily bombardments of stressors and toxins change our state of health. Staying ahead of the game is where extraordinary health is.

1. Decide you want to get well. The most important issue you will ever face regarding your health. The greatest power you have is in the palm of your hands, so choose wisely.

APPENDIX B
Asa's Top 10 Things to Avoid

These ten items should be eliminated from everyone's kitchen, diet, and lifestyle.

1. **Trans fats**—Trans fat increases blood levels of (LDL), or "bad" cholesterol, while lowering levels of (HDL), or "good" cholesterol. It can also cause the clogging of arteries, type 2 diabetes, and other serious health problems. There is no upper safety limit recommended for the daily intake of trans fat. The FDA has only said that "intake of trans fats should be as low as possible." Read your labels! Anything that says "partially hydrogenated" anything is a trans fat, and it only takes a miniscule amount of trans fat (1.3 milligrams) to do cell damage. Only cook with organic butter or extra-virgin coconut oil as all other oils will turn into trans fat when used for cooking (that includes olive oil).

2. **Artificial sweeteners**—Artificial sweeteners are contributing to the diabetes epidemic as much as processed sugar, because they prompt you to eat more. Alternatives are raw honey, stevia extract, agave nectar, and xylitol. Aspartame and sucralose (Splenda) should be avoided completely due to their toxic effects on the body. Saccharin is acceptable for use in moderate quantities. Artificial sweeteners are covered in more detail in chapter 8.

3. **High fructose corn syrup and processed sugars**—High fructose corn syrup is not metabolized the same as other sugars. Instead of being converted to glucose, which the body uses, it is removed by the liver. Because of this, fructose does not cause the pancreas to release insulin as it normally does. Fructose converts to fat more than any other sugar. This may be one of the reasons Americans continue to get fatter.

4. **Soy products.** Soy has been shown to depress thyroid function, block intake of enzymes that the body needs for protein digestion, and cause serious gastric distress, and can lead to chronic deficiencies in amino acid uptake. Soy creates hormonal imbalances in men and women by affecting estrogen levels. Instead of soy milk for drinks and for infants, use goat's milk. It's the closest

294

molecular structure to a human mother's milk and is highly anti-allergenic. Soy is covered in more detail in chapter 8.

5. **Pork products**—Pork was created to clean the waste off the ground. When we eat toxic meat such as the pig, it creates toxic cells. They were never meant for consumption.

6. **Shellfish**—These sea creatures perform much of the same functions as the pig does on land. Shellfish are also scavengers, ingesting countless toxins from the water in attempt to keep our oceans and lakes clean.

7. **Processed wheat and white flour**—Do you remember making **papier-mâché** in elementary school? You used flour and water to make a glue that was hard as concrete. It has a similar effect in the body. Processed flour blocks the absorption of nutrients in our digestive systems. If you are going to eat bread, choose sprouted grain bread such as Ezekiel bread or spelt bread. Remember, if the flour product is not frozen, it has been processed.

8. **Soft drinks**—Sodas, even diet drinks, poison the body. Calories from sugary soft drinks are not adequately controlled by the body's appetite regulation system. They don't reduce your hunger as solid food does, so your total caloric intake is even higher. Additionally, regular soft drinks are sweetened with high-fructose corn syrup, and diet drinks use artificial sweeteners, which should both be avoided. A great alternative to still have the fizz that you crave is to add fresh lime or lemon to sparkling water along with approved sweeteners such as stevia extract or saccharin.

9. **Unfiltered tap water**—Regular tap water is filled with chemicals and infused with chlorine. Always drink fresh spring water or filtered water, and use a water filter for your home (even for the water in which you bathe and wash your clothes).

10. **Non-organic dairy and meat products**—Animals that are not raised organically are fed chemical and hormone-laced foods from the day they are born. And by eating them, those harmful toxins go directly into you.

APPENDIX C
Asa's Natural Medicine Resource Guide

PHYSICIANS AND HEALTH CENTERS

A preferred local provider (PLP) is a health care professional (or company) in your area that has been personally chosen by Dr. Asa's team based on his or her integrity, professionalism, and experience. They are contractually obligated to share the same health and wellness philosophies that Asa imparts in this book and on his *Empowering Your Health* radio program. Below are a few excellent clinics that offer a more integrated apporach. To find a preferred local provider call 888-283-7272 or go to www.AsaAndrew.com and click on Preferred Local Provider.

The Center for Natural Medicine
Dr. Asa Andrew
4535 Harding Road, Ste C-210
Nashville, TN 37205
888-283-7272
www.AsaAndrew.com/wellnessclinic. htm

The Gesundheit Institute
Dr. Patch Adams
HC 64 Box 167
Hillsboro, WV 24946
www.patchadams.org

The Greenbrier Clinic
320 West Main Street
White Sulphur Springs, WV 24986
304-536-4870
www.greenbrierclinic.com

The Mayo Clinic
4500 San Pablo Road
Jacksonville, FL 32224
904-953-2000
www.mayoclinic.org/jacksonville

The Mayo Clinic
13400 East Shea Boulevard
Scottsdale, AZ 85259
480-301-8000
www.mayoclinic.org/scottsdale

The Mayo Clinic
200 First Street S.W.
Rochester, MN 55905
507-284-2511
www.mayoclinic.org/rochester

Chattanooga Health Center
Dr. Jeff Hall
423-614-7616
www.ocoeehealthcenter.com

Jody Jones DDS
615-259-5100
www.jodyjonesdds.com

American Council on Exercise (ACE)
888-825-3636
www.acefitness.org

Aerobic and Fitness Association of America (AFFFA)
877-968-7263
www.afaa.com

Optimal Wellness Center
Dr. Joseph Mercola
1443 W. Schaumburg, Ste 250
Schaumburg, IL 60194
(847) 985-1777
www.mercola.com

International Academy of Oral Medicine and Toxicology
www.iaomt.org

International College of Integrated Medicine
866-464-5226
www.icimed.com

PRODUCTS

Air Purifiers and Water Filters
Pionair Air Purifiers
866-746-6247
www.pionair.net

Venta Air Wash
888-333-8218
www.veta-airwasher.com

NEEDS
800-634-1380
www.needs.com

Gaiam Harmony Catalog
800-869-3446
www.gaiam.com

Wellness Filter
800-428-9419
www.wellnessfilter.com

Organic Personal Care Products
Aubrey Organics
800-282-7394
www.aubrey-organics.com

Organic Personal Care Products
Jason Natural Products Consumer
Relations
877-527-6601
www.jason-natural.com

Kiss My Face
845-255-4312
www.kissmyface.com

Organic Essentials
800-765-6491
www.organicessentials.com

Fitness
Optimum Performance Systems
561-393-3881
www.opsfit.com

Rebound Air
888-464-5867
www.reboundair.com

APPENDIX D—
Supplements and Nutritional Products

Nutritional supplementation is essential today because bodies are exposed to such an extreme level of toxins through poor soil, the air we breathe, the water we drink, and the foods we eat. We are bombarded with carcinogenic pollutants that the commercial agrochemical industry places within our food supply. It has become vital that we supplement our healthy diets with the highest quality nutritional formulas to make sure we are able to protect our health.

At the Center for Natural Medicine we promote and use Empower Nutritional Products. All of the supplements mentioned below can be purchased by going to www.AsaAndrew.com/shoppingcart.htm. I've also recommended two other websites to consider for the supplements below. Before taking any supplements check with your physician who can monitor your progress through some clinical testing. Please be cautious when purchasing nutritional supplements. They are not all the same.

Nutri-West   **Standard Process**
www.nutriwest.com   www.standardprocess.com

THE FOUNDATIONAL FOUR

1. Whole-Food Multivitamin: Start taking whole food multivitamins and you will literally feel the difference. Whole food multivitamins are generally clearly labeled as such. Empower Men's/Women's Multi-Balance is a whole-food multivitamin I recommend.

2. Digestive Enzymes: Enzymes help break down the food that we eat. Take one to two per meal enzyme supplements with every meal. Look for brands that contain chlorella, chlorophyllase, and pepsin and avoid brands that say they have been freezedried or frozen. Empower Enzyme Balance and HCL Balance are great digestive aids to incorporate into your diet.

3. Probiotics: Probiotics are dietary supplements containing beneficial bacteria. The bacteria used in probiotic formulas are able to convert sugars and other carbohydrates into lactic acid. In general, look for standardized or pharmaceutical grade probiotics. Empower Probiotic Balance is one of the better probiotics on the market.

4. Omega-3 Oils: Many of us are shockingly deficient in omega-3 fats, those found in sources like cod liver oil, most nuts, salmon, tuna, and flaxseeds. Omega-3 fat is called an essential amino acid because it is truly *essential* that you consume it. Our bodies do not produce essential amino acids on their own, but they are necessary for a multitude of functions in the body such as proper hormone function, brain function, and skin, hair, and nail health. Cod liver oil is the best choice for absorption. Empower Cod Liver Oil is one of the highest natural source of mercury-free omega-3 fatty acids available today.

ACTIVATED VITAMINS

Empower Activated Liquid Vitamins—to restore vital nutritional deficiencies. For example, the liquid B12 is the highest grade available today and available in the most active forms dependent on your genetic predispositions. Call the office to find out what specific versions will help prevent your genetic tendencies toward the top diseases.

ADRENAL HEALTH

Empower Adrenal Balance—designed to keep your stress glands working at their optimal levels and handle whatever life gives you.

ANTIOXIDANTS

Empower Vitamin C, E, CoQ10, and a full line of antioxidant blends—for maximum protection against free radicals.

BLOOD SUGAR REGULATION

Empower Blood Sugar Balance—to regulate our body's ability to manage insulin and restore proper function.

BONE HEALTH

Empower Bone Balance—combines all the essential nutrients including vitamin D3, which is critical for strengthening our structure and reducing the risk of osteoporosis.

Organic phosphorus—If you find yourself craving soft drinks, take organic phosphorus in a liquid form to replenish the levels and support proper bone health, which you will find at your local health food store. Check out Phos Drops at www.Nutri-west.com.

HEART HEALTH

Empower Homocysteine Balance—to help reduce the damaging effects of homocysteine in the body.

Empower Restore Balance—University-tested natural formula that will lower blood pressure naturally.

APPENDIX D—Supplements and Nutritional Products

HORMONE BALANCE AND RESTORATION

Empower Restore Balance—for losing weight, increasing energy, reducing cellulite, reducing body fat, and lowering blood pressure.

Empower HgH Balance—for restoring optimal hormone function, normalizing human growth hormone levels for cellulite reduction, and increased energy and stamina.

Empower Hormone Balance—helps maintain that critical balance between testosterone, estrogen, progesterone, and other critical hormone processes. Whether you are facing female menopause or male facing andropause, this will help keep you balanced.

LIVER DETOXIFICATION

Empower Detox Balance—to help eliminate toxins and decongest the liver to help normalize cholesterol production and liver function.

PHYTONUTRIENT POWDER

Empower Green Balance—a full spectrum green mix that equals up to twelve servings of vegetables per serving.

THYROID HEALTH

Empower Organic Iodine—the purest form of iodine available today. One of our most essential minerals, yet it highly depleted in our food supply. For optimal thyroid function, make sure to have your iodine levels checked and only use the purest form of organic iodine.

Empower Thyroid Balance—for those with challenges with the thyroid, a whole food blend designed to support all levels of thyroid function.

WEIGHT LOSS AND MANAGEMENT

Empower Restore Balance—for losing weight, increasing energy, reducing cellulite, reducing body fat, and lowering blood pressure.

Empower HgH Balance—for restoring optimal hormone function, normalizing human growth hormone levels for cellulite reduction, and increased energy and stamina.

Empower CLA Balance—Conjugated linoleic acid isdesigned to help drop 6 percent body fat in six to eight weeks.

NOTES

CHAPTER 1

1. Jerome Groopman, *The Anatomy of Hope: How People Prevail in the Face of Illness* (New York: Random House, 2003).

CHAPTER 3

1. Edward Bach, *Heal Thyself* (London: C. W. Daniel Company, 2004).
2. Dariush Mozaffarian and Eric B. Rimm, "Fish Intake, Contaminants, and Human Health: Evaluating the Risks and the Benefits," *JAMA;* 296 (October 18, 2006): 1885–1899.
3. Ahmedin Jemal, et al., "Trends in the Leading Causes of Death in the United States, 1970–2002," *JAMA;* 294 (September 14, 2005): 1255–1259.

CHAPTER 4

1. Zig Ziglar, *Over the Top* (Nashville: Thomas Nelson, 1997).
2. Earl Nightingale, *Earl Nightingale's The Strangest Secret* (Sarasota, FL: Keys Company, 1999).
3. Dennis Waitley, *Seeds of Greatness* (Old Tappan, NJ: Fleming H Revell Company, 1983), 29.

CHAPTER 5

1. R. F. Anda, et al., "Self-Perceived Stress and the Risk of Peptic Ulcer Disease. A Longitudinal Study of US Adults," *Archives of Internal Medicine;* 152 (Apr 1992): 829–833.
2. 2 Timothy 1:7, King James Version

CHAPTER 6

1. "Plasma Vitamin C Concentrations in Patients in a Psychiatric Hospital," *Human Nutrition-Clinical Nutrition;* 37:6 (Dec 1983): 447–52.
2. Robin G. McCreadie, et al., "Dietary Improvement in People with Schizophrenia: Randomized Controlled Trial," *Br. J. Psychiatry;* 187 (Oct 2005): 346–351.
3. Brian Vastag, "Decade of Work Shows Depression Is Physical," *JAMA;* 287 (Apr 2002): 1787–1788.
4. J. G. Henderson and A. A. Dawson, "Serum Vitamin-B12 Levels in Psychiatric Patients on Long-term Psychotropic Drug Therapy," *British Journal of Psychiatry;* 116 (Apr 1970): 439–442.

CHAPTER 7

1. "Trans Fatty Acids in Nutrition Labeling, Nutrient Content Claims, and Health Claims" or on display at the FDA's Dockets Management Branch (Dockets Management Branch, HFA-305, Food and Drug Administration, 5630 Fishers Lane, Room 1061, Rockville, MD 20852).
2. Eric Brunner, "Oily Fish and Omega 3 Fat Supplements," *BMJ;* 332 (Apr 2006): 739–740; http://www.bmj.com/cgi/rapidpdf/bmj.38798.680185.47v1.
3. Joseph Mercola, "Should You Take Vitamin Supplements?" [Available Online] Mercola.com [July 2002]; Available from http://www.mercola.com/2002/jul/10/vitamin_supplements.htm.
4. John H Cummings and Sheila A Bingham, "Fortnightly Review: Diet and the Prevention of Cancer," *BMJ;* 317 (Dec 1998): 1636–1640.
5. Paul D. Blanc, *How Everyday Products Make People Sick: Toxins at Home and in the Workplace* (Berkeley: University of California Press, 2007).
6. Westin A. Price, *Nutrition and Physical Degeneration,* (LA: Price-Pottinger Foundation, 1939, 1997).

7. Price, *Nutrition and Physical Degeneration*.

8. Joseph Mercola and Rachael Droeger, "Five Common Toxic Metals to Avoid, and Where You'll Find Them," [Available Online] Mercola.com [Dec 2003] Available from http :// www.mercola.com/2003/dec/27/ toxic_metals.htm.

9. US Environmental Protection Agency, *Recognition and Management of Pesticide Poisoning*, 5th ed. (US Environmental Protection Agency) 15: 151.

10. Janice K. Kiecolt-Glaser, et al., "Hostile Marital Interactions, Proinflammatory Cytokine Production, and Wound Healing," *Archives of General Psychiatry;* 62 (Dec 2005): 1377–1384.

CHAPTER 8

1. Digestion. Dictionary.com. *The American Heritage New Dictionary of Cultural Literacy*, 3rd ed. (Boston: Houghton Mifflin Company, 2005), http://dictionary.reference.com /browse/digestion (accessed: April 11, 2007).

2. Solomon H. Katz, "Food and Biocultural Evolution: A Model for the Investigation of Modern Nutritional Problems," *Nutritional Anthropology*, 1987; 50.

3. Sally Fallon & Mary G. Enig, "Newest Research On Why You Should Avoid Soy," [Available Online] http://www.mercola.com/article/soy/avoid_soy.htm.

4. T. L. Davidson and S.E. Swithers, "A Pavlovian Approach to the Problem of Obesity," *International Journal of Obesity;* 28:7 (July 2004): 933–935.

5. Council on Scientific Affairs, "Saccharin: Review of Safety Issues," JAMA; 254 (Nov 1985): 2622–2624.

6. John Henkel, "Sugar Substitutes: Americans Opt for Sweetness and Lite." FDA Consumer magazine (November-December 1999). [Available Online] http://www.fda.gov/fdac /features/1999/699_sugar.html.

7. Joseph Mercola, "Potential Dangers of Sucralose," [Available Online] Mercola.com [Dec 2003] Available from www.mercola.com/2000/dec/3/sucralose_dangers.htm.

8. *New England Journal of Medicine* 342 (April 27, 2000): 1250–1253.

9. A. Rivellese, et al., "Long Term Metabolic Effects of Two Dietary Methods of Treating Hyperlipidaemia," *BMJ;* 308 (Jan 1994): 227–231.

10. Richard Trubo, "Endocrine-Disrupting Chemicals Probed as Potential Pathways to Illness," *JAMA;* 294 (July 20, 2005): 291–293.

11. Catherine A. Richter, et al., "Estradiol and Bisphenol: A Stimulate Androgen Receptor and Estrogen Receptor Gene Expression in Fetal Mouse Prostate Mesenchyme Cells," *Environmental Health Perspectives;* 115 (June 2007): 6.

CHAPTER 9

1. Chug-Ahuja et al., *Journal of the American Dietetic Association*, (1993) 93:318, and Mangels et al., *Journal of the American Dietetic Association;* 93 (1993):284–296.

CHAPTER 10

1. Elaine O'Connor, "Toxins in Humans Go Unrecorded," *The Vancouver Province*, Friday, July 13, 2007.

2. Environmental Working Group, "Body Burden—The Pollution in Newborns: A benchmark investigation of industrial chemicals, pollutants and pesticides in umbilical cord blood," July 14, 2005. Available at http://archive.ewg.org/reports/bodyburden2/execsumm.php.

3. S. L. Zunt, et al., "Mouthwash and Oral Cancer," *Journal or the Indiana Dental Association;* 70:6 (Nov 1991): 16–9.

4. Linda Strega, "Perfume, Chemicals, and Cancer" *Off Our Backs* (Jun 1995).

5. Draft Toxicological Review of Dibutyl Phthalate (Di-n-Butyl Phthalate): In Support of the Summary Information in the Integrated Risk Information System (IRIS)," *Federal Register*: June 27, 2006 (Volume 71, Number 123): 36525-36526. From the Federal Register Online via GPO Access http://www.epa.gov/fedrgstr/EPA-MEETINGS/2006/June/Day-27/m10103.htm.

6. "Sodium Laureth Sulfate, Sodium Lauryl Sulfate," *Journal of the American College of Toxicology;* 2:5 (1983): 1–34.

7. M. Ema, E. Miyawaki, and K. Kawashima, "Further Evaluation of Developmental Toxicity of Dinbutyl Phthalate Following Administration During Late Pregnancy in Rats," *Toxicology Letter* (1998): 87–93.

8. Jodi K. Bryner et al., "Dextromethorphan Abuse in Adolescence: An Increasing Trend," *Arch Pediatr Adolesc Med*; 160 (Dec 2006): 1217–1222.

CHAPTER 11

1. Vicki Wade, "Adrenal Fatigue," [Available Online] Feb 2005, Available at http://www.bpharmacysolutions.com/patient/articles/2005/0202-7.asp.

2. "Report on Carcinogens," *National Toxicology* (May 15, 2000).

CHAPTER 12

1. *International Journal of Integrated Medicine*, 2: 6 (Nov–Dec 2000).

CHAPTER 13

1. Anne F. Reeves, et al., "Total Body Weight and Waist Circumference Associated With Chronic Periodontitis Among Adolescents in the United States," *Arch Pediatr Adolesc Med*; 160 (Sep 2006): 894–899.

2. Michael Gershon, *The Second Brain* (New York: Harper Collins, 1998).

CHAPTER 16

1. Eduardo E. Benarroch, "The Autonomic Nervous System: An Introduction to Basic and Clinical Concepts," *Arch Neurol*; 55 (Sep 1998): 1261–1262.

CHAPTER 18

1. Ecology Health Center, "Goat's Milk: Why it's a Better Choice For Adults and Children," [Available Online] http://www.crohns.net/Miva/education/aboutgoatsmilk.shtml.

2. K. Jolin, "Should I Consider Goat's Milk?" [Available Online] http://www.associatedcon tent.com/article/160408/should_i_consider_goat_milk.html.

CHAPTER 19

1. Lauren M. Sompayrac, *How the Immune System Works*, 2nd Ed. (Oxford: Blackwell Publishing Limited, 2002).

2. UK Cancer Research, "The Lymphatic System," [Available Online] http://www.cancerhelp.org.uk/help/default.asp?page=117.

3. Bruce Fife, *The Detox Book: How to Detoxify Your Body to Improve Your Health, Stop Disease, and Reverse Aging*, 2nd ed. (Colorado Springs: Picadilly Books Ltd, 1997).

CHAPTER 20

1. Guy Faguet, *The War on Cancer: An Anatomy of Failure, A Blueprint for the Future,* (New York: Springer, 2005)

2. *Canadian Medical Association Journal*; 57:77:106.

3. K. Kario, et. al., "Guidelines for Home- and Office-Based Blood Pressure Monitoring [Discussion of Jan A. Staessen and others, Antihypertensive treatment based on blood pressure measurement at home or in the physician's office]," *JAMA*; 291:19 (May 19 2004): 2315–2316.

4. W. B. Kannel, et al., "Epidemiologic Assessment of the Role of Blood Pressure in Stroke: The Framingham Study." *JAMA*; 276 (Oct 1996): 1269–1278.

5. Jeremiah Stamler et al., "Low Risk-Factor Profile and Long-term Cardiovascular and Noncardiovascular Mortality and Life Expectancy: Findings for 5 Large Cohorts of Young Adult and Middle-Aged Men and Women," *JAMA*; 282 (Dec 1999): 2012–2018.

6. M. E. Kahn, "Health and Labor Market Performance: The Case of Diabetes," *Journal of Labor Economics* (1998) Abstract available at http://ideas.repec.org/a/ucp/jlabec/v16y1998i4p878-99.html#abstract

7. Writing Group of the Premier Collaborative Research Group, "Effects of Comprehensive Lifestyle Modification on Blood Pressure Control: Main Results of the Premier Clinical Trial," *JAMA*; 283 (Apr 2003): 2083–2093.

8. J. Miriam, et al., "Dietary Intake of Phytoestrogens Is Associated with a Favorable Metabolic Cardiovascular Risk Profile in Postmenopausal U.S. Women: The Framingham Study," *The American Society for Nutritional Sciences J. Nutr*; 132 (2002): 276–282.

9. Karen Edwards et al., "Effect of Pistachio Nuts on Serum Lipid Levels in Patients with Moderate Hypercholesterolemia." Nephrology Division (K.E., I.K., I.K.), Bio-Statistics Department (J.M.), UCLA School of Medicine, Los Angeles, CA.

10. Killian Robinson et al., "Low Circulating Folate and Vitamin B6 Concentrations Risk Factors for Stroke, Peripheral Vascular Disease, and Coronary Artery Disease," American Heart Association Inc. (1998).

11. V. Digiesi et al., "Coenzyme Q10 in Essential Hypertension," *Mol Aspects Med*; 15 (1994): 257–263.

12. Katherine M. Flegal et al., "Prevalence and Trends in Obesity Among US Adults, 1999–2000," *JAMA*; 288: 14 (Oct 9, 2002): 1723–1727.

13. Steven V. Joyal, "A Perspective on the Current Strategies for the Treatment of Obesity," Bentham Science Publishers; 3:5 (Oct 2004): 341–356.

14. David B. West et al., "Effects of Conjugated Linoleic Acid on Body Fat and Energy Metabolism in Mice," *BJM* 275: 3 (September 1998): R667–R672.

15. Naomi Fisher et al., "Cocoa Flavanols and Brain Perfusion," *Journal of Cardiovascular Pharmacology* (June 2006): 47.

16. I. F. Douek, et al., "Diabetes in the Parents of Children with Type I Diabetes," Berlin: Springer; 45:4 (April, 2002): 495–501.

17. Carol Lewis, "Diabetes: A Growing Public Health Concern," U.S. Food and Drug Administration Report, *FDA Consumer Magazine* (Jan–Feb 2002).

CHAPTER 21

1. "The Exercise Prescription," *Post Graduate Medicine* (April 2005): 51.

2. "Wellness Health Care and the Architectural Environment," *Journal of Community Health*; 12:2–3 (June 1987): 163–175.

3. Hülya Akdur et al., "Comparison of Cardiovascular Responses to Isometric (Static) and Isotonic (Dynamic) Exercise Tests in Chronic Atrial Fibrillation," *Japanese Heart Journal*; 43:6 (2002): 621–629.

CHAPTER 22

1. M. J. Dauncey, "Thyroid Hormones and Thermogenesis," Proceedings of the Nutrition Society; 49:2 (July 1990): 203–215.

2. Steven W. J. Lamberts, "The Endocrinology of Aging and the Brain," *Arch Neurol*; 59 (Nov 2002): 1709–1711.

CHAPTER 23

1. Chip R. Bell and Bilijack R. Bell "Leading for Customer Service Ingenuity, *Leader to Leader*; 32 (Mar 2004): 12–15.

2. Maurice M. Ohayon, "Prevalence and Correlates of Nonrestorative Sleep Complaints," *Archives of Internal Medicine*; 165 (Jan 2005): 35–41.

3. C. S. Leonard and R. Llinás, "Serotonergic and Cholinergic Inhibition of Mesopontine Cholinergic Neurons Controlling REM Sleep: An In Vitro Electrophysiological Study," *Neuroscience*; 59:2 (Mar 1994): 309–330.

4. Fabio Barbone, et al., "A Case-Crossover Study of Sleep and Childhood Injury. *Pediatrics Official Journal of the American Academy of Pediatrics* (July 26, 2007).

5. F. M. Brouwers et al., "The Effect of a Polynutrient Supplement on Fatigue and Physical Activity of Patients with Chronic Fatigue Syndrome: A Double-Blind Randomized Controlled Trial," *QJM*; 95:10 (Aug 2001): 677–683.

6. Staff Editor, "Post-Polio Syndrome," *Scientific American* (April 1998): 1.

DR. ASA ANDREW

NATURAL MEDICINE®

The Center for Natural Medicine

Located in the heart of Nashville, Tennessee, the Center for Natural Medicine is a state-of-the-art facility designed to take on any health challenge. Through the extensive Natural Medicine testing evaluation, we will find any current or underlying health challenges.
- Learn how to beat genetics
- Evaluate your exact blood chemistry and restore any deficiencies
- Correct any mental instabilities concerning key neurotransmitters
- Reverse the aging process by looking and feeling 20 years younger
- Balance essential hormones in the body
- Reduce inflammation and detoxify the body
- Find the vitamins and minerals that are specific to your body chemistry

Natural Medicine Distance Program
The Center for Natural Medicine offers special programs for our out-of-state patients. Dr. Asa can take care of you right in your own home by following our Natural Medicine Protocol:
- The Asa Panel blood work (draw sites nationwide)
- A complete health evaluation
- Personalized phone consultation with Dr. Asa's Natural Medicine specialists
- The Extraordinary Health package
- Referral to a local Natural Medicine physician if needed
- Weight loss programs if applicable

For more information please call 888.28.DR.ASA (888.283.7272) or visit us online at AsaAndrew.com